MENTAL ILLNESSES AND TREATMENTS

INTELLECTUAL DISABILITY

MANAGEMENT, CAUSES AND SOCIAL PERCEPTIONS

MENTAL ILLNESSES AND TREATMENTS

Additional books in this series can be found on Nova's website
under the Series tab.

Additional E-books in this series can be found on Nova's website
under the E-book tab.

DISABILITY AND THE DISABLED-ISSUES, LAWS AND PROGRAMS

Additional books in this series can be found on Nova's website
under the Series tab.

Additional E-books in this series can be found on Nova's website
under the E-book tab.

MENTAL ILLNESSES AND TREATMENTS

INTELLECTUAL DISABILITY

MANAGEMENT, CAUSES AND SOCIAL PERCEPTIONS

DOMENICO F. MANCINI
AND
CARLO M. GRECO
EDITORS

Nova Science Publishers, Inc.
New York

For permission to use material from this book please contact us:
Telephone 631-231-7269; Fax 631-231-8175
Web Site: http://www.novapublishers.com

LIBRARY OF CONGRESS CATALOGING-IN-PUBLICATION DATA

Library of Congress Control Number: 2012932578

ISBN: 978-1-61942-298-8

Published by Nova Science Publishers, Inc. † New York

Contents

PREFACE

Intellectual disability occurs with a frequency of 1-3% within the general population. This impairment is frequently associated with additional features like multiple congenital anomalies and facial dysmorphisms. This book presents current research in the management, causes and social perceptions of mental retardation. Topics include chromosomal regions with a high diagnostic impact in mental retardation syndromes; psychosocial and psychopharmacological treatment of comorbid aggression in pediatric mental retardation; caring for children with Williams and Smith-Magenis syndromes; and cognitive skills enhancement in mental retardation.

Chapter 1 - The use of subtelomere screening procedures with regard to the analysis of patients with mental retardation, dysmorphic features and congenital malformations has permitted to detect cryptic imbalances. A clinical role of the subtelomeric endings, especially in patients with mental retardation, is due to the data of the last two decades without a doubt. This review article highlights the "evolution" of the subtelomere screening procedure and its results as well as the development of different analytical techniques over the last two decades. Thereby the gainful use of the array CGH technique in the screening procedure is clearly represented. Furthermore, the outcome of recognizable clinical pictures – identified in the subtelomere screening era – and their role in the pathogenesis of further disorders are highlighted. This includes the description of the 1p, 2q, 4p, 5p, 6p, 9q, 17p, 22q subtelomere deletion syndromes as well as the description of the involvement of these regions in holoprosencephaly, facioscapulohumeral muscular dystrophy, and the enrichment of the new identified *WASH* genes within these regions. Furthermore, the authors focussed on the increasing number of inherited benign subtelomeric alterations which also have been identified: numerous collective screenings have yielded similar, in some cases even higher detection quota for subtelomeric polymorphisms than for pathogenic imbalances. Thus, they currently count 35 polymorphic regions out of 41 relevant subtelomere endings (85.4%). The data presented in this review thus illustrates the important role of subtelomeric regions in the pathogenesis of various clinical pictures and diseases (nearly all associated with mental retardation) and the necessity of validated screening techniques on one hand and on the other hand, how much care must be taken in interpreting subtelomeric imbalances. The different illustrated data also demonstrate the need to formulate, for each subtelomere, the exact boundary between a benign subtelomeric rearrangement on the one hand and pathogenic imbalances on the other hand. "Standard measurements", which to date exist only for the endings of 20 chromosomes and two interstitially variants in 17p13.3 and in 18q23, are required. A "standard measure" would appear to be essential, considering that these diagnostic approaches are becoming increasingly important in parental diagnosis. More complete knowledge of the exact boundaries between polymorphisms and pathogenic imbalances will not only help to interpret the screening results more accurately but will also guarantee maximum benefit for the patients.

Chapter 2 - Children and adults with disabilities often require highly specialized instruction in order to acquire functional academic, social, adaptive, and vocational skills that will allow them to experience significantly independent lives upon graduation from special education programs. It follows that those responsible for teaching these skills must be able to engage in only the most efficacious instructional methods and curriculum development, given the amount of skills that must be directly taught, combined with the unique learning characteristics of those with significant disabilities. In other words, skills must be taught effectively and efficiently. Unfortunately, the field of education has consistently suffered from a marked gap between research and practice. Effective instructional procedures have been identified and vetted by the peer review process. However, they are consistently under-utilized in instructional environments. Likewise, federal education law mandates that those eligible for special education receive an individualized education plan (IEP), which contains measureable goals and objectives. It is known that instructional and curricular decisions should be based on data and measurement of learner performance. However, in implementation, what is known and what is practiced are quite different. In this case, the mandates for measures of learner performance are in place, but it is arguably more common than not to see goals and objectives that are unable to be measured objectively, and subsequent assessment reports that are subjective, or based on a "gut feeling," as opposed to truly objective performance. The end result of this set of circumstances is that learners are often unable to meet their potential. They may be subjected to ineffective instruction at one end of a continuum, or possibly move along at too slow a pace due to lack of adequate mastery criteria at the other end. They may suffer from educational plans that are poorly devised. They may also experience frustration when they are left to bear the burden of instructional problems that would be better placed on the systems responsible for providing such instruction. On another front, teachers who are not accustomed to students with disabilities achieving success may be more subject to frustration, "burnout," and eventual attrition or staff "turnover." The current situations call for a personnel training and performance feedback framework by which those responsible for both planning and implementing instruction and curriculum may effectively utilize those things that have been shown to work. At hand is the proposal to adopt data-based mechanisms for objectively evaluating and providing feedback on the practical output (implementation of evidence-based instructional practices; development of measurable goals and objectives) of personnel involved in teaching those with intellectual and developmental disabilities. The authors offer a systematic way to train, monitor, and evaluate personnel (across varied systems of service delivery) who are charged with instruction, which would lead to improved personnel performance, and – ultimately – improved outcomes for those with disabilities. This system includes both theoretical and behavioral underpinnings, as well as a technology of implementation that would allow for the development and deployment of sound programming.

Chapter 3 - For decades, psychologists, educationalists, even University faculty used to attach labels to describe persons deviating from what has been attributed to be normal. Yet, from the linguistic, communicative and psychological points of view the majority of these terms do not convey the aimed message. Obviously, this practice has resulted to serious problems of understanding the specific issues and developing the appropriate remedial measures. Consequently, there is a serious problem faced by all people with disabilities due to a variety of terms attached to such persons, for example handicapped, exceptional, retarded and other. Instead of these terms, the most authentic world organizations refer to persons with disabilities, which is, also, fully accepted by the unions of these persons. The United Nations Organization (UNO) in the convention of the rights for *persons with disabilities* (2006) support that the relative problems result from the interaction between persons with impairments and attitudinal and environmental barriers. The World Health Organization (WHO), in 2001 defined that *disability* is not something that only happens to a minority of people and recognizes the experience of disability as a universal human experience. The Council of Europe (2006) supports that the key target of the *Disability Action Plan* is to serve as a practical tool to develop and implement viable strategies to bring about full participation of *people with disabilities* in society. The employment and Social Affairs of EU27 (2010) defines *disability* as a right issue and not a matter of discrimination. The paradox about the terminology used so far is that most of the member-countries of these organizations, though signatory, continue to use terminology which was adopted many years ago. Additionally, the fact that gifted persons (another wrong term) are classified among the persons "with special needs" is beyond any logic concept. More specifically, the term *"mental retardation"* is not the appropriate one. *Mental* refers to the health or illnesses of the mind. *"retardation"* means reduction or delay of the rate of developing of something. Using this term to describe someone who has not developed mentally as much as most other people of the same age, is considered and really is *offensive*. The alternative term *" developmental disability"* or even "*Intellectual Disability",* is closer to the accurate description of these persons, since *"developmental"* means a person's (child's) growth and ability to learn things and *"disability"* denotes a condition in which someone *is not able to use a part of the body or mind properly.* On the other hand, intellectual denotes the ability to think in an intelligent way and understand things. This term is used in USA and Canada to describe almost life-long disabilities related to the condition of persons to perform in these areas. A supportive element is the definition of the American Association on Mental Deficiency (1973) relating mental retardation *to deficits manifested during the developmental period.* Based on these concepts, this chapter will discuss issues of management, causes and social perceptions of this disability and criticize the various definitions, the IQ testing, levels of severity, reliability of prevalence, future trends. Finally, recommendations suitable to provide solutions to this situation will be tabled.

Chapter 4 - Children with mental retardation and other pervasive developmental disorders are at increased risk of displaying aggressive behaviors (Brosnan & Healy, 2011; Matson & Rivet, 2008; Nevels, Dehon, Alexander, & Gontkovsky, 2010). Several clinical disorders occur comorbidly with aggression during childhood and adolescence. Attention-deficit hyperactivity disorder (ADHD), mood disorders (in particular bipolar disorders/pediatric mania), mental retardation (MR), schizophrenia, oppositional defiant disorder (ODD), conduct disorder (CD), and autism spectrum disorders (ASDs) most notably are characterized by aggressive behaviors (Barkley, 2003). Approximately 10 to 20% of individuals with intellectual disabilities, including ASDs and mental retardation, display behavior such as self-injury and aggression (McClintock, Hall, & Oliver, 2003). Aggressive behaviors related to

ASDs and MR often are compounded by higher rates of comorbid mood disorders, behavioral disorders, psychoses, or other intellectual disabilities. Pervasive developmental disorders (PDDs) and other clinical disorders frequently present with comorbid aggression, which is clinically challenging (Nevels et al., 2010). Pediatric aggression can be serious and costly, and while many children and adolescents display some form of aggression, aggressive displays do not necessarily indicate a psychiatric disorder. Aggressive children and adolescents, however, tend to exhibit hyperactive and impulsive traits as well as lower IQs when compared to their peers (Tremblay et al., 2004). Most children and adolescents who present for therapeutic intervention have some type of behavior problem, and approximately 5 to 14% of preschoolers engage in moderate to severe problem behaviors (Singh et al., 2006).

Chapter 5 - With improved diagnostic techniques, prevalence rates of genetic disorders are increasing steadily, and thus, the number of individuals providing care to affected children is growing. Medical advances have increased survival rates and extended the lifespan of individuals affected by these disorders, which has increased caregiving demands and caregiver burden. While many of these individuals' needs are medical in nature, most also have some degree of intellectual impairment that interferes with their ability to function independently. Specifically, children with Williams syndrome and Smith-Magenis syndrome typically struggle with intellectual disability, in addition to other syndrome complications, such as behavioral problems. As a result, these individuals are typically unable to live independently, which often means that their guardians will assume a caregiver role for the entirety of their lives. Coping with the burden of caring for an individual with such significant needs has been associated with a decline in self-care behaviors, negatively impacting not only the caregiver but also the child and family system as a whole. This chapter examines self-care behaviors among these caregivers and investigates the effects of caregiver well-being on the individuals affected by these syndromes. How these individuals impact an entire family system is also explored. Finally, current interventions aimed at maximizing adaptive family functioning in these populations are reviewed, and suggestions for future research are discussed.

Chapter 6 - Many labels refer to treatment for cognitive impairments. Most of them are referred to as "cognitive rehabilitation", "cognitive skills enhancement", "cognitive empowerment". Anyway the purpose of these treatments is to help an individual acquire the highest level of cognitive functioning and functional independence possible for that individual. The objectives of the present chapter are to study in depth the latest theoretical approaches to cognitive empowerment in intellectually disabled children and to show that modifiability can be applied despite the presence of severe impairments in the attention, memory, reasoning and language processes of an individual. This chapter begins with a theoretical overview on cognitive empowerment. The first part contains basic principles and theoretical standpoints of cognitive empowerment. Cognitive and biological bases of empowerment will be presented, connected to the concept of "neuroplasticity". The second part contains operational principles of cognitive empowerment and examples of applications on case studies. Methodologies presented show how to improve attention, memory, thinking, reasoning, and present statistical data that show trends in each of the considered processes.

Chapter 7 - Intellectual disability is a lifelong condition with multiple aetiologies (Harris, 1995). There are no specific personality or behavioural characteristics that are specific to intellectual disability (American Psychiatric Association, 1994). Severe levels of intellectual disability or syndromes may be associated with motor disability. In these cases there are even more limits in social and adaptive functioning. In Rett Syndrome for example initially the child looks normal and seems to follow a normal development. It is at about 18 months of age that a subtle regression in the evolutive acquisitions begins, opening the path to the clinical stages described by Hagberg and Witt-Engerström (1986). Loss of the previously acquired language skills and of purposeful hand use, increasing difficulties in motor abilities (dyspraxia), and mental retardation are the most clear signs of the regression involved in RS. Other typical signs of RS appear meanwhile: hand stereotypies - such as hand-washing, hand-wringing, hand-mouthing - breathing disorders (breath holding and hyperventilation), ataxia, agnosia, bruxism. Since persons with Rett Syndrome are not able to communicate occupational therapy can include assistive technology devices, such as pointers and switches that activate toys or a simple cause/effect computer activity (Pizzamiglio et al., 2008). Lack of expressive and receptive language is also a large part of Rett syndrome.

In: Intellectual Disability
Editors: Domenico F. Mancini and Carlo M. Greco
ISBN: 978-1-61942-298-8

Chapter 1

SUBTELOMERIC ENDINGS – CHROMOSOMAL REGIONS WITH A HIGH DIAGNOSTIC IMPACT IN MENTAL RETARDATION SYNDROMES: INSIGHTS FROM THE PAST TWO DECADES. TAKING A CLOSER LOOK AT CHROMOSOME TIPS

Andreas Roos[1][1], Eva Brauers[1], Stephan Buchkremer[1], Sabrina Spengler[2], Herdit Monika Schüler[2] and Gesa Schwanitz[3]

1Institute of Neuropathology, University Hospital RWTH Aachen, Aachen Germany

2Institute of Human Genetics, University Hospital RWTH Aachen, Aachen Germany

3Institute of Human Genetics, University Bonn, Bonn Germany

ABSTRACT

The use of subtelomere screening procedures with regard to the analysis of patients with mental retardation, dysmorphic features and congenital malformations has permitted to detect cryptic imbalances. A clinical role of the subtelomeric endings, especially in patients with mental retardation, is due to the data of the last two decades without a doubt. This review article highlights the "evolution" of the subtelomere screening procedure and its results as well as the development of different analytical techniques over the last two decades. Thereby the gainful use of the array CGH technique in the screening procedure is clearly represented. Furthermore, the outcome of recognizable clinical pictures – identified in the subtelomere screening era – and their role in the

[1] Andreas Roos, PhD. Institute of Neuropathology, University Hospital, RWTH Aachen. Pauwelsstr. 30, D-52074 Aachen. Phone: +49 241 8037084. Fax:+49 241 8082394. E-mail:aroos@ukaachen.de. roos@medbiol.de.

pathogenesis of further disorders are highlighted. This includes the description of the 1p, 2q, 4p, 5p, 6p, 9q, 17p, 22q subtelomere deletion syndromes as well as the description of the involvement of these regions in holoprosencephaly, facioscapulohumeral muscular dystrophy, and the enrichment of the new identified *WASH* genes within these regions. Furthermore, we focussed on the increasing number of inherited benign subtelomeric alterations which also have been identified: numerous collective screenings have yielded similar, in some cases even higher detection quota for subtelomeric polymorphisms than for pathogenic imbalances. Thus, we currently count 35 polymorphic regions out of 41 relevant subtelomere endings (85.4%). The data presented in this review thus illustrates the important role of subtelomeric regions in the pathogenesis of various clinical pictures and diseases (nearly all associated with mental retardation) and the necessity of validated screening techniques on one hand and on the other hand, how much care must be taken in interpreting subtelomeric imbalances. The different illustrated data also demonstrate the need to formulate, for each subtelomere, the exact boundary between a benign subtelomeric rearrangement on the one hand and pathogenic imbalances on the other hand. "Standard measurements", which to date exist only for the endings of 20 chromosomes and two interstitially variants in 17p13.3 and in 18q23, are required. A "standard measure" would appear to be essential, considering that these diagnostic approaches are becoming increasingly important in parental diagnosis. More complete knowledge of the exact boundaries between polymorphisms and pathogenic imbalances will not only help to interpret the screening results more accurately but will also guarantee maximum benefit for the patients.

INTRODUCTION

Mental retardation (MR) or developmental delay (DD; this term is used for children under five years of age) occurs with a frequency of 1-3% within the general population (Shaffer, 2005; Leonard and Wen, 2002). This impairment is frequently associated with additional features like multiple congenital anomalies (MCA) and facial dysmorphisms. The etiological diagnosis is very often difficult due to a variety of genetic and environmental causes resulting in this pathology. Nevertheless it is generally acknowledged that up to 50% of cases with MR arise from genetic disturbances. In the routine diagnostic procedures, GTG karyotyping is a cytogenetic method which identifies the genetic cause of the phenotype in up to 36% of cases (Schreppers-Tijdink et al., 1988). This method is able to detect chromosomal rearrangements with a minimum size of five megabases (Mb) (microscopic chromosomal aberration). However, there are also submicroscopic aberrations existing which very often occur in the chromosomal endings, the so called subtelomeric regions. The identification of submicroscopic rearrangements needs advanced molecular cytogenetic techniques like fluorescent in situ hybridization (FISH), multiplex ligation dependent probe amplification (MLPA) and nowadays array based comparative genomic hybridization (aCGH).

SUBTELOMERIC ARCHITECTURE

Subtelomeric regions are among the most structurally complex, variable and dynamic areas of the genome. They are evaluated as the gene-richest regions of the human genome (Saccone et al., 1992) and are organized as the transition zones between chromosome-specific sequences and the areas of the telomere repeats at the end of the chromosomes. The identity, arrangement and polymorphism of the blocks of subtelomeric sequence shared among multiple chromosomes (Mefford and Trask, 2002) suggest that subtelomeric duplications spread recently. The subtelomeric structure as well as their length is specific for each chromosome. Their lengths ranges from 8kb (subtelomere 7p) up to 300kb (subtelomere 8p). Structure of the telomeric flanking regions is presented in figure 1. In some cases the subtelomeric clusters of several chromosomes (4p, 4q, 16p, 18p, 20p, 22q) are separated into two domains due to interstitially localized, degenerating $(TTAGGG)_n$-sequences (Chute et al., 1997; Flint et al., 1997). The distally localized domain (see figure 1) contains short sequences with many homologies to other chromosomal areas, whereas the proximal domain (see figure 1) contains longer sequences with few homologies. In addition to the repetitive sequences some subtelomeres also present coding gene-sequences like the olfactory receptor genes (OR-genes). They are localized within the subtelomeric sequences of chromosome 4p, 5q, 6p, 6q, 8p, 10q and 11q (Trask et al., 1998). The proximally localized repetitive subtelomeric sequences border the subtelomeric regions specific for each chromosome (see figure 1) (Flint et al., 1996). These are exactly the regions which are mentioned and discussed in several studies or case reports presenting rearrangements which cause pathogenic consequences on their own. The precise function of the repetitive subtelomeric sequences is unknown so far. Nevertheless, one might speculate that the accumulation of homologue sequences were of evolutionary advantage, taking over the role of a “protecting cap” if the telomeric endings are lost due to mutations (i.e. deletions). Heterologous recombination processes between these regions are able to compensate these imbalances and therefore assure the stability of the chromosome (Dunham et al., 2000). Additionally, their plasticity and variability combined with the chromosomal specific gene dosage causes the genomic and phenotypic diversity (Freitas-Junior et al., 2000; Linardopoulou et al., 2001). It is postulated that these regions (even because of their molecular architecture as mentioned above) are more susceptible to rearrangements than other chromosomal areas (Saccone et al., 1992; Brown et al.; 2001).

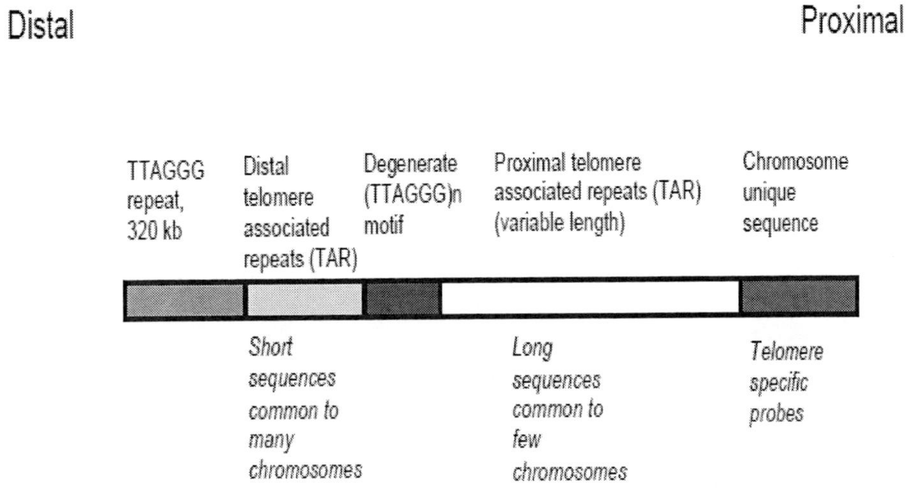

Figure 1. schematic overview of the subtelomeric region.

SUBTELOMERIC HAPLOTYPES

Lemmers and co-workers (2010) studied the human 4q and 10q subtelomeres. They share a high sequence similarity over a region of approximately 200 kilobases (kb) and contain the polymorphic macrosatellite repeat D4Z4. Sequence analysis of four markers in the African, European, and Asian HAPMAP panels identified 17 subtelomeric 4q and eight subtelomeric 10q haplotypes. In all three ethnic populations, there were also haplotypes which were composed of a combination of the 4q and 10q sequences (frequency >10%). This finding supports the assumption of a mechanism of ongoing interchromosomal substitution between the chromosomes 4 and 10. With the help of the construction of an evolutionary network, they identified the 4q haplotype ancestral to all 4q and 10q haplotypes. Their studies furthermore revealed that all subtelomeres originate from only four distinct sequence transfer events during the evolution of *homo sapiens*. Mixed haplotypes of 4q- and 10q-sequences denote intermediate structures in the conversion from the 4q to the 10q subtelomeres. Lemmers et al., (2010) suggest that the limited rate of interchromosomal sequence transfers results in an accumulation of haplotype-specific polymorphisms.

SUBTELOMERE SCREENING COHORTS

The first hint of a clinical significance and pathological role of these regions was already given in 1992 by Ledbetter. He described the phenomenon of "cryptic translocations" in probands and their parents as carriers of a balanced rearrangement. In the last two decades, rearrangements within these regions can be detected in approximately 5% of patients with MR/DD and additional clinical features. The detection rate thereby varies from 0-23% (Xu and Chen, 2003; Edelman and Hirschhorn 2009; Shao et al., 2008; Rooms et al., 2004; Northrop et al., 2005; Baroncini et al., 2005; Knight et al., 1999, Wu et al., 2010). Interestingly, substantially larger studies revealed a percentage of approximately 2.5% subtelomeric rearrangements in cases with idiopathic mental retardation (and additional clinical features) (Ravnan et al., 2006; Ballif et al., 2007; Shao et al., 2007) and therefore a lower frequency of these imbalances as estimated. Knight and co-workers (1999) as well as Ravnan and his group (2006) demonstrated that half or more of the patients inherited the unbalanced aberration from a phenotypically normal parent presented with a balanced translocation of the chromosome sections involved. However, sub-microscopic pure duplications generally occur less frequently than deletions. Their frequency is approximately 0.5% (Ruiter et al., 2007). Aberrations within the subtelomeres are not restricted to a certain ethnic cohort. Moreover, specific criteria were formulated in order to standardize the screening procedures for appropriate patients (De Vries et al., 2001b; Walter et al., 2004) and may help to choose patients with mental retardation and/or multiple congenital anomalies with a high probability of abnormal findings in this diagnostic approach. However, this method has also been applied in screening patients with congenital heart malformations (Schellberg et al., 2004), couples with recurrent miscarriages (Cockwell et al., 2003) or spontaneous miscarriages (Bruno et al., 2006) as well as patients presenting with clinical manifestations of the Silver-Russell syndrome (Eggermann et al., 2008) or cases with infantile epileptic encephalopathies (Ruiter et al., 2010). Wise and coworkers (2009) screened 565 apparently normal individuals in order to determine the frequency of carriers for cryptic balanced subtelomeric translocations.

SUBTELOMERE SCREENING PROCEDURES

Due to the detection of (cryptic) subtelomeric imbalances in at least 2.5% of cases with mental impairment (and additional clinical features) and normal karyotype, demonstrating their clinical significance, subtelomere screening procedures have become a "standard of care" diagnostic test with different technical approaches to perform the screening. However, many laboratories can only make use of one screening method due to their technical equipment.

Analyses of the subtelomeric regions with the help of microsatellite markers was one of the first techniques (Slavotinek et al., 1999), aside from the analysis of high resolution chromosomes (Knight et al., 2000; Ning et al., 1996), followed by fluorescence in situ hybridization (FISH) using clones for the 41 relevant subtelomeric regions. During the FISH era, advanced fluorescence in situ hybridization-based procedures like S-COBRA FISH (Engels et al., 2003) and the innovative 12-color FISH-assay called M-TEL (Brown et al., 2001) were developed in order to investigate these regions. Further techniques were multiplex amplifiable probe hybridization (MAPH) (Armour et al., 2000; Sismani et al., 2001) and multiplex ligation dependent probe amplification (MLPA) (Rooms et al., 2004) as well as quantitative PCR using SYBR-green dye (Boehm et al., 2004). Other methods were only applied in single screening studies, such as multiplex PCR/ liquid chromatography (Udaka et al., 2007), or optimized MLPA (Ahn et al., 2007). In the "evolution" of subtelomere screening procedures, the array based comparative genome hybridization (aCGH) is the latest and most promising technique (Veltman et al., 2002; Vissers et al., 2003; Harada et al., 2004; Kok et al., 2005). It allows – beside the detection of the aberration – a precise localization of the breakpoints and therefore an overview of the genes involved in the rearrangement. Furthermore, the array technique allows the detection of tandem-duplications. Over the last years, this procedure has rapidly replaced the other techniques for subtelomere screening and now seems to be the method of choice for assessing the integrity of the chromosomal endings in patients with idiopathic mental retardation (and associated clinical features like congenital anomalies and facial dysmorphisms) as an adjunct to conventional chromosome analysis. The effort of the aCGH technique for the detection of subtelomeric imbalances was thus demonstrated in two large-sclae studies: Shaffer et al., (2006) analyzed 1,500 children with idiopathic mental retardation with the help of a targeted BAC-array (126 targets, including all telomeric regions) and identified relevant genomic imbalances in 5.6% of cases. More than half of these imbalances involved the telomeric regions. Ballif and co-workers (2007) investigated a large cohort of 7,000 patients by aCGH (BAC clone average every 500 kb for the ~5 Mb of each telomere region) and identified telomeric imbalances in 2.4% of cases. DeScipio and co-workers (2008) moreover developed a special TEL-array CGH system with a coverage of the most distal 10 Mb of each chromosomal ending (1.5x BAC coverage of the last 1 Mb, 0.5x BAC coverage of the following 1 Mb to 5 Mb proximal region and 0.25x

BAC coverage for the 5 Mb to 10 Mb proximal region). The tiling path of the most distal regions allowed the group for the first time the investigation of subtelomeric regions, which were not covered in aCGH analysis before and showed first promising results. Furthermore, a combination of two different systems, e.g. aCGH and MLPA, was applied (Kirchhoff et al., 2005). All these investigations revealed similar frequencies of imbalances within the different screening studies and can therefore be equalized. They disclosed cryptic or semicryptic (in terms of complex rearrangements; Davies et al., 2003) imbalances as structural aberrations. They include pure terminal deletions, double-deletions, duplications, and unbalanced translocations resulting in partial deletions and/or duplications, interstitial deletions and an inserted duplication in one family case. Besides, an increasing number of inherited polymorphisms have been characterized (see below).

Conclusion

Pathologic Subtelomeric Aberrations and Syndromes

Up to now, more than 25,000 patients with different clinical conditions and healthy persons have been investigated to determine the frequency and type of subtelomeric imbalances and aberrations that were reported for every subtelomeric region (see figure 2).

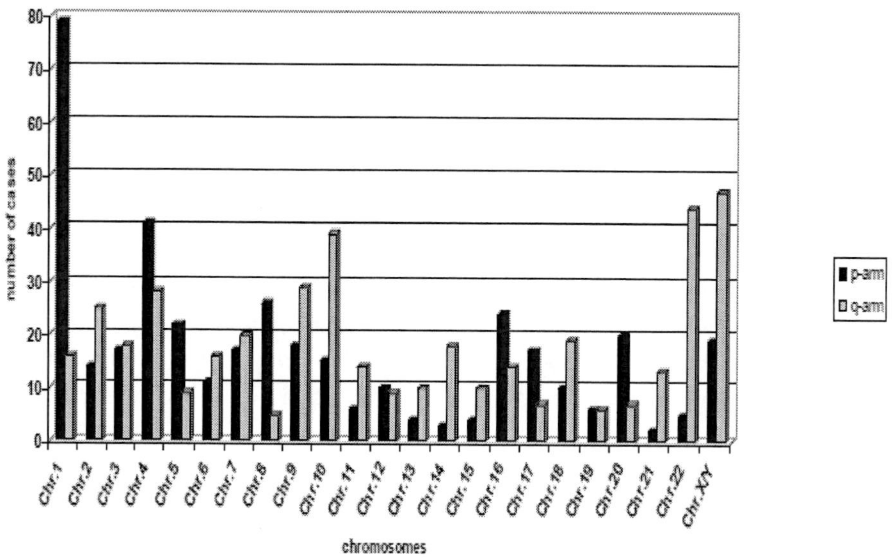

Figure 2. frequency of pathogenic subtelomeric imbalances (modified according to Ledbetter and Martin, 2007). Data from four large-scale studies (Ravnan et al., 2006; Ballif et al., 2007; Shao et al., 2008; Wu et al., 2010) are included. Number of aberration thereby includes the number of times each subtelomere was involved in any type of rearrangement (deletion, duplication, unbalanced translocations, etc.).

Thereby, the frequency of involvement of subtle subtelomeres varies surprisingly. The subtelomeric regions of 1p followed by 22q, 4p, 9q, 8p, 2q and 20p are most frequently involved (see figure 2). Other subtelomeres are very rarely involved in imbalances like 8q, 17q, 19q and 20q (see figure 2; Wu et al., 1996; De Vries et al., 2001a). However, just a closer look on the subtelomeric imbalances shows recognizable phenotypes; among them are also chromosomal endings which are less frequently involved in rearrangements (like 5p and 17p; see figure 2). The so-called subtelomeric syndromes, which could or should be suspected in a patient based on the clinical presentation, are listed below.

Monosomy 1p36

Monosomy 1p36 is characterized by a heterozygous terminal deletion of the short arm of chromosome 1p. This aberration presents a frequency of 1:5000 (Shaffer and Lupski, 2000) and is therefore the most frequent terminal deletion in human beings (Gajecka et al., 2007). No common breakpoint could be identified, but a deletion of 10.5 Mb genomic material is recurrent. The phenotype is characterized by typical craniofacial features consisting of straight eyebrows, deep-set eyes, midface hypoplasia, broad and flat nasal root/bridge, long philtrum, pointed chin, large, late-closing anterior fontanel, microbrachycephaly, epicanthal folds, and posteriorly rotated, low-set, abnormal ears (Battaglia and Shaffer, 2008). Mental retardation/ developmental delay (with variable degree) is present in all cases. Majority of cases also suffers from hypotonia. Seizures occur in approximately 50% of affected individuals (Battaglia and Shaffer, 2008). Other findings include structural brain abnormalities (like polymicrogyria; Saito et al., 2011), cardiac malformations, ophthalmologic disturbances, hearing impairmant, skeletal anomalies, abnormalities of the external genitalia as well as renal malformations (Battaglia and Shaffer, 2008). Within this subtelomeric region, *PLCH2*, a gene encoding the phosphoinositide-specific phospholipase C (PI-PLC ŋ2), which is expressed in the brain after birth and plays a significant role in axon growth and retraction, growth cone guidance, synapse formation, and responses to neurotransmitters, is discussed as the candidate gene for the neurodevelopmental delay associated with the 1p36 deletion (Lo Vasco 2011).

Monosomy 2q37.3

The majorities of the 2q37.7 deletion cases are associated with hereditary Albright-ostodystrophy (AHO; OMIM: 600430) and very often show a mild mental impairment, and sleep disturbances (Shrimpton et al., 2004). The clinical picture also includes facial dysmorphisms, heart defects (20% of cases), and in some cases epilepsy, Wilms tumors and urogenital anomalies, eczema, autism, situs abnormalities as well as holoprosencephaly (Aldred et al., 2004; Williams et al., 2010). Molecular genetic studies performed by Williams and coworkers (2010) identified *HDAC4*, encoding a histone deacetylase that regulates genes important in bone, muscle as well as neurological, and cardiac development, as the striking gene responsible for the deletion phenotype. Their finding was highlighted by the detection of *de novo* mutations within this gene in cases suffering from brachydactyly mental retardation syndrome (BDMR) (Williams et al., 2010).

Monosomy 4p16.3

The Wolf-Hirschhorn syndrome (WHS; OMIM: 194190), caused by terminal deletions at 4p16.3, is characterized by mental retardation, growth delay, developmental delay, congenital malformations, hypotonia, seizures, feeding problems and distinctive facial features (De Vries et al., 2003; South et al., 2007; Thomson, 1998). Smaller deletions lead to a milder phenotype (Zollino et al., 2000). Subtelomeric deletions of 100-300 kb from the telomeric end are not associated with a WHS phenotype (De Vries et al., 2003; Gandelman et al., 1992; Estabrooks et al., 1992; Van Buggenhout et al., 2004) indicating that the genes responsible for the WHS phenotype are located proximal to the subtelomeric region of 4p and probably more than 300 kb from the terminus of 4p (South et al., 2007). To manifest a WHS phenotype, a deletion of either of two critical regions – WHSCR and WHSCR-2 – is necessary (South et al., 2007). WHSCR is located proximal to the *FGFR3* and *LETM1* genes (South et al., 2007) and includes the *WHSC2* gene as well as the 3′end of the *WHSC1* gene. WHSCR-2 which is more definitive comprises the *LETM1* gene localized between 1.78 and 1.825 Mb from the terminus of 4p, and the 5′ end of the *WHSC1* gene (South et al., 2007). Ravnan and coworkers (2006) described seven cases with a proven subtelomeric 4p deletion. All cases revealed clinical abnormalities such as mental retardation and/ or developmental delay. South and coworkers (2007) present two patients with *de novo* terminal microdeletions in 4p16.3 who show mild developmental delays and some unspecific manifestations of WHS like feeding problems but their facial features were not typical for WHS. One of the patients presented with a terminal deletion of around 1.78 Mb distal to WHSCR, and with the breakpoint next or within the distal boundary for WHSCR-2. As seizures could be detected in this patient, one might speculate that *LETM1*, located in WHSCR-2, plays a direct role in the development of seizures (Endele et al., 1999) and confirm that characteristics of the WHS phenotype can be seen in cases with deletions distal to the known boundaries of the two proposed critical regions: this means that hemizygosity for genes in this interval lead to mild growth delay, mild developmental delay and some minor facial abnormalities seen in WHS.

Monosomy 5p15.33

Deletions of the end of chromosome 5p causes Cri-du-chat syndrome (CdCS; OMIM: 123450). Common phenotypic features are the cat-like cry probably due to laryngomalacia, mental retardation, microcephaly, hypertelorism and epicanthic folds as well as micrognathia and transverse flexion creases (Cerruti Mainardi, 2006). Cardiac complications are also common with about 30% of the patients presenting heart malformations. With the help of a "phenotype dissection" study of Wu and coworkers (2005), *FLJ25076/ UBE2QL1* (5p15.31), encoding an ubiquitine-conjugated enzyme E2Q family-like 1 which is locally expressed in thoracic and scalp tissues, could be identified as the critical gene for the cat-like cry. Further phenotype-genotype correlation studies suggest that larger deletions tend to cause a more severe developmental delay phenotype compared to smaller ones (Cornish et al., 1999). In this context, loss of the more proximally located *CTNND2* gene (5p15.2) is discussed as to cause the severe intellectual disabilities (Medina et al., 2000). The fact that smaller deletions of 5p (involving the subtelomeric region) lead to a more "unspecific 5p minus phenotype" is highlighted by a publication of Stathopulu et al., (2003) who described a case with a small deletion in 5p15.33 and a phenotype suggesting Lujan-Fryns syndrome (OMIM: 309520)

Monosomy 6p25

More than 30 cases of monosomy 6p25 are described so far, where by a minimum of 11 cases show pure subtelomeric deletions. Manifestation of the phenotype seems to be independent from the size of deletion; *ergo* the 6p25 cytoband represents the critical region for the corresponding phenotype (DeScipio et al., 2008). *FOXC1, FOXF2* and *FOXQ1* are thereby discussed as candidate genes. Monosomy 6p25 shows significant clinical overlappings with the Ritscher-Schinzel syndrome (OMIM: 220210). Mental retardation, deafness, heart-, hand- and feet-anomalies are also common clinical findings as (cranio)facial dysmorphisms (frontal bossing, hypoplastic midface, epicanthus, ptosis, extern ear-anomalies, deep root of the nose, and high palate) (Lin et al., 2005; DeScipio et al., 2008). Typical anomalies of the eyes are posterior embryotoxon, disturbed refraction power and disturbed mobility of the eyes (Lin et al., 2005; DeScipio et al., 2008).

Monosomy 9q34

Up to now, more than 50 cases of monosomy 9q34 are published (Stewart and Kleefstra, 2007), among them two cases with cytogenetic visible deletions. These patients died at the age of 4-5 month due to respiratory insufficiency. There are three sections discussed as the possible critical deletion-region (3 Mb; 2.5 Mb; 1.4 Mb; 0.8 Mb). *EHMT1* (OMIM: 607001) is discussed as the critical candidate gene. Therefore, Stewart and Kleefstra (2007) propose first subtelomere screening followed by sequencing of the *EHMT1* gene in patients with 9q34 minus phenotype which includes mental retardation, brachycephaly, hypertelorism, synophris, a hypoplstic midface, short nose, protruding tongue, and downward curved corners of the mouth, congenital heart anomalies, epilepsy and sleeping disturbances. The authors declare the 9q34 minus clinical picture as confused with Down syndrome (DS; OMIM: 190685) and Smith-Magenis syndrome (SMS; OMIM: 182290) (Stewart and Kleefstra, 2007).

Monosomy 17p13.3

Monosomy of the 17p13.3 region (including the *PAFAH1B1* gene which encodes LIS1) causes lissencephaly with reduced gyration of the cerebral surface and an increased cortical thickening. Thereby the phenotype can vary from isolated lissencephaly (ILS; OMIM: 607432) to the Miller-Dieker lissencephaly syndrome (MDS; OMIM: 247200) according to the size to the deletion. Patients with MDS present with a more severe brain phenotype combined with characteristic dysmorphic features and malformations (Dobyns et al., 1993). The "MDS critical region", differentiating ILS from MDS is approximately 400 kb (Cardoso et al., 2003). Novel co-locating microdeletions affecting the same subtelomere but not leading to ILS or MDS have been described (Mignon-Ravix et al., 2010; Bruno et al., 2010). The studies of Bruno and coworkers (2010) identified eight patients with 17p13.3 microdeletions (two terminal, five interstitial and one terminal deletion with concurrent duplication) not involving the *PAFAH1B1* gene and presenting growth retardation, facial dysmorphisms and developmental delay. A molecular comparison of these patients with previous published cases furthermore identified a new 258 kb critical region encompassing six genes (including *CRK* and *YWHAE*). Interestingly one patient with an interstitial deletion (involving *CRK* but not *YWHAE*) presented with only subtle facial dysmorphisms. This finding suggests that a 109 kb genomic region (encompassing *TUSC5* and *YWHAE*) is responsible for the facial phenotype (Bruno et al., 2010).

Monosomy 22q13

The 22q13.3 deletion syndrome, also called Phelan-McDermid syndrome (OMIM: 606232) or speech-disability syndrome, is a subtelomeric microdeletion syndrome characterized by neonatal hypotonia, global developmental delay, normal to accelerated growth, absent to severely delayed speech, and minor dysmorphic features as well as autistic-like behaviour (Phelan, 2008). Less is known about the exact metal status of the patients suffering from the deletion 22q13.3 syndrome but Misceo and coworkers (2011) described a patient with a mental retardation (IQ 34-49). The microdeletion, ranging from cryptic 100 kb up to cytogenetic visible 9Mb can result from a simple deletion, translocation, ring chromosome formation and less common structural changes in the region containing the *SHANK3* gene located on the long arm of chromosome 22 (22q13.33) (Phelan, 2008) and seems to be the second most frequent subtelomeric imbalance with mental retardation after 1p36 deletion (Ravnan et al., 2006). Equal frequencies of the deletion are detected in male and female. The syndrome is underdiagnosed at laboratory and clinical level nevertheless the detection rate can be improved by additional FISH, aCGH, MLPA and sequencing. In all cases of hyptonia of unknown etiology and in individuals with absent speech, diagnosis of monosomy 22q13.3 should be taken into consideration.

There Is No Specific Molecular Mechanism for Subtelomeric Rearrangements

The composition of the subtelomeric architecture with their flanking regions – segmental duplications with high sequence homology between non-homologous chromosomes – suggests a common mechanism for subtelomeric disturbances due to non-homologous recombination (Linardopoulou et al., 2005). But this assumption is not in line with the observation of missing “hotspots” for subtelomeric rearrangements as for example demonstrated for the most common subtelomeric imbalance, the 1p36 deletion (Heilstedt et al., 2003). Furthermore, the hypothesis subtelomeric-repeat mediated rearrangements is confuted by the dataset of Ravnan et al. (2006). In his large scale study, he identified 112 derivative chromosomes involved in translocation events but failed to identify frequent recurrences involving the same partner chromosomes (Ledbetter and Martin, 2007).

Subtelomeric Rearrangements and Holoprosencephaly (HPE)

Two of the main four HPE genes are located within the sutelomeric regions (*SHH* in 7q and *TGIF* in 18p). Bendavid et al., (2007) therefore proposed that subtelomere screening should be a part in the diagnostic procedure of HPE patients. A MLPA study of 372 patients with HPE furthermore identified imbalances in already known HPE-candidate loci (1q, 20p and 21q) as well as in new loci (1p, 5q, 8p, 17q, 18q, 22q and Xp). This multi-hit result on one hand outlines the multi-hit origin of HPE with a broad phenotypic spectrum and on the other hand implicates a significant role of the subtelomeres in the pathogenesis of this disorder.

Subtelomeric Rearrangements and Facioscapulohumeral Muscular Dystrophy

Facioscapulohumeral muscular dystrophy (FSHD) is an autosomal dominant myopathy and the most common inherited disease of muscle (FSH Consortium, 1998). Almost all FSHD patients carry deletions/ contractions of an integral number of the tandem 3.3 kb tandem repeats D4Z4, located in 4q35 (Van Deutekom et al., 1993). Thereby, Gabellini and coworkers (2002) could show that the genes located upstream of the repeat element are inappropriately overexpressed, and that a regulative multiprotein-complex binds to D4Z4 and mediates transcriptional repression of genes located within 4q35. Although the 4q subtelomere harboring the FSHD locus is specifically anchored with peripheral heterochromatin and generates a reproducible chromosome orientation related to gene expression profiles, the investigation of heterozygous FSHD myoblasts demonstrated no significant displacement of the mutant allele from the periphery (Tam et al., 2004). However, this finding supports a potential role in regulating the heterochromatic state (Tam et al., 2004). Funakoshi and coworkers (1998) described epilepsy and/or mental retardation as a further clinical finding in part of FSHD patients carrying large deletion of FSHD locus. Hence, some FSHD cases represent a syndrome rather than a distinct myopathy (FSH Consortium, 1998). Interestingly, deletions of 4q35.2 are associated with co-morbid psychiatric illness and mental retardation (Pickard et al., 2004), but not with FSHD (Tupler et al., 1996; Pickard et al., 2004).

Subtelomeric Rearrangements and WASH Genes

The human subtelomeric *WASH* genes are concentrations of large interchromosomal duplications and are the third subclass of the Wiskott-Aldrich syndrome protein (WASP) family (OMIM: 301000) (Linardopoulou et al., 2007). Among the latter ones, N-WASP, the neuronal Wiskott-Aldrich syndrome protein, regulates the formation of dendritic spines and synapses in hippocampal neurons (Wegner et al., 2008). It is a known fact that changes in number, size, and shape of dendritic spines are associated with synaptic plasticity and therefore underlies the mental ability (Wegner et al., 2008). Such a connection between mental ability or rather mental impairment and the physiological role of the corresponding gene product couldn't rule out for the *WASH* genes. Rather, investigations of flies lacking the *WASH* genes demonstrated that this subgroup of genes is critical for survival and hence indicate that WASH is functionally distinct from the other two WASP subclasses (Linardopoulou et al., 2007). However, the consequence of the localization of apparently essential genes within rearrangement-prone regions is currently poorly understood.

Differentiation between Pathologic Imbalance and Polymorphism

Beside the identification of pathologic subtelomeric aberrations, the investigation of hitherto more than 25,000 probands as mentioned above revealed also the presence of benign rearrangements of the chromosomal endings. Thus we were able to delineate more general conclusions on this relevant type of structural chromosome alteration: polymorphisms and pathogenic imbalances may often be difficult to differentiate. Clinical features in patients with comparable subtelomeric alterations show a wide variability due to differences in extent, number and functional role of genes involved. Even epigenetic factors might have an influence on phenotypic spectrum. However, in the last years a growing number of persons with subtelomeric alterations without phenotypic effect, classified as subtelomeric polymorphisms, could be observed. Furthermore, the differentiation between patients with *de novo* and familial alterations has changed its diagnostic relevance and clinical assessment in the course of the last years. According to the literature, in the beginning *de novo* imbalances appeared to be more often pathogenic than familial ones. But the diagnosis of polymorphisms occurring *de novo* is increasing and familial cases show a significant change from polymorphism to pathogenic imbalance when inherited. This means that there are some subtelomeric rearrangements that have incomplete penetrance and/or variable expressivity that make some family members with the same imbalance more or less affected. Furthermore, in the scientific literature the two abbreviations "copy number variant" (CNV) and "copy number polymorphism" (CNP) are existing for the benign subtelomeric alterations. The definition of a polymorphism is a benign variant present at a frequency of 1% in the population. This is just the case for few subtelomeric polymorphisms (like 2q; see below) and most subtelomeric imbalances have a lower frequency and must therefore be classified as CNVs (see below) or as regions of the genome that are not sensitive to dosage changes. In order to simplify the description of the benign subtelomeric imbalances within this chapter, we use the abbreviation CNV for all rearrangements without a phenotypic effect.

Frequencies of Subtelomeric Polymorphisms in Different Study Groups

Of the sequence organization of the human chromosome 2q telomere identified a first DNA polymorphism specific to this region (Macina et al., 1994). Knight et al. delineated this common subtelomeric polymorphism in their first large-scale study in 1999, namely a repeat-reduction involving the subtelomeric region 2q37.3 (Knight et al., 1999). In 2001, Fan et al. ascertained a frequency of 6% for the deletion of this locus D2S2986 (Fan et al., 2001). Jalal et al. (2001) reported a frequency of 9.4% for this variant in a population of mentally retarded patients. The 2q subtelomeric polymorphism has been estimated to occur at a frequency of 5% through studies using commercial probes of a larger size as compared to earlier versions (Ballif et al., 2000). In our lab we found a pick-up rate of 10% for the benign 2q deletion within a study group presenting developmental delay, facial dysmorphisms and congenital malformations (unpublished data).

The subtelomeric region 10q is highly polymorphic as well: Martin et al. first described a deletion in a patient and his healthy mother (Martin et al., 2002). A gain in this region was observed by Koolen et al. in a frequency of 2.4% in patients with MR (Koolen et al., 2004). A similar pick-up rate (1.9%) in patients with mental retardation and dysmorphic features was described by Kirchhoff et al. in 2005 (Kirchhoff et al., 2005). Further investigations confirmed the occurrence of deletions and duplications of different size in patients with mental retardation for this polymorphic region (Ravnan et al., 2006).

One might speculate that these two polymorphisms occur very frequently in routine diagnoses and oftentimes are not published due to widespread tacit acceptance of their existence. Hence, their real frequency may be much higher.

The frequency of pathogenic aberrations and polymorphisms is not the same in the general population as compared to selected groups of patients. The majority of investigated individuals have hitherto been analyzed on account of mental retardation combined with other clinically relevant features. So it was indeed a surprise when Ballif et al. detected a subtelomere polymorphism rate of 7% versus 2.6% pathogenic imbalances in a cohort of 154 patients presenting with mental retardation and dysmorphic features (Ballif et al., 2000). Joyce et al. (2001) detected no pathogenic aberrations in a screening study of 200 patients with idiopathic mental retardation, but two polymorphisms (deletion 4q and duplication 17q) in a cohort of 150 healthy subjects (pick-up rate of 1.3%). Other cohort screening procedures in patients and controls have resulted in equal detection rates for both polymorphisms and pathogenic imbalances. In some cases, benign variants have even achieved higher pick-up rates. For example, Rooms et al. used MLPA to examine their cohort of 275 unselected patients presenting with idiopathic mental retardation and found 1.8% de novo rearrangements, 1.1% familial cases of alterations which were probably causing the phenotype and 1.5% polymorphisms (Rooms et al., 2006). Shao et al. screened 5380 consecutive clinical cases using DNA array tests and found copy number changes in 591 patients (pick-up rate 11%), among whom pathogenic aberrations were observed in 238 patients (4.4% of total) (Shao et al., 2007). These data imply that 6.6% of copy number changes were subtelomeric polymorphisms and thus were found more often than imbalances of pathogenic character.

The studies summarized above illustrate the differences in the frequencies of pathogenic imbalances and polymorphisms in different patient cohorts and in the general population obviously caused by the ascertainment bias, but they also show that the results are independent of the investigation method applied.

Characterization of Distal Subtelomeric Polymorphisms

The descriptions mentioned below are based on 50 publications (studies or case reports) over a period of 17 years. They include a total of 220 patients presenting clinical hallmarks and a characterized polymorphism, 155 transmitting parents or further healthy family members with the same polymorphism as wells as 82 healthy individuals also carrying a subtelomeric polymorphism. Most of the screening studies – identifying the patients with polymorphisms and the transmitting parents – were performed within study cohorts with isolated mental retardation or mental impairment in addition with congenital malformations and facial dysmorphisms.

To date, 41 subtelomeric endings have been investigated and polymorphisms were identified for 35 regions (85.4%) (Adeyinka et al., 2005; Baker et al., 2002a+b; Balikova et al., 2007; Ballif et al., 2000; Barber 2005; Barber 2008; Bejjani et al., 2005; Bonaglia et al., 2003; Bonaglia et al., 2007; Bonaglia et al., 2008; Dawson et al., 2002; DeScipio et al., 2008; Erjavec-Škerget et al., 2006; Fan et al., 2001; Flint and Knight, 2003; Gersh et al., 1995; Gignac et al., 2006; Gilmore et al., 2001; Harada et al., 2004; Hengstschläger et al., 2005; Horsley et al., 1998; Horsley et al., 2001; Isidor et al., 2008; Jalal et al., 2001; Jalal et al., 2003; Joyce et al., 2001, Kirchhoff et al., 2005; Knight et al., 1995; Knight et al., 1999; Koolen et al., 2004; Martin et al., 2002; Martin et al., 2007, Morales et al., 2007; Pettenati et al., 1992, Ravnan et al., 2006; Reddy, 1999; Riegel et al., 2001; Rio et al., 2002; Rooms et al., 2006, Roos et al., 2008; Rosenberg et al., 2001; Shaffer et al., 1999; Shuib et al., 2009; Stegmann et al., 2008; Van Bon et al., 2008; Van Karnebeek et al., 2002; Zahed et al., 2008). 31 of these regions are listed in the existing database: The Transmitted Sub-Telomeric Imbalance collection; *http://www.ngrl.org.uk/Wessex/subtel_collection.htm*, which was unfortunately updated for the last time in August 2008. From our point of view, some specific cases should not be included in the imbalance collection in which affected child and transmitting parent show similar clinical abnormalities affecting the subtelomeres 6q (Adeyinka et al., 2005; Rooms et al., 2006), and 18p (Adeyinka et al., 2005) as well as 18q (Koolen et al., 2004). Contrariwise other cases of a 6q (Balikova et al., 2007) and a 18p subtelomeric deletion (Horsley et al., 2009) should be included, as the aberration is inherited from a healthy parent to an affected child. Additional polymorphic regions which should be included in the register are benign deletions of 5p (Gersh et al., 1995; Bejjani et al., 2005); 7p (Jalal et al., 2003; Adeyinka et al., 2005); 7q (Rosenberg et al., 2001) and a benign duplication of 19p (Stegmann et al., 2008). Besides, the data base is still incomplete regarding a number of very relevant polymorphisms: these are deletions of 8p (Adeyinka et al., 2005; Gilmore et al., 2001; Pettenati et al., 1992 and Reddy, 1999); 15q (Adeyinka et al., 2005) and 16q (Koolen et al., 2004) as well as duplications of 9p (Baker et al., 2002; Kichhoff et al., 2005); 16p (Stegmann et al., 2008) and 17p (Morales et al., 2007; Ravnan et al., 2006). Some of these polymorphisms appear to be very widespread within the general population (e.g. deletions of 2q, 10q and Xp) while others are based on single or few reports (for example duplications of 5q (Rooms et al., 2006), 8q (Ravnan et al., 2006), 11q (Balikova et al., 2007), 16p (Stegmann et al., 2008), 19p (Stegmann et al., 2008), 21q (Bonaglia et al., 2007) and deletions of 6q (Balikova et al., 2007), 11p (Koolen et al., 2004), 16q (Koolen et al., 2004), 17q (Balikova et al., 2007), 18p (Horsley et al., 2009). Furthermore, there is still missing documentation on subtelomeric regions showing the combination of a cryptic deletion and duplication at the same time.

With regard to the growing list of subtelomeric polymorphisms we postulate that screening procedures based on a single test locus do not provide enough information to allow an unambiguous characterization. In this context, the above-mentioned multitude of newly developed medium-throughput analysis systems seems to be a positive development: using these systems, large-scale studies can and should be carried out with healthy subjects – perhaps subdivided into different ethnic cohorts – and/or with other various large cohorts involving, for example, patients with infertility disorders or couples with a history of recurrent miscarriages. The use of large collectives such as the EPR (Environmental Polymorphisms Registry), a well characterized and diverse DNA resource (Chulada et al., 2008) would be instrumental in screening the general population on the one hand and clinic patients on the other hand in order to determine the frequency of individual subtelomeric polymorphisms.

In the pre-microarray era, this has only been done for two relatively small groups. Cockwell et al. analyzed 50 couples with a history of recurrent miscarriages (Cockwell et al., 2003). Bejjani et al. (2005) investigated a group of 50 healthy individuals in order to validate their DNA array test and detected length polymorphisms for 5q (deletion in 3 cases = 6%), 6p (duplication in 15 cases = 30%) and 14q (deletion in 30 cases = 60%). Anyway, the current use of genome-wide microarrays – also detecting subtelomeric aberrations – was also utilized for a broad spectrum of different studies. Some of them were performed on normal populations and allowed the coverage of subtelomeric imbalances as being polymorphic and are collected in the database of genomic variants (*http://projects.tcag.ca/variation/*) and DECIPHER (http://decipher.sanger.ac.uk/application/). However, further screening studies, like the Sanger-project performed at this stage, will even more extend our knowledge on the number of polymorphic subtelomeric regions as well as the magnitude of the tolerable segments by determining the exact boundaries between subtelomeric polymorphism and pathogenic imbalance and allow to complete and to precise the list (see table 1). Hence, in the near future the constitution of a microarray-data supplemented list of benign subtelomeric aberrations will be possible.

Inherited (subtelomeric) alterations are usually assumed to be non-causative for a diagnosed phenotype (Thuresson et al., 2007). However, it is difficult to determine whether such rearrangements are of no pathological significance, or if they contribute to the phenotype by other mechanisms such as non-penetrance (Yobb et al., 2005), intrafamilial variance of the imbalances at the molecular level (Joyce et al., 2001) or genomic imprinting (Thuresson et al., 2007). Adeyinka and co-workers reported on a family with a cryptic 20p deletion (Adeyinka et al., 2005). This imbalance was present in two siblings, both of whom had mild to moderate developmental delay, severe headaches, small hands and minor anomalies. The same cryptic terminal deletion was identified in the mother, who had merely experienced headaches and hearing loss. Adeyinka and co-workers (2005) postulated a chromosomal anticipation mechanism involving an increasing size of the deletion, which would in turn cause the differing phenotypes. However, without analysis of deletion size/ breakpoint characterization, the assumption of an increasing size of the deletion is a very hypothetical explanation and an undetected mosaicism in a mildly affected or healthy parent should also be considered in this context.

Tab. 1: Survey on tolerable subtelomeric polymorphisms in size and the identified benchmark genes

Sub-telomere	sizes of tolerable gains and losses	Number of affected genes	Boundary gene(s)	References
1q	Gain of 2.9 Mb*	83	n.d.	Balikova et al., 2007
	Loss of 1.6 Mb	n.d.	*CIAS1*	Roos et al., 2008
	Loss of 0.4 Mb	n.d.	n.d.	Van Bon et al., 2008
2p	Loss of 0.14-0.33 Mb	n.d.	n.d.	Gignac et al., 2006
2q	Loss of 0.24-0.29 Mb	n.d.	n.d.	Van Karnebeek et al., 2002
	Loss of 1.7 Mb	37	n.d.	Balikova et al., 2007
3p	Gain of 1.5 Mb	n.d.	n.d.	Martin et al., 2007
	Loss of 2.8 Mb	8	n.d.	Balikova et al., 2007
	Loss of 1.0 Mb	n.d	*(CHL1)*	DeScipio et al., 2008
	Loss of 8.6 Mb	n.d..	*SRGAP3*	Shuib et al., 2009
4p	Loss of 0.4 - 0.5 Mb	11-8	n.d.	Balikova et al., 2007
	Loss of>1.11 Mb	n.d.	n.d.	Zahed et al., 2008
4q	Gain of 1.15 - 1.3 Mb*	22	n.d.	Balikova et al., 2007
	Gain of 1.2 Mb	n.d.	n.d.	Martin et al., 2007
	Loss of 1.15-1.3 Mb	22	n.d.	Balikova et al., 2007
	Loss of 1.0 Mb	n.d.	n.d.	Martin et al., 2007
6p	Gain of 0.2 Mb	2 (both are olfactory receptor genes)	n.d.	Bonaglia et al., 2003, 2007
6q	Loss of 0.8 - 0.6 Mb	9	n.d.	Balikova et al., 2007
9p	Loss of 0.3 Mb	n.d.	n.d.	Martin et al., 2007
10q	Gain of 7.8 Mb*	78	n.d.	Balikova et al., 2007
	Gain of 0.17 Mb	n.d.	n.d.	Martin et al., 2007
	Loss of 3.6 Mb	59	n.d.	Balikova et al., 2007
	Loss of 1.3 Mb	n.d.	n.d.	Martin et al., 2007
	Loss of 0.1 Mb	n.d.	n.d.	Martin et al., 2007
11q	Gain of 0.34 Mb	3	n.d.	Balikova et al., 2007
12p	Loss of 1.65 Mb	10	n.d.	Baker et al., 2002a+b
15q	Gain of 0.54 Mb	n.d.	n.d.	Martin et al., 2007
16p	Loss of0.27 Mb	15	n.d.	Horsley et al., 2001
17p	Loss of 0.6 Mb	n.d.	n.d.	Martin et al., 2002
17p13.3 (interstitial)	Loss of 0.27 - 0.36 Mb*	4	n.d.	Balikova et al., 2007
	Loss of 0.65 Mb	n.d.	n.d.	Barber, 2008
17q	Loss of 0.8 Mb*	16	n.d.	Balikova et al., 2007
18q23 (interstitial)	Gain of 0.45 Mb	7		Isidor et al., 2008
20q	Gain of 0.3 Mb	n.d.	n.d.	Bonaglia et al., 2003, 2007
21q	Gain of 0.25 Mb	n.d.	n.d.	Bonaglia et al., 2007
	Loss of 1.6 Mb	n.d.	n.d.	Martin et al., 2007
Xp	Loss of 1.15 - 1.3 Mb*	6-7	n.d.	Balikova et al., 2007
Yq	Loss of0.15/ >0.16 Mb	6/5	n.d.	Balikova et al., 2007
	Loss of0.32 Mb	a.d.	n.d.	Martin et al., 2007

Characterization of Interstitial Subtelomeric Polymorphisms

Up to now, interstitial subtelomeric polymorphisms seem to be rare imbalances as only single cases are reported. In their presentation of the TEL-array method, DeScipio and his group (2008) described a case in which the FISH analysis seemed to indicate a terminal deletion of the 14q subtelomere combined with a duplication of 19q. Further characterization of this imbalance using the TEL-array method revealed that the deletion is smaller and located more proximately than expected after FISH studies, i.e. an interstitial imbalance, which has previously been shown to be a benign variant (DeScipio et al., 2008). Furthermore, Barber (2008) reported on an affected boy and his *inconspicuous* mother who carried a 0.65 Mb interstitial deletion in 17p13.3 which included the *RPH3AL* and *GEMIN4* genes, distal to the Miller-Dieker region. Isidor and coworkers (2008) published the case of a fetus with multiple congenital anomalies and its healthy father; both individuals presented an interstitial amplification in 18q23 detected by subtelomere MLPA, FISH and were further characterized by DNA array-testing. This duplicated region of 0.45Mb contained seven genes (*Q8N7E7*, *CTDP1*, *Q6ZVY3*, *KCNG2*, *PQLC1*, *TXNL4A* and *C18orf22*). Telomeric located to the duplication eighteen probes showed normal intensity ratios in the array testing indicating that the duplication was interstitial.

These cases imply that sometimes firstly expected terminal polymorphisms betimes can be disclosed as interstitial subtelomeric polymorphisms after DNA array testing and occasionally represent CNVs (copy number variations) commonly detected using this method.

Boundaries between Polymorphisms and Pathogenic Imbalance and the Role of the Size of Variants

Upon reviewing reports of subtelomeric polymorphisms, Martin et al. established their so-called molecular ruler concept which the authors applied to the endings of chromosome 16p and 17p (Martin et al., 2002). The results of these investigations on the defined regions enabled them to detect the exact boundary between pathogenic rearrangements and benign variants: the largest deletion in their investigation with no apparent phenotypic effect had an extent of approximately 600 kb on 17p. The monosomy for 17p affected several genes for which haploinsufficiency was apparently not associated with clinical consequences. The situation changed dramatically when the partial monosomy 17p encompassed 1-2 Mb. It is then associated with the characteristic clinical picture of the Miller-Dieker syndrome and/or lissencephaly (see above). Baker et al. (2002a+b) used the same strategy in order to characterize the boundary between a benign variant and a pathogenic aberration for the subtelomeric region of chromosome 12p. In their case, the loss of 1.65 Mb genomic material was compatible with a normal phenotype which was detected in the mother, who transmitted this alteration to her affected son while herself presenting "only" with learning difficulties. The region for which haploinsufficiency seems to be without any serious consequences in the mother includes 10 genes (among them *SLC6A12* and *WNT5B*). According to this study, more proximally located genes within the flanking gene-rich region appear to be candidates for the specific 12p-deletion phenotype. In 2007, Balikova et al. described gains and losses, including the sizes which can be tolerated without phenotypical consequences, for 15 subtelomeres in 12 families (duplications of 1q, 4q, 10q, 11q and deletions of 2q, 3p, 4p, 4q, 6q, 10q, 17p, 17q, Xp, Yq; see table 1) (Balikova et al., 2007). In their study they identified five imbalances without apparent phenotypic effects. However, they were not able to identify a candidate gene for the boundary between polymorphism and pathogenetic aberration among the subtelomeres they characterized in their study. For chromosome 1q, a comparison of the breakpoints identified in two case reports was instrumental in determining the exact boundary line separating pathogenic imbalance from benign subtelomeric variant (Roos et al., 2008). We were able to show that deletions of the terminal 1.6 Mb are without phenotypical consequences, and to identify *CIAS1* as the critical gene for clinical manifestation of the imbalanced karyotype (see table 1; Roos et al., 2008). Concerning the determination of a polymorphism boundary for each subtelomeric ending, 3q is a very challenging chromosomal part: DeScipio et al. (2008) described a patient with a 3p deletion 1 Mb in size, detected by TEL-array CGH, and pinpointed the *CHL1* gene as the first clinically relevant gene within the deleted interval. Rooms et al. (2006) published a familial case of a putative partial 3pter monosomy in an affected boy and his healthy mother. Due to a polymorphism within the *CHL1* gene, ligation of the MLPA probe was inhibited, preventing amplification of the region in the patient and his healthy mother. The resulting pseudo deletion in both cases further emphasizes the caution needed in interpreting screening results, especially with regard to its broad application in diagnostic procedures. Taking into account other reports, Endris et al., (2002) and Takagishi et al., (2006) reported on patients with terminal cytogenetic visible 3p deletions and minimal phenotypic features. In case of the patients described by Takagishi and his group (2006), the breakpoint for the terminal deletion could be located between 8.65 and 10.16 Mb. Knight et al. (1995) published a report on a family (mother and daughter) carrying a cytogenetically visible 3p interstitial deletion not associated with any pathogenic consequences. In 2005, Adeyinka and co-workers reported a further case involving a cytogenetically visible deletion on 3p. Their patient presented with mild to moderate developmental delay, macrocephaly, minor anomalies and a single seizure episode. Her father carried the same deletion but showed no clinical features apart from macrocephaly. The authors suggested a mechanism of reduced penetrance for 3p deletion phenotypes in some of the carriers (Adeyinka et al., 2005). In 2009, Shuib and co-workers reported about a patient carrying a ~8.6 Mb deletion without any signs of a 3p minus syndrome. Genes deleted in this patient included *ITPR1*, *CNTN4*, *CHL1*, *LRRN1*, *SETMAR*, *IL5RA* and *TRNT1*. Hence, *CHL1* seems not to be the candidate for a polymorphism boundary as postulated by DeScipio et al., (2008). With regard to the other phenotypically unaffected cases mentioned above, Shuib concluded that the candidate genes for terminal 3p minus associated mental retardation should map centromeric to their detected deletion breakpoint (~8,6 Mb) (Shuib et al., 2009). *SRGAP3* (*MEGAP*) maps approximately 9 Mb from the telomere and is therefore retained in the patients published by Shuib et al., (2009) and Takagishi et al., (2006). Endris and co-workers (2002) described a disruption of the *SRGAP3* gene in a patient with a constitutional chromosomal translocation, which presented with hypotonia and severe mental retardation. Furthermore, *SRGAP3* was deleted in 13 patients with terminal 3p deletions and mental retardation as one of their clinical features (Shuib et al., 2009). All this data makes the *SRGAP3* gene a plausible candidate at least for the mental retardation in 3p minus cases (see table 1; Endris et al., 2002; Shuib et al., 2009).

In interpreting these boundaries it is essential to keep in mind that the results are based on single case studies. Thus, the degree to which the gain or loss of subtelomeric genomic material can be tolerated may be even higher, and more genes may be tolerant of a haploinsufficiency than has previously been assumed. For example, DeScipio et al. (2008)

described a 1.0 Mb region for 3p which may be lost without apparent phenotypic consequences, whereas Balikova et al. (2007) identified a haploinsufficient tolerant region of 2.8 Mb size for the same region (see table 1) and Shuib et al., (2009) highlighted the tolerance for a 3p haploinsufficency with their report of a 8.6 Mb acceptable loss. Furthermore, in their same study, Balikova et al. (2007) established a 0.27-0.36 Mb region for 17p which may be deleted without effect, whereas Martin et al. (2002) described a 0.6 Mb polymorphic region for the 17p subtelomere (see table 1). These observations further emphasize that the real size of gains and losses which may be tolerated as benign variants can only be detected with the help of large-scale screening studies and breakpoint mapping, based on molecular karyotyping. The collection of these results in the database of genomic variants *(http://projects.tcag.ca/variation/)* and DECIPHER (database of chromosomal imbalance and phenotype in humans using Ensembl resources; https://decipher.sanger.ac.uk/application/) allows each one an accurate genotype-phenotype correlation by interpreting and validation of detected subtelomeric imbalances.

Furthermore, this type of screening of the general population – like the Sanger-genome-wide array project, performed at this stage – enables the research community to collect the data required for a reliable interpretation also of subtelomeric imbalances and for the completion of the existing database (The Transmitted Sub-Telomeric Imbalance Collection; *http://www.ngrl.org.uk/Wessex/subtel_collection.htm*), a tool which will be valuable in determining the exact boundaries between polymorphisms and pathogenic imbalances.

Currently, subtelomere screening in some laboratories is used before genome-wide molecular karyotyping is carried out. A reason could be availability, but on the other hand the data presented in this review stresses the necessity of proving the subtelomere screening results by molecular karyotyping. A selective investigation of the subtelomeric regions therefore seems not to guarantee the most benefit for the patients before the exact boundaries are defined and the probes used in discriminatory subtelomere screening procedures are revalidated.

Subtelomere Screening in Prenatal Diagnosis

Subtelomere screening is becoming ever more popular in prenatal diagnosis, still using FISH techniques (Cotter et al., 2003; Gignac et al., 2006) and MLPA (Roselló et al., 2010; Kjaergaard et al., 2010), despite the many gaps in our knowledge about benign imbalances. Therefore, a standard procedure must be developed and for all investigated subtelomeric regions a precise definition is required on alterations that can be tolerated as neutral dosage imbalances on the genetic relevance or irrelevance of a subtelomeric alteration. Especially in this diagnostic context, it has to be considered that decisions must be made within a very short time, as they might result in the termination of a pregnancy.

A particularly important aspect at prenatal diagnosis are subtelomeric changes that are subject to intrafamilial variance on the molecular level (Adeyinka et al., 2005; Kirchhoff et al., 2005), unequal crossing over at pachytene or genes affected by imbalance following genomic imprinting (Thuresson et al., 2007).

References

Adeyinka A, Adams SA, Lorentz CP, Van Dyke DL, Jalal SM 2005. Subtelomere deletions and translocations are frequently familial. *Am J Med Genet,* 2005 135(1): 28-35.

Ahn JW, Ogilvie CM, Welch A, Thomas H, Madula R, Hills A, Donaghue C, Mann K 2007. Detection of subtelomere imbalance using MLPA: validation, development of an analysis protocol, and application in a diagnostic centre. *BMC Med Genet,* 2007 8: 9.

Aldred MA, Sanford RO, Thomas NS, Barrow MA, Wilson LC, Brueton LA, Bonaglia MC, Hennekam RC, Eng C, Dennis NR, Trembath RC 2004. Molecular analysis of 20 patients with 2q37.3 monosomy: definition of minimum deletion intervals for key phenotypes. *J Med Genet,* 41(6):433-439.

Armour JA, Sismani C, Patsalis PC, Cross G 2000. Measurement of locus copy number by hybridisation with amplifiable probes. *Nucleic Acids Res,* 28(2): 605-609.

Baker E, Hinton L, Callen DF, Altree M, Dobbie A, Eyre HJ,Sutherland GR, Thompson E, Thompson P, Woollatt E, Haan E 2002a. Study of 250 children with idiopathic mental retardation reveals nine cryptic and diverse subtelomeric chromosome anomalies. *Am J Med Genet,* 107(4): 285-293.

Baker E, Hinton L, Callen DF, Haan EA, Dobbie A, Sutherland GR 2002b. A familial cryptic subtelomeric deletion 12p with variable phenotypic effect. *Clin Genet,* 61(3): 198-201.

Barber JC 2005. Directly transmitted unbalanced chromosome abnormalities and euchromatic variants. *J Med Genet,* 42(8): 609-629.

Battaglia A and Shaffer LG 2008. 1p36 deletion syndrome. *Gene Reviews,* PMID: 20301370.

Balikova I, Menten B, de Ravel T, Le Caignec C, Thienpont B, Urbina M, Doco-Fenzy M, de Rademaeker M, Mortier G, Kooy F, van den Ende J, Devriendt K, Fryns JP, Speleman F, Vermeesch JR 2007. Subtelomeric imbalances in phenotypically normal individuals. *Hum Mutat,* 28(10): 958-967.

Ballif BC, Kashork CD, Shaffer LG 2000. The promise and pitfalls of telomere region-specific probes. *Am J Hum Genet,* 67(5): 1356-1359.

Ballif BC, Sulpizio SG, Lloyd RM, Minier SL, Theisen A, Bejjani BA, Shaffer LG 2007. The clinical utility of enhanced subtelomeric coverage in array CGH. *Am J Med Genet,* 143A(16): 1850-1857.

Barber JC 2005. Directly transmitted unbalanced chromosome abnormalities and euchromatic variants. *J Med Genet,* 42(8): 609-629.

Barber JC 2008. Chromosomal copy number variation. *European Cytogeneticists Association Newsletter* 22: 6-14.

Baroncini A, Rivieri F, Capucci A, Croci G, Franchi F, Sensi A, Battaglia P, Aiello V, Calzolari E 2005. FISH screening for subtelomeric rearrangements in 219 patients with idiopathic mental retardation and normal karyotype. *Eur J Med Genet,* 48(4): 388-396.

Bejjani BA, Saleki R, Ballif BC, Rorem EA, Sundin K, Theisen A, Kashork CD, Shaffer LG 2005. Use of targeted array-based CGH for the clinical diagnosis of chromosomal imbalance: is less more? *Am J Med Genet,* 134(3): 259-267.

Bendavid C, Dubourg C, Pasquier L, Gicquel I, Le Gallou S, Mottier S, Durou MR, Henry C, Odent S, David V 2007. MLPA screening reveals novel subtelomeric rearrangements in holoprosencephaly. *Hum Mutat,* 28(12): 1189-1197.

Boehm D, Herold S, Kuechler A, Liehr T, Laccone F 2004. Rapid detection of subtelomeric deletion/duplication by novel real-time quantitative PCR using SYBR-green dye. *Hum Mutat*, 23: 368-378.

Bonaglia MC, Giorda R, Cavallini A, Pramparo T, Rocchi M, Borgatti R, Zuffardi O 2003. Distal trisomy 6p and 20q owing to the concurrent transposition of distal 6p and 20q to the 22q telomere: a genomic polymorphism? *J Med Genet,* 40(8): e94.

Bonaglia MC, Marelli S, Gottardi G, Zucca C, Pramparo T, Giordo R, Grasso R, Borgatti R, Zuffardi O 2007. Subtelomeric trisomy 21q: a new benign chromosomal variant. *Eur J Med Genet,* 50(1): 54-59.

Bonaglia MC, Giorda R, Beri S, Peters GB, Kirk EP, Hung D, Ciccone R, Gottardi G,Zuffardi O 2008. Concurrent transposition of distal 6p and 20q to the 22q telomere: a recurrent benign chromosomal variant. *Eur J Med Genet,* 51(2): 148-155.

Brown J, Saracoglu K, Uhrig S, Speicher MR, Eils R, Kearny L 2001. Subtelomeric chromosome rearrangements are detected using an innovative 12-color FISH assay (M-TEL). *Nat Med,* 7: 497-501.

Bruno DL, Anderlid BM, Lindstrand A, van Ravenswaaij-Arts C, Ganesamoorthy D, Lundin J, Martin CL, Douglas J, Nowak C, Adam MP, Kooy RF, Van der Aa N, Reyniers E, Vandeweyer G, Stolte-Dijkstra I, Dijkhuizen T, Yeung A, Delatycki M, Borgström B, Thelin L, Cardoso C, van Bon B, Pfundt R, de Vries BB, Wallin A, Amor DJ, James PA, Slater HR, Schoumans J 2010. Further molecular and clinical delineation of co-locating 17p13.3 microdeletions and microduplications that show distinctive phenotypes. *J Med Genet,* 47(5): 299-311.

Bruno DL, Burgess T, Ren H, Nouri S, Pertile MD, Francis DI, Norris F, Kenney BK, Schouten J, Choo KHA, Slater HR 2006. High-throughput analysis of chromosome abnormality in spontaneous miscarriage using an MLPA subtelomere assay with an ancillary FISH test for polyploidy. *Am J Med Genet,* 140A: 2786-2793.

Cardoso C, Leventer RJ, Ward HL, Toyo-Oka K, Chung J, Gross A, Martin CL, Allanson J, Pilz DT, Olney AH, Mutchinick OM, Hirotsune S, Wynshaw-Boris A, Dobyns WB, Ledbetter DH 2003. Refinement of a 400-kb critical region allows genotypic differentiation between isolated lissencephaly, Miller-Dieker syndrome , and other phenotypes secondary to deletions of 17p13.3. *Am J Hum Genet*, 72(4): 918-930.

Chute I, Le Y, Ashley T, Dobson MJ 1997. The telomere -associated DNA from human chromosome 20p contains a pseudotelomere structure and shares sequences with the subtelomeric regions of 4q and 18p. *Genomics,* 46(1): 51-60.

Cerruti Mainardi P 2006. Cri-du-chat syndrome. *Orphanet J Rare Dis,* 5(1): 33.

Chulada PC, Vahdat HL, Sharp RR, Delozier TC, Watkins PB, Pusek SN, Blackshear PJ 2008. The Environmental Polymorphisms Registry: a DNA resource to study genetic susceptibility loci. *Hum Genet,* 123(2): 207-214.

Cockwell AE, Jacobs PA, Beal SJ, Crolla JA 2003. A study of cryptic terminal chromosome rearrangements in recurrent miscarriage couples detects unsuspected acrocentric pericentromeric abnormalities. *Hum Genet,* 112(3): 298-302.

Cornish KM, Cross G, Green A, Willatt L, Bradsh JM 1999. A neurophysiological-genetic profile of atypical Cri-du-chat syndrome: implications for prognosis. *J Med Genet*, 36: 567-570.

Cotter PD, Musci TJ, Norton ME 2003. Rapid prenatal diagnosis in translocation carriers by interphase FISH with chromosome-specific subtelomere probes. *Am J Med Genet,* 122A(1): 1-5.

Davies AF, Kirby TL, Docherty Z, Ogilvie CM 2003. Characterization of terminal chromosome anomalies using multisubtelomere FISH. *Am J Med Genet,* 120A(4): 483-489.

Dawson AJ, Putnam S, Schultz J, Riordan D, Prasad C, Greenberg CR, Chodirker BN, Mhanni AA, Chudley AE 2002. Cryptic chromosome rearrangements detected by subtelomere assay in patients with mental retardation and dysmorphic features. *Clin Genet,* 62(6): 488-494.

DeScipio C, Spinner NB, Kaur M, Yaeger D, Conlin LK, Ambrosini A, Hu S, Shan S, Krantz IDRiethman H 2008. Fine-mapping subtelomeric deletions and duplications by comparative genomic hybridization in 42 individuals. *Am J Med Genet,* 146A(6): 730-739.

De Vries BB, Lees M, Knight SJ, Regan R, Corney D, Flint J, Barnicoat A, Winter RM 2001a. Submicroscopic 8pter deletion, mild mental retardation, and behavioral problems caused by a familial t(8;20)(p23;p13). *Am J Med Genet,* 99: 314-319.

De Vries BBA, White SM, Knight SJL, Regan R, Homfray T, Young ID, Super M, McKeown C, Splitt M, Quarrell OWJ, Trainer AH, Niermeijer MF, Malcolm S, Flint J, Hurst JA, Winter RM 2001b. Clinical studies on submicroscopic subtelomeric rearrangements: a checklist. *J Med Genet,* 38(3): 145-150.

De Vries BBA, Winter R, Schinzel A, van Ravenswaaij-Arts C 2003. Telomeres: A diagnosis at the end of the chromosomes. *J Med Genet,* 40: 385-398.

Dobyns WB, Reiner O, Carrozzo R, Ledbetter DH 1993. Lissencephaly. A human brain malformation associated with deletion of the LIS1 gene located at chromosome 17p13.*JAMA, 270*(23): 2838-2842.

Dunham MA, Neumann AA, Fasching CL, Reddel RR 2000. Telomere maintenance by recombination in human cells. *Nat Genet,* 26(4): 447-450.

Edelmann L and Hirschhorn K 2009.Clinical utility of array CGH for the detection of chromosomal imbalances associated with mental retardation and multiple congenital anomalies. *Ann N Y Acad Sci,* 1151: 157-166.

Eggermann K, Schönherr N, Ranke MB, Wollmann HA, Binder G, Eggermann T 2008. Search for Subtelomeric Imbalances by Multiplex Ligation-Dependent Probe Amplification in Silver-Russell Syndrome. *Genet Test,* 12(1): 111-113.

Endele S, Fuhry M, Pak SJ, Zabel BU, Winterpacht A 1999. LETM1, a novel gene encoding a putative EF-hand Ca(2+)-binding protein, flanks the Wolf-Hirschhorn syndrome (WHS) critical region and is deleted in most WHS patients. *Genomics,* 60(2): 218-225.

Endris V, Wogatzky B, Leimer U, Bartsch D, Zatyka M, Latif F, Maher ER, Tariverdian G, Kirsch S, Karch D, Rappold GA 2002. The novel Rho-GTPase activating gene MEGAP/srGAP3 has a putative role in severe mental retardation. *Proc Natl Acad Sci USA*, 99: 11754-11759.

Engels H, Ehrbrecht A, Zahn S, Bosse K, Vrolijk, H, White S, Kalscheuer V, Hoovers JMN, Schwanitz G, Propping P, Tanke HJ, WiegantJ, Raap AK 2003. Comprehensive analysis of human subtelomeres with conbined binary labelling fluorescence in situ hybridisation. *Eur J Hum Genet,* 11: 643-651.

Erjavec-Škerget A, Stangler-Herodez S, Zagorac A, Zagradisnik B, Kokalj-Vokac N 2006. Subtelomeric chromosome rearrangements in children with idiopathic mental retardation: applicability of three molecular-cytogenetic methods. *Croat Med J,* 47(6): 841-850.

Estabrooks LL, Lamb AN, Kirkman HN, Callanan NP, Rao KW 1992. A molecular deletion of distal chromosome 4p in two families with a satellited chromosome 4 lacking the Wolf-Hirschhorn syndrome phenotype. *Am J Hum Genet,* 51(5): 971- 918.

Fan YS, Zhang Y, Speevak M, Farrell S, Jung JH, Siu VM 2001. Detection of submicroscopic aberrations in patients with unexplained mental retardation by fluorescence in situ hybridization using multiple subtelomeric probes. *Genet Med,* 3(6): 416-421.

Freitas-Junior LH, Bottius E, Pirrit LA, Deitsch KW, Scheidig C, Guinet F, Nehrbass U, Wellems TE, Scherf A 2000. Frequent ectopic recombination of virulence factor genes in telomeric chromosome clusters of P. falciparum. *Nature,* 407(6807): 1018-1022.

FSH Consortium 1998. Facioscapulohumeral dystrophy: a distinct regional myopathy with a novel molecular pathogenesis. *Ann. Neurol,* 43: 279-282.

Flint J, Bates GP, Clark K, Dorman A, Willingham D, Roe BA, Micklem G, Higgs DR, Louis EJ 1997. Sequence comparison of human and yeast telomeres identifies structurally distinct subtelomeric domains. *Hum Mol Genet,* 6(8): 1305-1313.

Flint J and Knight S 2003. The use of telomere probes to investigate submicroscopic rearrangements associated with mental retardation. *Curr Opin Genet Dev,* 13(3): 310-316.

Flint J, Rochette J, Craddock CF, Dodé C, Vignes B, Horsley SW, Kearney L, Buckle VJ, Ayyub H, Higgs DR 1996. Chromosomal stabilisation by a subtelomeric rearrangement involving two closely related Alu elements. *Hum Mol Genet,* 5(8): 1163-1169.

Funakoshi M, Goto K, Arahata K 1998. Epilepsy and mental retardation in a subset of early onset 4q35-facioscapulohumeral muscular dystrophy. *Neurology,* 50: 1791-1794.

Gabellini D, Green MR, Tupler R 2002. Inappropriate gene activation in FSHD: a repressor complex binds a chromosomal repeat deleted in dystrophic muscle. Cell, 110: 339-348.

Gajecka M, Mackay KL, Shaffer LG 2007. Monosomy 1p36 deletion syndrome *Am J Med Genet,* 145C(4): 346-356.

Gandelman KY, Gibson L, Meyn MS, Yang-Feng TL 1992. Molecular definition of the smallest region of deletion overlap in the Wolf-Hirschhorn syndrome. *Am J Hum Genet,* 51(3): 571-518.

Gersh M, Goodart SA, Pasztor LM, Harris DJ, Weiss L, Overhauser J 1995. Evidence for a distinct region causing a cat-like cry in patients with 5p deletions. *Am J Hum Genet,* 56: 1404-1410.

Gignac J, Danis K, Tihy F, Lemyre E 2006. Prenatal detection of subtelomeric rearrangements by multi-subtelomere FISH in a cohort of fetuses with major malformations. *Am J Med Genet,* 140A: 2768-2775.

Gilmore L, Cuskelly M, Jobling A, Smith S 2001. Deletion of 8p: a report of a child with normal intelligence. *Dev Med Child Neurol,* 43(12): 843-846.

Harada N, Hatchwell E, Okamoto N, Tsukahara M, Kurosawa K, Kawame H, Kondoh T, Ohashi H, Tsukino R, Kondoh Y, Shimokawa O, Ida T, Nagai T, Fukushima Y, Yoshiura K, Niikawa N, Matsumoto N 2004. Subtelomere specific microarray based comparative genomic hybridisation: a rapid detection system for cryptic rearrangements in idiopathic mental retardation. *J Med Genet,* 41(2): 130-136.

Heilstedt HA, Ballif BC, Howard LA, Kashork CD, Shaffer LG 2003. Population data suggest that deletions of 1p36 are a relatively common chromosome abnormality. *Clin Genet,* 64(4): 310-316.

Hengstschläger M, Prusa A, Repa C, Deutinger J, Pollak A, Bernaschek G 2005. Subtelomeric rearrangements as neutral genomic polymorphisms. *Am J Med Genet,* 133A(1): 48-52.

Horsley SW, Knight SJ, Nixon J, Huson S, Fitchett M, Boone RA, Hilton-Jones D, Flint J, Kearney L 1998. Del(18p) shown to be a cryptic translocation using a multiprobe FISH assay for subtelomeric chromosome rearrangements. *J Med Genet,* 35(9): 722-726.

Horsley SW, Daniels RJ, Anguita E, Raynham HA, Peden JF, Villegas A, Vickers MA, Green S, Waye JS, Chui DH, Ayyub H, MacCarthy AB, Buckle VJ, Gibbons RJ, Kearney L, Higgs DR 2001. Monosomy for the most telomeric, gene-rich region of the short arm of human chromosome 16 causes minimal phenotypic effects. *Eur J Hum Genet,* 9(3): 217-225.

Isidor B, Winer N, Joubert M, Boisseau P, Le Caignec C, Bocéno M, Fallet C, David A, Rival JM 2008. Inherited 18q23 duplication in a fetus with multiple congenital anomalies. *Eur J Med Genet,* 51(3): 231-238.

Jalal SM, Harwood AR, Anderson MH, Skehon GS, Ketterling RP, Michels VV 2001. Analysis by telomere specific FISH probes of 191 karyotypically normal patients with nonspecific dysmorphic features or developmental delay, or history of multiple miscarriages. *Am J Hum Genet,* 69(suppl): A879.

Jalal SM, Harwood AR, Sekhon GS, Pham Lorentz C, Ketterling RP, Babovic-Vuksanovic D, Meyer RG, Ensenauer R, Anderson Jr. MH, Michels VV 2003. Utility of subtelomeric fluorescent DNA probes for detection of chromosome anomalies in 425 patients. *Genet Med,* 5(1): 28-34.

Joyce CA, Dennis NR, Cooper S, Browne CE 2001. Subtelomeric rearrangements: results from a study of selected and unselected probands with idiopathic mental retardation and control individuals by using high-resolution G-banding and FISH. *Hum Genet,* 109(4): 440-451.

Kirchhoff M, Gerdes T, Brunebjerg S, Bryndorf T 2005. Investigation of patients with mental retardation and dysmorphic features using comparative genomic hybridization and subtelomeric multiplex ligation dependent probe amplication. *Am J Med Genet,* 139(3): 231-233.

Kjaergaard S, Sundberg K, Jørgensen FS, Rohde MD, Lind AM, Gerdes T, Tabor A, Kirchhoff M 2010. Diagnostic yield by supplementing prenatal metaphase karyotyping with MLPA for microdeletion syndromes and subtelomere imbalances. *Prenat Diagn,* 30(10): 995-999.

Knight SJ, Lese CM, Precht KS, Kuc J, Ning Y, Lucas S, Regan R, Brenan M, Nicod A, Lawrie NM, Cardy DL, Nguyen H, Hudson TJ, Riethman HC, Ledbetter DH, Flint J 2000. An optimized set of human telomere clones for studying telomere integrity and architecture. *Am J Hum Genet,* 67(2): 320-32.

Knight SJ, Regan R, Nicod A, Horsley SW, Kearney L, Homfray T, Winter RM, Bolton P, Flint J 1999. Subtle chromosomal rearrangements in children with unexplained mental retardation. *Lancet,* 354(9191): 1676-1681.

Knight LA, Yong MH, Tan M, Ng IS 1995. Del(3) (p25.3) without phenotypic effect. *J Med Genet,* 32(12): 994-995.

Kok K, Dijkhuizen T, Swart YE, Zorgdrager H, van der Vlies P, Fehrmann R, te Meerman GJ, Gerssen-Schoorl KB, van Essen T, Sikkema-Raddatz B, Buys CH 2005. Application of a comprehensive subtelomere array in clinical diagnosis of mental retardation. *Eur J Med Genet,* 48(3): 250-262.

Koolen DA, Nillesen WM, Versteeg MH, Merkx GF, Knoers NV, Kets M, Vermeer S, van Ravenswaaij CM, de Kovel CG, Brunner HG, Smeets D, De Vries BB, Sistermans EA 2004. Screening for subtelomeric rearrangements in 210 patients with unexplained mental retardation using multiplex ligation dependent probe amplification (MLPA). *J Med Genet,* 41(12): 892-899.

Ledbetter DH 1992. Minireview: cryptic translocations and telomere integrity. *Am J Hum Genet,* 51(3): 451-456.

Ledbetter DH, Martin CL 2007. Cryptic telomere imbalance: a 15-year update. *Am J Med Genet,* 145C(4): 327-334.

Lemmers RJLF, van der Vliet P, van der Gaag KJ, Zungia S, Frants RR, de Knijff P, van der Maarel SM 2010. Worldwide population analysis ofthe 4q and 10q subtelomeres identifies only four discrete interchromosomal sequence transfers in human evolution. *Am J Hum Genet,* 86: 364-377.

Leonard H and Wen X 2002. The epidemiology of mentaal retardation: challenges and opportunities in the new millenium. *Ment Retard Dev Disabil Res Rev,* 8: 117-134.

Lin RJ, Cherry AM, Chen KC, Lyons M, Hoyme HE, Hudgins L 2005. Terminal deletion of 6p results in a recognizable phenotype. *Am J Med Genet,* 136A(2): 162-168.

Linardopoulou E, Mefford HC, Nguyen O, Friedman C, van den Engh G, Farwell DG, Coltrera M, Trask BJ 2001. . Transcriptional activity of multiple copies of a subtelomerically located olfactory receptor gene that is polymorphic in number and location. *Hum Mol Genet,* 10(21): 2373-2383.

Linardopoulou EV, Parghi SS, Friedman C, Osborn GE, Parkhurst SM, Trask BJ 2007. Human subtelomeric WASH genes encode a new subclass of the WASP family. *PLOS Genet,* 3(12): e237.

Linardopoulou EV, Williams EM, Fan Y, Friedman C, Young JM, Trask BJ 2005. Human subtelomeres are hot spots of interchromosomal recombination and segmental duplication. *Nature,* 437(7055): 94-100.

Lo Vasco VR 2011. Role of phosphoinositide- specific phospholipase C ŋ2 in isolated and syndromic mental retardation. *Eur Neurol,* 65(5): 264-269.

Macina RA, Negorev DG, Spais C, Ruthig LA, Hu XL, Riethman HC 1994. Sequence organization of the human chromosome 2q telomere. *Hum Mol Genet,* 3(10): 1847-1853.

Martin CL, Waggoner DJ, Wong A, Uhrig S, Roseberry JA, Hedrick JF, Pack SD, Russell K, Zackai E, Dobyns WB, Ledbetter DH 2002. "Molecular rulers" for calibrating phenotypic effects of telomere imbalance. *J Med Genet,* 39(10): 734-740.

Martin CL, Nawaz Z, Baldwin EL, Wallace EJ, Justice AN, Ledbetter DH 2007. The evolution of molecular rulers analysis for characterizing telomere imbalances: from fluorescence in situ hybridization to array comparative genomic hybridization. *Genet Med,* 9(9): 566-573.

Medina M, Marinescu RC, Overhauser J, Kosik KS 2000. Hemizygosity of delta-catenin (CTNND2) is associated with severe mental retardation in Cri-du-chat syndrome. *Genomics,* 63(2): 157-164.

Mefford HC and Trask BJ 2002. The complex structure and dynamic evolution of human subtelomeres. *Nat Rev Genet,* 3: 91-102.

Mignon-Ravix C, Cacciagli P, El-Waly B, Moncla A, Milh M, Girard N, Chabrol B, Philip N, Villard L 2010. Deletion of YWHAE in a patient with periventricular heterotopias and pronounced corpus callosum hypoplasia. *J Med Genet,* 47(2): 132-136.

Misceo D, Rødningen OK, Barøy T, Sorte H, Mellembakken JR, Strømme P, Fannemel M, Frengen E 2011. A translocation between Xq21.33 and 22q13.33 causes an intragenic SHANK3 deletion in a woman with Phelan-McDermid syndrome and hypergonadotropic hypogonadism. *Am J Med Genet,* 155A(2): 403-408.

Morales C, Soler A, Margarit E, Madrigal I, Sánchez A 2007. Trisomy of 19.4 Mb region of chromosome 22 and subtelomeric 17p identified in a male without clinical affectation. *Am J Med Genet,* 143A(20): 2423-2429.

Ning Y, Roschke A, Smith ACM, Macha M, Precht K, Riethman H, Ledbeetter DH, Flint J, Horsley S, Regan R, Kearney L, Knight S, Kvaloy K, Brown WRA 1996. A complete set of human telomeric probes and their clinical application, National Institutes of Health and Institute of Molecular Medicine collaboration. *Nat Genet,* 14(1): 86-89.

Northrop EL, Ren H, Bruno DL, McGhie JD, Coffa J, Schouten J, Choo KH, Slater HR 2005. Detection of cryptic subtelomeric chromosome abnormalities and identification of anonymous chromatin using a quantitative multiplex ligation-dependent probe amplification (MLPA) assay. *Hum Mutat,* 26(5): 477-486.

Pettenati MJ, Rao N, Johnson C, Hayworth R, Crandall K, Huff O, Thomas IT 1992. Molecular cytogenetic analysis of a familial 8p23.1 deletion associated with minimal dysmorphic features, seizures, and mild mental retardation. *Hum Genet,* 89(6): 602-606.

Phelan MC 2008. 22q13.3 syndrome. Orphanet J Rare Dis, 14.

Pickard BS, Hollox EJ, Malloy MP, Porteous DJ, Blackwood DH, Armour JA, Muir WJ 2004. A 4q35.2 subtelomeric deletion identified in a screen of patients with co-morbid psychiatric illness and mental retardation. BMC *Med Genet*, 5: 21.

Ravnan JB, Tepperberg JH, Papenhausen P, Lamb AN, Hedrick J, Eash D, Ledbetter DH, Martin CL 2006. Subtelomere FISH analysis of 11 688 cases: an evaluation of the frequency and pattern of subtelomere rearrangements in individuals with developmental disabilities. *J Med Genet,* 43(6): 478-489.

Reddy KS 1999. A paternally inherited terminal deletion, del(8)(p23.1)pat, detected prenatally in an amniotic fluid sample: a review of deletion 8p23.1 cases. *Prenat Diagn,* 19(9): 868-872.

Riegel M, Baumer A, Jamar M, Delbecque K, Herens C, Verloes A, Schinzel A 2001. Submicroscopic terminal deletions and duplications in retarded patients with unclassified malformation syndromes. *Hum Genet,* 109(3):.

Rio M, Molinari F, Heuertz S, Ozilou C, Gosset P, Raoul O, Cormier-Daire V, Amiel J, Lyonnet S, Le Merrer M, Turleau C, de Blois MC, Prieur M, Romana S, Vekemans M, Munnich A, Colleaux L 2002. Automated fluorescent genotyping detects 10% of cryptic subtelomeric rearrangements in idiopathic syndromic mental retardation. *J Med Genet,* 39(4): 266-270.

Rooms L, Reyniers E, van Luijk R, Scheers S, Wauters J, Ceulemans B, Van Den Ende J, Van Bever Y, Kooy RF 2004. Subtelomeric deletions detected in patients with idiopathic mental retardation using multiplex ligation-dependent probe amplification (MLPA). *Hum Mutat,* 23(1): 17-21.

Rooms L, Reyniers E, Wuyts W, Storm K, Van Luijk R, Scheers S, Wauters J, Van Den Ende J, Biervliet M, Eyskens F, Van Goethem G, Laridon A, Ceulemans B, Courtens W, Kooy RF 2006. Multiplex ligation-dependent probe amplification to detect subtelomeric rearrangements in routine diagnostics. *Clin Genet,* 69(1): 58-64.

Roos A, Eggermann T, Zerres K, Schüler HM 2008. Polymorphic subtelomeric deletion 1q demonstrates the need to reevaluate subtelomere screening methods: determination of the boundary between pathogenic deletion and benign variant for subtelomere 1q. *Am J Med Genet,* 146A(6): 795-798.

Roselló M, Ferrer-Bolufer I, Monfort S, Oltra S, Quiroga R, Martinez F, Gonzalvo M, Benac A, Perales A, Orenalla C 2010. Prenatal study of common submicroscopic "genomic disorders" using MLPA with subtelomeric/microdeletion syndrome probe mixes, among gestations with ultrasound abnormalities in the first trimester. *Eur J Med Genet,* 53(2): 76-79.

Rosenberg MJ, Killoran C, Dziadzio L, Chang S, Stone DL, Meck J, Aughton D, Bird LM, Bodurtha J, Cassidy SB, Graham Jr. JM, Grix A, Guttmacher AE, Hudgins L, Kozma C, Michaelis RC, Pauli R, Peters KF, Rosenbaum KN, Tifft CJ, Wargowski D, Williams MS, Biesecker LG 2001. Scanning for telomeric deletions and duplications and uniparental disomy using genetic markers in 120 children with malformations. *Hum Genet,* 109(3): 311-318.

Ruiter EM, Koolen DA, Kleefstra T, Nillesen WM, Pfundt R, de Leeuw N, Hamel BC, Brunner HG, Sistermans EA, de Vries BB 2007. Pure subtelomeric microduplications as a cause of mental retardation. *Clin Genet,* 72: 362-368.

Ruiter M, Pfundt R, Koolen DA, Sistermans EA, Nillessen WM, van Ravenswaaij CM, De Vries BBA, Willemsen MAAP 2010. Subtelomeric chromosomal anomalies in infantile epileptic encephalopathies. *J Pedia Neuro,* 8(4): 391-396.

Saccone S, De Sario A, Della Valle G, Bernardi G 1992. The highest gene concentrations in the human genome are in telomeric bands of metaphase chromosomes. *Proc Nat Acad Sci USA,* 89(11): 4913-4917.

Saito Y, Kubota M, Kurosawa K, Ichihashi I, Kaneko Y, Hattori A, Komaki H, Nakagawa E, Sugai K, Sasaki M 2011. Polymicrogyria and infantile spasms in a patient with 1p36 deletion syndrome *Brain Dev,* 33(5): 437-441.

Schellberg R, Schwanitz G, Grävinghoff L, Kallenberg R, Trost D, Raff R, Wiebe W 2004. New trends in chromosomal investigation in children with cardiovascular malformations. *Cardiol Young,* 14(6): 1-8.

Schreppers-Tijdink GA, Curfs LM, Wiegers A, Kleczkowska A, Fryns JP 1988. A systematic cytogenetic study of a population of 1170 mentally retarded and/or behaviourly disturbed patients including fragile X-screening. The Hondsberg experience. *J Genet Hum,* 36: 425-446.

Shaffer LG 2005. American college of medical genetics professional practice and guidelines committee: American college of medical genetics guideline on the cytogenetic evaluation of the individual with developmental delay or mental retardation. *Genet Med,* 7: 650-654.

Shaffer LG, Kashork CD, Bacino CA, Benke PJ 1999. Caution: telomere crossing. *Am J Med Genet,* 87(3): 278-280.

Shaffer LG, Kashork CD, Saleki R, Rorem E, Sundin K, Ballif BC, Bejjani BA 2006. Targeted genomic microarray analysis for identification of chromosome abnormalities in 1500 consecutive clinical cases. *J Pediatr,* 149(1): 98-102.

Shaffer LG, Lupski JR 2000. Molecular mechanisms for constitutional chromosomal rearrangements in humans. *Annu Rev Genet,* 34: 297-329.

Shao L, Shaw CA, Lu X, Patel A, Sahoo T, Bacino CA, Lalani S, Stankiewicz P, Chinault AC, Beaudet AL, Jupski JR, Cheung SW 2007. Identification of abnormalities in subtelomeric regions by microarray analysis: a study of 5380 cases. *Abstract Band ASHG 57th annual meeting* 2007, 1640/T: 324.

Shao L, Shaw CA, Lu XY, Sahoo T, Bacino CA, Lalani SR, Stankiewicz P, Yatsenko SA, Li Y, Neill S, parsley AN, Chinault AC, Patel A, Beaudet AL, Lupski JR, Cheung SW 2008. Identification of chromosome abnormalities in subtelomeric regions by microarray analysis: a study of 5380 cases. *Am J Med Genet*, 146A: 2242-2251.

Shrimpton AE, Braddock BR, Thomson LL, Stein CK, Hoo JJ 2004. Molecular delineation of deletions on 2q37.3 in three cases with an Albright hereditary osteodystrophy-like phenotype. *Clin Genet,* 66(6): 537-544.

Shuib S, McMullan D, Rattenberry E, Barber RM, Rahman F, Zatyka M, Chapman C, Macdonald F, Latif F, Davison V, Maher ER 2009. Microarray based analysis of 3p25-p26 deletions (3p- syndrome). *Am J Med Genet,* 149A: 2099-2105.

Sismani C, Armour JA, Flint J, Girgalli C, Regan R, Patsalis PC 2001. Screening for subtelomeric chromosome abnormalities in children with idiopathic mental retardation using multiprobe telomeric FISH and the new MAPH telomeric assay. *Eur J Hum Genet,* 9(7): 527-532.

Slavotinek A, Rosenberg M, Knight S, Gaunt L, Fergusson W, Killoran C, Clayton-Smith J, Kingston H, Campbell RH, Flint J, Donnai D, Biesecker L 1999. Screening for submicroscopic chromosome rearrangements in children with idiopathic mental retardation using microsatellite markers for the chromosome telomeres. *J Med Genet,* 36(5): 405-411.

South ST, Bleyl SB, Carey JC 2007. Two unique patients with novel microdeletions in 4p16.3 that exclude the WHS critical regions: implications for critical region designation. *Am J Med Genet,* 143A(18): 2137-2142.

Stathopulu E, Mackie Ogilvie C, Flinter FA 2003. Terminal deletion of chromosome 5p in a patient with phenotypical features of Lujan-Fryns syndrome. *Am J Med Genet,* 119A: 363-366.

Stegmann APA, Jonker LMH, Engelen JJM 2008. Prospective screening of patients with unexplained mental retardation using subtelomeric MLPA strongly increases the detection rate of cryptic unbalanced chromosomal rearrangements. *Eur J Med Genet,* 51(2): 93-105.

Stewart DR, Kleefstra T 2007. The chromosome 9q subtelomere deletion syndrome. *Am J Med Genet,* 145C(4): 383-392.

Takagishi J, Rauen KA, Drumheller T, Kousseff B, Sutcliffe M 2006. Chromosome 3p25 deletion in mother and daughter with minimal phenotypic effect. *Am J Med Genet,* 140A: 1587-1593.

Tam R, Smith KP, Lawrence JB 2004. The 4q subtelomere harboring the FSHD locus is specifically anchored with peripheral heterochromatin unlike most human telomeres. *J Cell Biol,* 167(2): 269-279.

Thomson P 1998. Wolf-Hirschhorn syndrome. Review of the literature and three case studies. *J Am Podiatr Med Assoc,* 88(4): 192-197.

Thuresson AC, Bondeson ML, Edeby C, Ellis P, Langford C, Dumanski JP, Annerén G 2007. Whole-genome array-CGH for detection of submicroscopic chromosomal imbalances in children with mental retardation. *Cytogenet Genome Res,* 118(1): 1-7.

Trask BJ, Friedman C, Martin-Gallardo A, Rowen L, Akinbami C, Blankenship J, Collins C, Giorgi D, Iadonato S, Johnson F, Kuo WL, Massa H, Morrish T, Naylor S, Nguyen OT, Rouquier S, Smith T, Wong DJ, Youngblom J, van den Engh G 1998. Members of the olfactory receptor gene family are contained in large blocks of DNA duplicated polymorphically near the ends of human chromosomes. *Hum Mol Genet,* 7(1): 13-26.

Tupler R, Berardinelli A, Barbierato L, Frants R, Hewitt JE, Lanzi G, Maraschio P, Tiepolo L 1996. Monosomy of distal 4q does not cause facioscapulohumeral muscular dystrophy. *J Med Genet,* 33: 366-370.

Udaka T, Imoto I, Aizu Y, Torii C, Izumi K, Kosaki R, Takahashi T, Hayashi S, Inazawa J, Kosaki K 2007. Multiplex PCR/Liquid Chromatography assay for screening of subtelomeric rearrangements. *Genet Test,* 11(3): 241-248.

Van Bon BW, Koolen DA, Borgatti R, Magee A, Garcia-Minaur S, Rooms L, Reardon W, Zollino M, Bonaglia MC, De Gregori M, Novara F, Grasso R, Ciccone R, Van Duyvenvoorde HA, Aalbers AM, Guerrini R, Fazzi E, Nillesen WM, McCullough S, Kant SG, Marcelis CL, Pfundt R, De Leeuw N, Smeets D, Sistermans EA, Wit JM, Hamel BC, Brunner HG, Kooy F, Zuffardi O, De Vries BB 2008. Clinical and molecular characteristics of 1qter microdeletion syndrome: delineating a critical region for corpus callosum agenesis/ hypogenesis. *J Med Genet,* 45(6): 346-354.

Van Buggenhout G, Melotte C, Dutta B, Froyen G, Van Hummelen P, Marynen P, Matthijs G, de Ravel T, Devriendt K, Fryns JP, Vermeesch JR 2004. Mild Wolf-Hirschhorn syndrome: micro-array CGH analysis of atypical 4p16.3 deletions enables refinement of the genotype-phenotype map. *J Med Genet,* 41(9): 691-698.

Van Deutekom, JC, Wijmenga C, Tienhoven EA, Gruter AM, Hewitt JE, Padberg GW, van Ommen GJ, Hofker MH, Frants RR 1993. FSHD associated DNA rearrangements are due to deletions of integral copies of a 3.2 kb tandemly repeated unit. *Hum Mol Genet,* 2: 2037-2042.

Van Karnebeek CD, Koevoets C, Sluijter S, Bijlsma EK, Smeets DF, Redeker EJ, Hennekam RC, Hoovers JM 2002. Prospective screening for subtelomeric rearrangements in children with mental retardation of unknown aetiology: the Amsterdam experience. *J Med Genet,* 39(8): 546-553.

Veltman JA, Schoenmakers EF, Eussen BH, Janssen I, Merkx G, Van Cleef B, Van Ravenswaaij CM, Brunner HG, Smeets D, Van Kessel AG 2002. High-throughput analysis of subtelomeric chromosome rearrangements by use of array-based comparative genomic hybridization. *Am J Hum Genet,* 70(5): 1269-1276.

Vissers LE, De Vries BB, Osoegawa K, Janssen IM, Feuth T, Choy CO, Straatman H, van der Vliet W, Huys EH, van Rijk A, Smeet D, van Ravenswaaij-Arts CM, Knoers NV, van der Burgt I, de Jong PJ, Brunner HG, van Kessel AG, Schoenmakers EF, Veltman JA 2003.

Array based comparative genomic hybridization for the genomwide detection of submicroscopic chromosomal abnormalities. *Am J Hum Genet,* 73: 1261-1270.

Walter S, Hinkel KSG, Mitulla B, Ounap K, Sims G, Sitska M, Utermann B, Viertel P, Kalscheuer V, Bartsch O 2004. Subtelomere FISH in 50 children with mental retardation and minor anomalies, identified by a checklist, detects 10 rearrangements including a de novo balanced translocation of chromosomes 17p13.3 and 20q13.33. *Am J Med Genet,* 128A(4): 364-373.

Wegner AM, Nebhan CA, Hu L, Majumdar D, Meier KM, Weaver AM, Webb DJ 2008. N-WASP and the Arp2/3 complex are critical regulators of actin in the development of dendritic spines and synapses. *J Biol Chem*, 283(23): 15912-15920.

Williams SR, Aldred MA, Der Kaloustian VM, Hala F, Gowans G, McLeod DR, Zondag S, Toriello HV, Magenis HE, Elsea SH 2010. Haploinsufficiency of HDAC4 causes brachydactyly mental retardation syndrome, with brachydactyly type E, developmental delays, and behavioral problems. *Am J Hum Gent,* 87(2): 219-228.

Wise JL, Crout RJ, McNeil DW, Weyant RJ, Marazita ML, Wenger SL 2009. Cryptic subtelomeric rearrangements and X chromosomemosaicism: a study of 565 apparently normal individuals with fluorescent in situ hybridization. *PLOS one,* 4(6): e5855.

Wu Y, Ji T, Wang J, Xiao J, Wang H, Li J, Gao Z, Yang Y, Cai B, Wang L, Zhou Z, Tian L, Wang X, Zhong N, Qin J, Wu X, Jiang Y 2010. Submicroscopic subtelomeric aberrations in Chinese patients with unexplained developmental delay/mental retardation. *BMC Med Genet,* 11: 72.

Wu Q, Niebuhr E, Yang H, Hansen L 2005. Determination of the "critical region" for cat-like cry of Cri-du-chat syndrome and analysis of candidate genes by quantitative PCR. *Eur J Hum Genet,* 13(4): 475-485.

Wu BL, Schneider GH, Sabatino DE, Bosovic LZ, Cao B, Korf BR 1996. Distal 8p deletion (8)(p23.1): an easily missed chromosomal abnormality that may be associated with congenital heart defect and mental retardation. *Am J Med Genet,* 62: 77-83.

Xu J and Chen Z 2003. Advances in molecular cytogenetics for the evaluation of mental retardation.*Am J Med Genet,* 117C(1): 15-24.

Yobb TM, Somerville MJ, Willatt L, Firth HV, Harrison K, MacKenzie J, Gallo N, Morrow BE, Shaffer LG, Babcock M, Chernos J, Bernier F, Sprysak K, Christiansen J, Haase S, Elyas B, Lilley M, Bamforth S, McDermid HE 2005. Microduplication and triplication of 22q11.2: a highly variable syndrome. *Am J Hum Genet,* 76(5): 865-876.

Zahed L, Sismani C, Ioannides M, Saleh M, Koumbaris G, Kenj M, Abdallah A, Ayyache M, Patsalis P 2008. Molecular and clinical description of a girl with a 46,X,t(Y;4)(q11.2;p16)/ 45,X,der(4)t(Y;4)(q11.2;p16) karyotype and a small cryptic 4p subtelomeric deletion. *Am J Med Genet,* 146(7): 893-898.

Zollino M, Di Stefano C, Zampino G, Mastroiacovo P, Wright TJ, Sorge G, Selicorni A, Tenconi R, Zappalà A, Battaglia A, Di Rocco M, Palka G, Pallotta R, Altherr MR, Neri G 2000. Genotype-phenotype correlations and clinical diagnostic criteria in Wolf-Hirschhorn syndrome. *Am J Med Genet,* 94(3): 254-261.

In: Intellectual Disability
Editors: Domenico F. Mancini and Carlo M. Greco
ISBN: 978-1-61942-298-8

Chapter 2

INCREASING OUTCOMES FOR INDIVIDUALS WITH INTELLECTUAL AND DEVELOPMENTAL DISABILITIES THROUGH DATA-BASED MECHANISMS FOR STAFF TRAINING AND PERFORMANCE FEEDBACK

Thomas P. Kitchen and Phillip J. Belfiore
Mercyhurst College

ABSTRACT

Children and adults with disabilities often require highly specialized instruction in order to acquire functional academic, social, adaptive, and vocational skills that will allow them to experience significantly independent lives upon graduation from special education programs. It follows that those responsible for teaching these skills must be able to engage in only the most efficacious instructional methods and curriculum development, given the amount of skills that must be directly taught, combined with the unique learning characteristics of those with significant disabilities. In other words, skills must be taught effectively and efficiently. Unfortunately, the field of education has consistently suffered from a marked gap between research and practice. Effective instructional procedures have been identified and vetted by the peer review process. However, they are consistently under-utilized in instructional environments. Likewise, federal education law mandates that those eligible for special education receive an individualized education plan (IEP), which contains measureable goals and objectives. It is known that instructional and curricular decisions should be based on data and measurement of learner performance. However, in implementation, what is known and what is practiced are quite different. In this case, the mandates for measures of learner performance are in place, but it is arguably more common than not to see goals and objectives that are unable to be measured objectively, and subsequent assessment reports that are subjective, or based on a "gut feeling," as opposed to truly objective performance. The end result of this set of circumstances is that learners are often unable to meet their potential. They may be subjected to ineffective instruction at one end of a continuum, or possibly move along at too slow a pace due to lack of adequate mastery criteria at the other end. They may suffer from educational plans that are poorly devised. They may also experience frustration when they are left to bear the burden of instructional problems that would be better placed on the systems responsible for providing such instruction. On another front, teachers who are not accustomed to students with disabilities achieving success may be more subject to frustration, "burnout," and eventual attrition or staff "turnover."

The current situations call for a personnel training and performance feedback framework by which those responsible for both planning and implementing instruction and curriculum may effectively utilize those things that have been shown to work. At hand is the proposal to adopt data-based mechanisms for objectively evaluating and providing feedback on the practical output (implementation of evidence-based instructional practices; development of measurable goals and objectives) of personnel involved in teaching those with intellectual and developmental disabilities. The authors offer a systematic way to train, monitor, and evaluate personnel (across varied systems of service delivery) who are charged with instruction, which would lead to improved personnel performance, and – ultimately – improved outcomes for those with disabilities. This system includes both theoretical and behavioral underpinnings, as well as a technology of implementation that would allow for the development and deployment of sound programming.

Section One – Introduction and Relevance

In the United States of America, all persons aged 3-21 years are entitled (by law) to a free, appropriate public education provided in the least restrictive environment where adequate yearly progress may be made. Many of these students face learning and behavioral challenges that may prohibit them from benefiting from their education, without individualized programs and procedures that are designed to meet their specific needs. In other words, they require specialized education. Specialized education, from here forward referred to as "special education," is essentially defined by the Individuals with Disabilities Education Act (IDEA) as specialized and free education that is aimed to meet the unique needs of children with disabilities through instruction in a variety of settings, and with provision of necessary related services, including speech-language pathology services, travel training, and vocational education (IDEA 20 U.S.C. §1401 (26)(A), (29)(A)(B)).

During the 2008-2009 school year (the most recent year for which broad statistics are published and readily available), approximately 6.5 million students aged 3-21 were provided with special education services across 14 disability categories. This figure accounts for approximately 13.2 percent of all students enrolled in public schools in prekindergarten through 12th grade programs in public schools (U.S. Department of Education, 2011). The United States federal government, through the U.S. Department of Education, has proposed a $12.8 billion expenditure toward the increased costs of special education for these students during the 2011 fiscal year. This provides only approximately 17 percent of the national average per pupil expenditure (APPE), thereby providing an estimated average of $1,750 per student (U.S. Department of Education, 2010). The fiscal burden of the remaining 83 percent of the funding required for special education falls upon state and local governments, bringing the combined expenditure for special education services in this country to approximately $75.3 billion.

Given these figures, several salient considerations may be derived: 1) Millions of children in the United States have demonstrated learning problems that are significant enough that they require individualized programming, the outcome of which will lead (presumably) to differences in the independence and subsequent quality of life they will experience throughout their lifetimes; 2) Enormous amounts of public (taxpayer) funding supports the provision of special education services, through all tiers of government; and 3) Because of the first two considerations, United States citizens have vested financial and social interests in the success of special education programs for those students receiving these services. As a result, it would follow that there should be a collective concern about the quality and efficacy of special education.

Aside from the rather clear-cut definition of special education however, there are often debates regarding the factors that comprise the characteristics of effective special education. Rather than engage in a "this approach is better than that approach" style of debate, this chapter will instead focus on a few characteristics that have evidentiary support, and provide suggestions regarding how such concepts may be applied with fidelity in a consistent manner. The premises of many of the approaches to effective special education discussed later may be aligned with four basic assumptions offered by Heward (2003) as the foundation for his exploration of best and worst practices, from a research-supported standpoint, which are as follows:

> "1) Students with disabilities have a right to an effective education; 2) Special education instruction should be individualized, intensive, and goal-directed; 3) Research has produced a useful and reliable knowledge base for special education; and 4) Research-based instructional tools are under-used in special education" (p. 186).

Each of these assumptions carries with it implications for how providers of specialized instruction and services should go about their business. First, the concept of "effective" should be examined closely in several regards: What exactly does it meanto say that an education is or has been effective? How does one determine whether or not the criteria for effectiveness have been met? It would not be surprising if many individual professionals would give almost as many definitions of "effective," as used in the phrase "effective education." Fortunately, there is a paradigm of teaching and learning that aims to superimpose a degree of objectivity and precision over concepts related to the quality of human performance. As human performance encompasses all of the things that are done by students within the process of learning and performing skills as a result of special education - and as it also encompasses all of those things that providers of special education do to occasion such skill acquisition - a pedagogical model that aims to quantify and measure human performance is of utmost value to the field of special education. This paradigm is a central tenet of the science of Applied Behavior Analysis (ABA, which is defined by Cooper, Heron, and Heward (2007) as "the science in which tactics derived from the principles of behavior are applied systematically to improve socially significant behavior and experimentation is used to identify the variables responsible for behavior change" (p. 20).

Skinner (1938) defined "behavior" as "the movement of an organism or of its parts in a frame of reference by the organism or by various external objects or fields" (p.6). An alternate, simpler definition is "any interaction of the muscles and glands of an organism and its environment (Gulick and Kitchen, 2007, p.43). Perhaps the simplest definition is the common notion that behavior is basically "everything we do." There are many characteristics that describe the science of ABA , a few of which will be provided here. ABA is *applied*, for it seeks to study behaviors that are important to society; it is *behavioral*, in that it aims to study the actual things people do that are in need of improvement, in measurable terms; it is *analytic*, in that clear cause:effect relationships are discovered primarily via the vehicle of single subject research (which will be expounded upon in following sections); it is *technological,* meaning that it provides tools and procedures to effect and document behavior change; and it is effective, meaning that the changes produced by the application of behavioral techniques must be of practical importance (Baer, Wolf, and Risley, 1968). Essentially, ABA is a science of human behavior which aims to specifically identify the things people do (behavior), identify sound methods to arrange the environment to maintain, increase, or decrease the things people do; and demonstrate empirically that those methods were indeed responsible for the corresponding changes in those behaviors. The above discussion is relevant, for it shows how the science of ABA, based on several of its most widely accepted foundational properties, can be useful in operationalizing, documenting, and encouraging change in behaviors associated with both teaching and learning; behaviors of both teacher and student. Further, it gives us a framework by which we may finally grant measurability to the concept of "effective," as it relates to provision of special education.

The second of the previously mentioned assumptions - that special education should be individualized, intensive, and goal directed – seems to speak about the very foundation of special education's legal requirements. According to special education law, all students receiving special education must have an Individualized Education Plan (IEP) that contains measurable annual goals, as well as statements of the education and services that will be provided to the child thatare both based on peer-reviewed research to the extent practicable and, will help the student "advance appropriately toward attaining the annual goals" (IDEA 20 U.S.C. §1414 (d)(1)(A)(i)(I-IV)). For practitioners and teachers to satisfy the above quoted text in a truly objective and consistent manner, this implies that there is a necessity to develop this document in a way that allows for measurement of student progress toward his or her goals.

The third and fourth assumptions, that there exists a body of research-based knowledge of effective special education practices – and that this knowledge is under-used – is both aligned with and in juxtaposition to special education law. As stated previously, the law stipulates that, to the greatest degree possible, the education and related services provided should be based on peer reviewed research. This addresses the third assumption. The fourth assumption, though, is startling, for in following sections of this chapter, it will be demonstrated that there is evidence that a gap exists between research and practice. From an outcomes standpoint, educators should be embracing the idea that what is practiced has peer-reviewed support. Practicing within the profession of special education in such a manner will lead to the greatest successes for recipients of such services, and this alone should serve as the primary motivation for doing so. That said however, providing services and educational strategies that are not based on peer-reviewed research is not simply a matter of educator preference – it is in direct contradiction with federal education law.

What then, are the best options for overcoming this gap between research and practice? First, those responsible for program design and implementation will simply have to "do their homework" by researching evidence-based best practice prior to adopting particular approaches. This concept will be discussed further as this chapter progresses. Additionally, simply being presented with information alone may not lead to the adoption and successful implementation of well-researched practices. For example, in reviewing reasons for why those responsible for implementing best practices for children with autism do not adhere to recommended treatment protocols, Cautilli and Santilli-Connor (2000) offer a functional analysis of resistance on the part of implementers. Two of the reasons proposed are that even when the implementation skill has been presented, the implementer has not had the adequate time to practice the skill under supervision, and/or the opportunities to practice the skill in "real world" conditions. Further, some researchers have taken a behavioral approach to solving such problems of implementing recommended practice by identifying these problems as generalization issues (Tillman, 2000). Such an approach implores that the examiner remain objective regarding reasons for practitioners' failure to implement evidence-based practice. It would be of more utility to view external antecedent variables - including past learning histories on the part of the teacher, therapist, or other implementer – as the culprit, as opposed to internal, personality-driven factors that manifest themselves as "resistance." Behavior analysis, as a scientific discipline, can be of help in the case of determining why certain behavioral repertoires on the part of the practitioner are either present or absent. Individuals are much more likely to engage in behaviors that have, in the past, been followed by consequences that change the environment in ways that make the behavior more frequent (Skinner, 1953). If those changes involve something being added or increased following the behavior, and then make the behavior more likely to occur again, then this is known as positive reinforcement. If those changes involve something being taken away or decreased following the behavior, but still make the behavior more likely to occur again, then this is known as negative reinforcement. Both types of reinforcement strengthen the behavior(s) they follow. Skinner (1974) discussed the role of cumulative contingencies leading not just to singular behaviors, but behavioral repertoires. These repertoires comprise patterns of behaviors that eventually allow one to establish himself or herself as a distinctive "self." In the case of the teacher or practitioner, there is a reinforcement history for each individual, and this history plays a crucial role in determining the likelihood of engagement in certain types of teaching behaviors. In other words, it is reinforcement for certain types of teaching behaviors that leads to the creation of the teacher's professional self. If a teacher has been reinforced positively (by obtaining praise, financial incentives, smiling students, etc.) or negatively (by reducing his or her exertion of effort, by avoiding being ostracized by other professionals, by avoiding complaints from students, etc.) for engaging in non-research-based practice in the classroom or therapeutic environment, then he or she will be likely to continue to engage in non-research-based practice. If, on the other hand, he or she has been reinforced positively or negatively for engaging in evidence-based practice, then it is far more likely that he or she will continue to engage in evidence-based practice. And, unfortunately, if the teacher has not been provided with opportunities to be reinforced for engaging in effective practice through adequate training, he or she is likely to experience frustration regarding the learning progress and behavioral challenges demonstrated by his or her students. Lack of adequate training, in addition to lack of effective approaches to student behavioral problems, are two factors that have been correlated to higher rates of teacher attrition (Greiner and Smith, 2009).

The task at hand, therefore, is threefold. First, a framework by which practitioners are able to identify evidence-based practice must be developed. Second, a system must be established that allows for adequate, competency-based training of repertoires consisting of specific teacher behaviors that are based in peer-reviewed literature. Third, to assist in the continued strengthening of the desired behavioral repertoires of teachers and other professionals providing special education services, systems must be employed that allow for monitoring, reinforcement, and correction of these specific behaviors, via data collection methods that yield accurate, objective, measurable, and graphable results. The resulting performance feedback information may then be used to further shape the behavior of the education professional toward more effective and efficient teaching practices.

SECTION TWO - THE ROLE OF SINGLE SUBJECT RESEARCH IN EFFECTIVE UTILIZATION OF EVIDENCE-BASED PRACTICES

Teaching individuals with developmental disabilities requires professionals in the field to differentiate (individualize) instruction to meet the unique characteristics of those with developmental disabilities, and identify highly specialized instructional strategies designed to increase independence in such curricular areas as functional academics, social skills, vocational skills, and communication. This should be done while simultaneously determining the most appropriate educational environment beyond that of the more traditional school classroom setting.

More recently, professionals in the field of special education are also instructed to select and implement those instructional strategies that have an evidence-based, or research-validated, history of yielding positive results (Odom, Brantlinger, Gersten, Horner, Thompson, and Harris, 2005; Schlosser, 2009). Evidence-based instructional practices may be defined as the integration of research validated instructional strategies with practical educational/clinical expertise (Schlosser and Raghavedra; 2004). Essentially, evidence-based practice refers to educators or clinicians in the field engaging in instructional practices derived from a body of research, with the understanding that the research must have met standards of professional acceptability (i.e., peer reviewed process of publication, demonstrated experimental control) as well as demonstrate evidence of applied effectiveness (Kitchen, Belfiore, and Kitchen, 2010; Shriver and Watson, 2005).

While the field of special education recognizes the need for evidence-based instructional practices, educational researchers warn that these practices, validated by sound research, are at one level being ignored completely or at another, equally troubling level, being implemented inconsistently in educational and clinical settings (Belfiore, Fritts, and Herman, 2008; Odom et. al., 2005; Shriver, 2007). The result of either inconsistent implementation of evidence-based practices, or a complete disregard of such practices, creates a disconnection between research validated, evidence-based instruction and the utilization of that evidence-base in educational or clinical practices. Neither professional option, inconsistency of delivery or disregard of evidence, serves the field of special education or our student population to the maximum extent possible. In fact, failure to implement best practices, and to do so with consistency (fidelity), has proven to be detrimental. As an example, it has been shown that teachers' lack of fidelity corresponded to rates of inappropriate behaviors from students (DiGennaro, Martens and Kleinman, 2007; DiGennaro, Martens, and McIntyre, 2005; Wilder, Atwell and Wine, 2006).

In addition to the resistance and generalization issues discussed in the chapter introduction, two other sets of variables may be at play, resulting in this gap between documented evidence-based practices and the utilization of those practices in the classroom or clinic. First, *contextual variables,* resulting from a lack of recognition by educational researchers to the real world, day-to-day realities of the classroom teacher or clinician, may adversely influence the implementation of evidence-based practices (Lee, Belfiore, and Budin; 2008). More specifically, Shriver and Watson (2005) and McIntyre, Gresham, DiGennaro, and Reed, (2007) suggest that contextual variables such as operational budgets, instructional materials, equipment, personnel level of expertise, complexity of intervention, organizational resources, and daily instructional time may impede the smooth transition from educational research to educational practice. Most classrooms and clinics do not have the luxury of additional graduate students serving as trained interventionists and data collectors, teacher/clinician release time from daily operations to implement specialized strategies with a select population of students who have been removed from the general classroom, or direct and sustained interactions with professional researchers operating out of institutions of higher education.

Second, *methodological variables* such as research design may have an equally significant impact on the gap between educational research and classroom/clinical practice. Several researchers (e.g., Detrich, Keyworth and States, 2005; Schlosser, 2009; Zhan and Ottenbacher, 2001) suggest that although randomized control trial designs may be considered the "gold standard" for determining evidence, an educational or therapeutic decision based on a sample of many participants may not be valid when applied to the field of special education. In large sample random control trials, where progress is usually assessed only once in the form of a posttest, and where some students show considerable improvement while others deteriorate, average improvement may be statistically significant, but therapeutically or educationally weak (Barlow, Nock, and Hersen, 2009). It has been argued that if the purpose of evidence-based practices are to inform therapeutic/educational decisions (Horner, Carr, Halle, McGee, Odom, and Wolery, 2005; Kratochwill et al., 2010; Odom et al., 2005; Schlosser, 2009; Zhan and Ottenbacher, 2001), then single subject research maybe a more effective research methodology than random control trials. In single subject research within subject variability (i.e., the clinical or educational course of a specific individual during no intervention-intervention) is of great practical concern to the teacher, clinician, and/or care-giver (Barlow, Nock, and Hersen, 2009).

Single subject research, which is the vastly accepted model of research design within the field of ABA, may be briefly defined as a class of research designs (within series, between series and combined series designs) that involve repeated measures on a dependent measure (e.g. behavior) and the introduction of one or more interventions (Kratochwill and Mace, 1984).

The logical rationale of single subject research, often referred to as "baseline logic" (c.f. Cooper et al., 2007) allows for the repeated, direct assessment within each research phase [baseline and intervention(s)] to: 1) describe current behavior within a specific phase; 2) contrast current behavior within a specific phase to behavior from a previous phase; 3) predict, given the current behavior within a specific phase, future behavior within a specific phase; and 4) validate previous predictions. The goal of single subject research is to establish experimental control (i.e., demonstrate through replication a functional/cause-effect relationship between the independent and dependent variables), while ruling out extraneous threats to validity by replication of baseline and intervention(s) phases.

Table 1. Comparison of Research to Practice and Behavior Analytic Action Research as practical options for moving Evidence-Based Practices into real world classrooms/clinics

Research to Practice (Detrich, et al., 2007; Shriver, 2007; Shriver and Watson, 2005)	Behavior Analytic Action Research (Belfiore, et al., 2002; Belfiore, et al., 2008)
1. Based on a relatively large and robust body of applied and basic research 2. Conducted in applied settings under typical day-to-day conditions 3. Demonstrates successful implementation of the practice 4. Provides a clear description of the procedures so that the practice can be implemented by other educators/clinicians 5. Improves and/or extends practice	1. Predicated on a practical problem 2. Linked to behavioral theory and research 3. Carried out exclusively by classroom staff/clinicians within the context of the general classroom/clinic 4. Utilizes direct methods of data collection, collected within the structure of a typical classroom/clinic 5. Implemented usually within a single subject research methodology 6. Establishes experimental control via demonstrating a functional relationship Additionally, practitioners working in the context of behavioral analytic action research can 1. Further extend the external validity of applied behavioral research, allowing for expanded dissemination of results 2. Call to question some aspects of behavioral research that does not ''hold up'' when applied within the real world classroom/clinic by classroom/clinic staff

While single subject research employs superior methodologies for enhancing the link between educational research and clinical/classroom practice, Shriver and Watson (2005) note a continued concern between applied single subject research, and replication of that research in the real, day-to-day classroom or clinic. In light of these concerns, the authors suggest several parameters for research to practice studies (See Table 1), in an attempt to move applied research to education or clinical practices (Shriver and Watson, 2005). Belfiore, Lee, Scheeler, and Klein (2002) note a similar disconnection, arguing for what they describe as behavior analytic action research as a single subject research methodology that addresses both the need for practicality of intervention in real world situations (i.e., teacher/clinician-friendly), and experimental control (i.e., functional relation) allowing for more widespread dissemination. This expectation of demonstrated experimental control as a parameter of behavior analytic action research is one of the biggest differences between research-to-practice studies and behavior analytic action research. Table 1 shows a comparison between research to practice studies (e.g. Shriver and Watson, 2005) and behavior analytic action research (e.g. Belfiore, Pulley Basile, and Lee, 2008). Both are practical strategic options for moving evidence-based practices into real world classrooms and clinics.

Section Three - Evidence-Based Practices, Staff Training, and Systems Support

As the field of special education, through single subject research methodologies, begins to close the gap between well documented evidence-based practices and the utilization of those practices in the classroom and clinic, the field must begin to address the systematic training of direct-care teachers, staff, and clinicians. The questions turns from one of "Are we engaging our students in evidence-based practices?" to "Now that I am utilizing evidence-based practices, am I delivering them with a level of daily consistency?" As Belfiore et al., (2008) suggest, *intervention accountability* (i.e. "Was the intervention effective, efficient, and socially valid?") has been established via a documented body of applied research in the field (i.e., emerging evidence-based strategies). What is currently the pressing issue for the field of special education is *treatment fidelity/procedural integrity* (were the evidence-based practices delivered in a consistent manner, as prescribed?) (Belfiore et al., 2008).

In a review of evidence-based practices, using single subject research designs, with children with autism, Odom, Brown, Frey, Karasu, Smith-Canter, and Strain (2003) identified two strategies; teacher-directed instruction and differential reinforcement, as having a well-established body of evidence of effectiveness. One specific intervention that incorporates both of these evidence-based strategies (teacher-directed instruction and differential reinforcement), and is currently used with students with autism is discrete trial instruction (Leblanc, Ricciardi, and Luiselli, 2005; Schoen, 2003). Discrete Trial Instruction (DTI) has been defined as a strategy that places emphasis on the teacher-directed systematic presentation of learning opportunities, prompting response accuracy, delivery of positive reinforcement, and correcting response errors (Leblanc et al., 2005). Given the extensive applied research foundation, discrete trial instruction would be considered an evidence-based practice, meeting *intervention accountability* as defined by Belfiore et al., (2008).

Although DTI has established a research body of effectiveness showing benefits to students with autism and ASD diagnoses, inadequately trained staff delivering ill-defined procedural steps may have a negative impact on student's educational progress (Belfiore et al., 2008). Once evidence-based practices have been adequately defined for the classroom or clinic, it is the responsibility of educational communities to ensure that those strategies are consistently implemented as previously defined. The best way to ensure accurate application of evidence-based intervention is to directly measure the extent to which that intervention is delivered as operationally described (McIntyre et al., 2007). Without such ongoing, direct assessment of evidence-based practices, the conclusions about instructional effectiveness (i.e., the functional relationship between the dependent target behavior and the independent intervention) may be suspect (Peterson, Homer, and Wonderlich, 1982). Additionally, McIntyre et al. (2007) suggests that student problem behavior negatively correlates with intervention accuracy, such that low levels of problem behavior are associated with high levels of consistency of intervention delivery.

As the first step in the consistent utilization of evidence-based practices, multiple authors have advocated the increased role of procedural integrity or treatment fidelity in single subject research (Auld, Belfiore, Scheeler, 2010; Belfiore et al., 2008; Lane, Bocian, MacMillan, and Gresham, 2004; McIntyre et al., 2007). Belfiore et al. (2008) defined procedural integrity as the measure of whether intervention procedures were delivered as prescribed. Evidence-based practices cannot be considered effective in the classroom or clinic unless they can be documented as being delivered as defined on an ongoing basis (DiGennaro et al., 2005). Additionally, when professional development and staff training require an understanding and implementation of evidence-based practices and procedures, teachers, clinicians, and staff can increase the amount of instructional time provided to students, thereby maximizing student engagement and learning. Although monitoring procedural integrity in the delivery of evidence-based practices is critical, Shriver and Watson (2005) and others (Belfiore et al., 2008; Leblanc et al., 2005) stress the need that staff training should be: 1) practical and efficient given the time constraints of the typical classroom or clinic; 2) viewed as favorable by teachers, clinicians, and staff; and 3) maintained long-term through intermittent follow-up documentation.

For example, Belfiore et al., (2008) demonstrated the effectiveness of video and self-monitoring checklist on staff procedural integrity when implementing DTI when working with students with autism. In this single subject (a multiple baseline design across persons) research study, instructional staff were exposed to a training package consisting of written information, practice and coaching, 5-step self-monitoring DTI protocols, and individualized performance feedback. Results of this study showed that all staff, when required to monitor and score videotapes of their daily instruction, increased the consistent procedural accuracy of their teaching practices. The authors suggested that consistency in the delivery of the DTI sequence was an important criterion for the successful classroom application of evidence-based practices (Belfiore et al., 2008).

Continuing a line of staff training research that demonstrate that evidence-based practices can be learned quickly, and maintained consistently, by classroom teachers and support staff (e.g., Belfiore and Browder, 1992; Belfiore et al., 2008; Lavie and Sturmey, 2002; Leblanc et al., 2005; Sarakoff and Sturmey, 2004), Auld and colleagues (Auld et al., 2009; Auld et al., 2010) measured the effects of providing direct instruction in the use of Differential Reinforcement of an Alternative Behavior (DRA), defined as placing one behavior on extinction (e.g. student talking out in class without being called on) while another, alternative behavior is reinforced (e.g. student hand raising to answer a question or to ask for assistance) (Vollmer and Iwata, 1992). The evidence-based practice of DRA, when applied in a consistent manner, is commonly and successfully used in classroom and clinical settings as an educational management strategy. Providing direct instruction and performance feedback to teachers, clinicians, and support staff, as well as pre-service teachers in the use of DRA helps reduce problem behaviors in the classroom and clinic, while increasing more academically engaging behaviors. As such, DRA procedures offer educators an essential, evidence-based practice for successful school-based intervention (Lane et al., 2004).

The purpose of the Auld and Belfiore (2010) study was to assess the effect of a brief instructional workshop for implementing evidence-based practices (DRA) for three pre-service teachers during their student teaching internship. First pre-service teachers met in a one-time, one-hour workshop to discuss problem student behavior, recognize the laws governing special education, identify specific DRA strategies they could use to help students learn more appropriate ways of responding, and practice using DRA strategies. Second, pre-service teachers met individually with the researcher weekly after the initial intervention workshop for follow-up sessions. Those sessions included a review of the observational data sheets and specific discussion on student behaviors within their classroom. Following the initial intervention workshop for each participant, weekly meetings (fifteen to thirty minutes in length) were held with each participant individually to review progress throughout the pre-service teacher's remaining student teaching experience. Specific concerns with the use of DRA were addressed in individual sessions (e.g., if a student teacher was experiencing difficulty ignoring attention seeking behaviors such as talking while raising a hand, the teacher was coached to practice identifying another student whose hand was raised by name and commenting to that student how pleased she was that he had raised his hand). The results of this study showed increases in pre-service teacher use of attention to student hand-raising, and in student hand-raising behavior in the classroom, as well as decreases in teacher attention to student talking out behavior, and in student talk-outs in the classroom.

In a similar study Auld et al., (2010) assessed the integrity with which pre-service teachers using a differential reinforcement of alternate behavior (DRA) strategy taught to them during their student teaching experience. Seven student teachers in general education settings participated. Teaching assignments ranged from early elementary through high school in urban, suburban, and rural settings. Intervention consisted of a 1-hr workshop and individual feedback meetings following direct classroom observation. Results showed that student teachers increased their number of correct DRA responses as measured by accurate teacher feedback to students, and students showed increased hand-raising and decreased talk-outs. Implications for helping pre-service general education teachers to teach more consistently and effectively in inclusive settings are discussed.

Auld, Belfiore, and Scheeler (2007) and McIntyre et al, (2007) make the case for school-wide assessment of procedural integrity when utilizing evidence-based practices and single subject research based on the assertion that recent education laws are increasingly requiring that schools be held accountable for the progress of their students (individual student, disaggregate groups, and school-wide), requiring an increased focus on demonstration of accurate plan implementation over time. Establishing the consistent delivery of evidence-based practices through school-wide procedural integrity protocols, assessed through single subject design methodologies positions the field of special education at what Levin, O'Donnell, and Kratochwill (2003) identify as Stage 4, *informed classroom practice*. Odom, et al. (2005) suggest that at this final stage of a 4-stage model (Levin et al., 2003), evidence-based class-wide practices would be adopted a school system models, monitored under naturally occurring existing conditions.

SECTION FOUR - MANAGEMENT OF TEACHER BEHAVIOR

As noted before, Applied Behavior Analysis, as a science of human behavior, provides a way to understand how and why people do the things that they do, how personal and professional habits are formed and reversed, and how environmental contingencies may be engineered to effect a change in one's behavior, if the change is needed for that person's success. Therefore, ABA is truly a science of teaching and learning, and the teacher whose behavior is subject to change has simultaneously become a learner himself or herself. When the time comes to modify the environment and subsequent behavior of a professional in the field, behavior analysts turn to the sub-field of Organizational Behavior Management, specifically to the tools and processes associated with Performance Mangagement (PM). In short, Performance Mangagement is "a technology for creating a workplace that brings out the best in people while generating the highest value for the organization" (Daniels and Daniels, 2006, p.7). In the case of applying this technology to teachers, the workplace becomes the school or other therapeutic environment, and the employee whose behavior is to change is the teacher or provider of related services. A hallmark of behavior analysis and any of its applications is the use of data collection and analysis tools (Baer et al., 1968) to monitor changes in behavior, and – as previously mentioned - to demonstrate experimental control over these changes through the utilization of single subject research. When applied to teachers and teaching behaviors, there is a necessity to first operationalize (provide specific examples of) the exact behavioral repertoires that are desired. Each of these repertoires likely consist of smaller behavioral units that are linked together sequentially to form a larger, more complex skill. When this complex skill is broken down into smaller, teachable units, a "task analysis" has been conducted (Cooper et al., 2007).

Task analyses have been conducted to teach a multitude of behaviors to individuals in many settings, comprising basic life skills through complex recreational and professional skills. For example, individuals have been taught how to make a bed (McWilliams, Nietupski, and Hamre-Nietupski, 1990), how to insert hearing aids (Tucker and Berry, 1980), how to engage in hygiene tasks (Kissel, Whitman, and Reid, 1983), how to learn mathematics skills (Resnick, Wang, and Kaplan, 1973), and even how to become better golfers (Simek and O'Brien, 1981) through task-analytic approaches to instruction. More applicable to the current discussion, though, are approaches where teaching or training behaviors are broken down, and often placed into checklist format for the purposes of providing staff training and performance feedback to teachers, therapists, trainers, or other professional and paraprofessional staff working with individuals with developmental disabilities. For example, Seligson-Petscher and Bailey (2006), as part of a training package for newly-hired implementers of school programming for children diagnosed with behavior problems, used a self-monitoring form that included lists of skills associated with managing problem behaviors, delivering reinforcement, and providing prompting to engage in tasks. Similarly, self-recording via a monitoring checklist was implemented by Plavnick, Ferreri, and Maupin (2010) to monitor and improve staff's adherence to a token economy procedure to reinforce appropriate behavior. For individuals with developmental disabilities many researchers (e.g., Arco, 1991; Kissel, et al, 1983; Reid and Whitman, 1983; Repp, Felce, and de Kock, 1987; DiGennaro, Martens and Kleinman, 2007; Richman, Riordan, Reiss, Pyles, and Bailey, 1988) have incorporated or described some type of written description or checklist of desired staff behaviors in their successful staff training and monitoring programs. An added benefit of using checklists for describing desired implementer behavior is that the resulting data may support changes in staff behavior as dependent variables for experimental research. This research may then be designed in such a manner that control may be demonstrated via single-subject methodology.

However, as a standalone technology, written descriptions of desired staff behaviors, whether in checklist or narrative form, may be unlikely to be effective (Smith, 1995). That said, though, when utilized as a way to monitor progress in such a way that they are able to be combined with (and be the basis for) data-based performance feedback strategies, checklists may be the first step toward improvements in staff behavior. Synthesized from Balcazar, Hopkins, and Suarez (1985) and Peterson (1982), Arco (1991, p. 231) states: "Performance feedback provides staff with information on past performance and effectively acts as a positive or negative reinforcer." Performance feedback may be conducted via self monitoring, or – most commonly – by supervisors, consultants, or researchers. It may be delivered verbally, in writing, or via graphic displays of performance data, usually at regular intervals.

Daniels and Daniels (2006) list ten characteristics of effective performance feedback:

1. Give specific how-to information regarding behaviors that should be exhibited or changed;
2. Feedback should be related to performance that the person can control;
3. Feedback should be provided during or immediately after the performance;
4. Feedback should be individualized;
5. Feedback should be self-monitored when possible;
6. If not self-monitored, then feedback should be delivered by the person in charge;
7. Feedback should be focused on improvement;
8. Feedback should be easily understood;
9. Feedback should be graphed;
10. Feedback should be used as an antecedent to reinforcement.

Section Five – Real-World Implementation of Data-Based Performance Monitoring and Feedback Systems

The previous discussions have expounded upon the importance of fidelity to teaching programs and procedures, the need to actually implement (with accuracy) practices that are based on peer-reviewed literature and the law, the need to monitor the performance of all individuals involved in the educational process, the utility of task analyses and performance checklists, and the delivery of performance feedback. How then can supervisory staff begin to take the first steps to incorporate these concepts into educational and therapeutic environments? The remainder of this chapter will be committed to providing real-world, practical examples of how the first author's data-based performance management and performance feedback strategies have been applied within the context of supervision of and consultation with multi-level staff working within varied human service and educational settings. The first example is a performance monitoring checklist that was first utilized in an intensive, ABA-based school program for children with autism. As the program developer and director, the first author had the responsibility of designing the general curriculum, instructional methodologies, physical space arrangement, and assigning staff responsibilities for the program. For teaching any new skills involving discrimination, such as learning object labels, categories, action words, letter sounds, colors, shapes, instruction-following, etc., the program utilized a well-researched best practice, Discrete Trial Instruction, which was discussed previously in the chapter. In teaching this instructional methodology, the first author implemented a comprehensive training package that consisted of a didactic presentation that included video examples of the technique. Following this presentation, the staff members completed an activity in which they were assigned to groups of two, given nonsense word cards, and had to teach the made-up words to each other utilizing DTI and selected accompanying prompting and error correction procedures. Following this activity, which was closely monitored by the trainer and practiced until all trainees demonstrated proficiency, the trainer conducted live skills training via DTI to a student from the program.

The skills taught were from the student's current curriculum. Following this additional modeling, the trainees were required to select a skill from the learner's current program list and teach it. Trainer feedback was present initially, and faded until the trainee was able to implement the instructional technique independently and without error. Several program students were in attendance, and each trainee had the opportunity to engage in this supported, "real life" practice of the newly trained instructional technique. These training activities were conducted in professional development workshops that were held in the two days prior to the beginning of the school year. Once the school year was underway, the trainer continued to support accurate implementation of DTI, but beyond the first week, this support model shifted from a training-based paradigm to a supervisory one. Instructional staff were provided with a checklist detailing the important behaviors associated with DTI. Many of the elements of the form, as well as its physical layout, were adapted from forms shared with the first author by Vincent Carbone, Ed.D, BCBA-D, whose similar program was toured in the previous year. The form used for monitoring the performance of staff conduction of DTI (Table 2) is found below:

Table 2. Performance Management checklist for discrete trial instruction (Some elements of form layout and content adapted from the clinical work of Vincent Carbone, Ed.D.)

Effective Teaching Procedures Evaluation Form – Discrete Trial Instruction

Staff:___________________________________ circle one:
Observer:________________________________Date:__________ ___________
Announced Unannounced
Time of observation: from________until__________

Mark a "+" if skill occurred or was met. Mark a "-" if skill did not occur or was not met. Write "N/A" if the skill was not evaluated or appropriate for evaluation given circumstances. Do not count "N/A" when developing %.

Area One: General Instructional Considerations

Instructional area is neat and clean (no food other than reinf., no extraneous materials)	
Necessary materials are organized and ready	
Session begins promptly – no time is wasted (begins within five sec. of student in chair)	
Instruction is appropriately intense	
Staff carries out instruction with professionalism (see "Professional Considerations" in handbook)	
Skill data are collected and graphed when appropriate	

Area Two: Instructional Delivery

Instructional control is established (child is facing instructor or materials and responds to instruction, no inappropriate behaviors – see BIP)	
MO of learner is confirmed and captured	
Begins session with pairing or manding	
Stimulus prompts are used if necessary	
Learning trials are kept discrete (S^D– Response – Consequence. . . .no variation)	
Instructional delivery is natural (no exaggerated inflection)	
Instructional delivery is enthusiastic when appropriate	
Content is interspersed appropriately, including verbal operants	
Response requirement is interspersed appropriately	

Stimulus prompting is implemented when necessary	
Effective prompting strategies are selected	
Prompt fading is implemented when appropriate	
Pace of instruction is appropriate	
S^D topography is varied when appropriate	

Area Three: Error Correction

Appropriately selects error correction procedures	
If using N-N-P, remains faithful to sequence	
Allows no more than two cycles of NNP before return to errorless procedures	
Fades prompting if NNP was reverted to	
Refrains from backing up to easier tasks after S^D delivery, unless topographically related to shaping/successive approximations	
Re-presents instructional target at an adequate ratio	
Repeats target after prompted trial of NNP until independent, conducts distractor trials, and quickly returns to target at an adequate ratio (expanding or collapsing model)	

Area Four: Reinforcement

Delivers reinforcers immediately	
Teacher controls access to reinforcers	
Schedule of reinforcement is appropriate	
Reinforcement is differentiated	
Effort is made to make S^{r+} compete with S^{r-}	
Social reinforcement is paired with tangibles reinforcement	
Reinforcement type is varied to reflect MO	

Area Five: Behavior Management

Extinction procedures are implemented	
Composure is maintained during problem behavior (no change in inflection or affect)	
Agreed-upon intervention is implemented when problem behaviors occur	
Behavior data are recorded when behavior occurs	

Total "+" : _____

Number of areas evaluated (do not count "N/A"): _____
% of criteria met: _____
Graph % on performance graph

Avg.: _________
Rate (per minute): _________

Teaching Samples:
Opportunities to respond – 30 second timing:
1. ______________________________ total: _________
2. ______________________________ total: _________
3. ______________________________ total: _________

Correct responses per minute – 1 minute timing:
Correct: ___________________ Incorrect: ___________________

Strengths:

Targets / Constructive Suggestions / Suggested Timelines:

Signature of observer: ______________________________ Date: ____________

Signature of Staff: ______________________________ Date: ____________

Once or twice per month, supervisory staff observed the teaching staff while engaged in DTI. With this form, supervisors were able to instantly record the presence or absence of desired staff behaviors across five essential areas: General instructional considerations, instructional delivery, error correction, reinforcement, and behavior management.

At the end of the observation, a percentage of observed behaviors, relative to the total desired behaviors, could be calculated, thereby yielding a graphable datum. Additionally, time-sampling of teacher and learner behavior was also conducted, providing a measurement of instructional intensity and student engagement by producing rates of both opportunities to respond (teacher stimulus presentation) and correct responses on the part of the learner.

Following this observation, the supervisors graphed the percentage data on a corresponding graph, and immediately met with program staff toreview both the completed performance monitoring form and graph, adhering as closely as possible to the characteristics of effective feedback provided by Daniels and Daniels (2006), and described above. The performance monitoring graph (Figure 1) is found below:

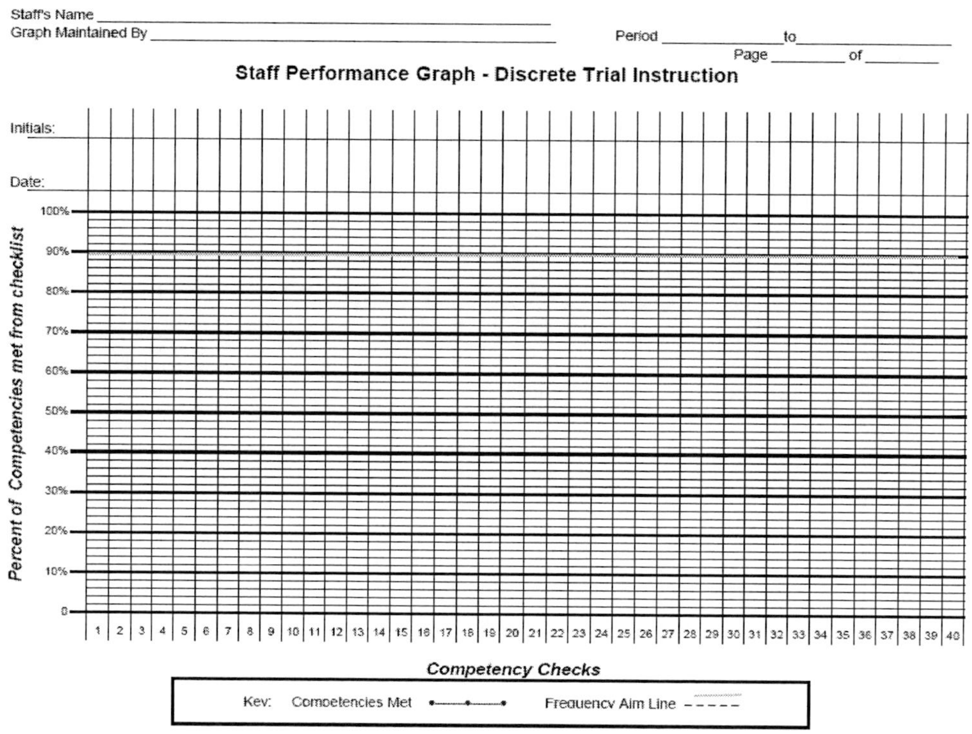

Figure 1. Performance Graph to accompany DTI Checklist.

The above DTI monitoring forms and graphs provided an ongoing record of staff improvement. In addition to providing individualized data regarding each staff member's areas of proficiency and need, it also provided the basis for a substantive annual performance review.

While the performance review form adopted by the school's human resources department was a simple series of questions, each accompanied by a rather subjective, five-point likert scale with possible responses ranging from unsatisfactory to excellent (and varying degrees in between), the use of the above-mentioned performance feedback system allowed these questions to be answered with a degree of objectivity, for the supervisor had the performance graph available to provide empirical substantiation to any item rating on the evaluation.

The first author has also adapted this system for supervising staff who work within home, and community, based behavioral services. Additionally, it has been adopted by the same as a means to provide performance feedback within consultative relationships, where educational and human service organizations are looking for effective and efficient methods to ensure that their employees are implementing the recommendations of the visiting consultant.

While the DTI performance monitoring checklist has already been described, the basic training model of the trainer first telling or showing, then providing prompting while the trainee begins to demonstrate the skill, fading out prompting and providing immediate feedback while the trainee performs the skill independently, and finally providing follow-up feedback or self-monitored feedback via a task checklist – may be employed to train, assess, and improve performance in almost any application of teaching methodology or educational plan development. Other skill checklists that the authors have utilized in school and human service settings include a similar checklist for small group instruction, shown below:

The preceding checklist is very similar in design and content to the DTI checklist, with some adaptations to make it relevant to group instruction. As with all of the checklists that have been and will be discussed in this chapter, its use produces a graphable datum that can be used to track teacher performance over time, and also used as the basis for visual analysis-based performance feedback delivered to the staff whose performance is being monitored.

As mentioned previously, special education consists of more than implementation of teaching technology; it also requires substantial individualization and goal planning. If performance management and feedback mechanisms are able to lend measurability to the behaviors associated with teaching, then why can they not also be applied to behaviors associated with instructional planning and organization? Christie and Yell (2010) completed a review of research conducted on IEP development and compared what they found to legal requirements regarding the same. An important distinction that was made in their review was to categorize studies conducted according to whether or not they focused on policies and procedures or intervention. In the case of special education, these distinctions may be characterized in another way as "procedural" vs. "substantive" issues in IEP development. If either one is lacking, however, an IEP and the education agency who developed it are possibly subject to due process litigation. Yell, Katsiyannis, and Hazelkorn (2007) indicated that the most effective IEPs are developed according to research-based practice, contain truly measurable goals, and use data to monitor progress and inform instructional changes. Smith (1990) concluded that, among other things, poor IEP development could be attributed to factors including a lack of adequate teacher training.

The chapter authors contend that the same issues, above, that play roles in the effectiveness of an IEP in a school setting also play roles in the effectiveness of a behavior intervention plan aimed at reducing problem behaviors and teaching replacement skills. In addition, the authors contend that the same lack of adequate training would contribute to poor treatment plan development. After directing a school-based program, the first author became employed as a director for a program that provided Behavioral Health Rehabilitation Services (BHRS) to individuals with autism at a large organization that served nearly 4,000 total clients through many programs across two states. BHRS is a state-specific program, funded by the state government that provides individualized programming and therapy to children who exhibit behavioral needs. The services are based on medical necessity and prescribed by a licensed psychologist or psychiatrist. Service delivery is carried out in the home, school, and/or community by clinical staff led by behavior specialists. The behavior specialists are responsible for the development of treatment procedures, consultation with the family, providing liaise between the treatment team and the family or school, training therapeutic staff, reviewing progress data, and submitting data reports to prescribing professionals. Under the behavior specialists, and working more frequently and directly with the client and his or her family, are direct-care therapists who are responsible for day-to-day plan implementation with the client, recording of data, and transfer of treatment plan skills to the client or the client's family or school personnel. Essentially, there are hundreds of hours of service provided to many clients each month, all based on the development of a clinical treatment plan. As these services are state-funded, those responsible for the disbursement of funds to reimburse provider agencies have imposed a mandate of accountability for such fund release, and – more specifically – have the prerogative to decline payment if the treatment plan is written in such a way that measurable progress is elusive.

Table 3. Performance Management Checklist – Small group instruction (Some elements of form layout and content adapted from the clinical work of Vincent Carbone, Ed.D.)

Effective Teaching Procedures Evaluation Form – Small Group Instruction

Staff:______________________________ circle one:
Observer:______________________________
Date:______________________________ Announced Unannounced
Time of observation: from________until__________

Mark a "+" if skill occurred or was met. Mark a "-" if skill did not occur or was not met. Write "N/A" if the skill was not evaluated or appropriate for evaluation given circumstances. Do not count "N/A" when developing %.

Area One: General Instructional Considerations

Instructional area is neat and clean (no food other than reinf., no extraneous materials)	
Necessary materials are organized and ready	
Session begins promptly – no time is wasted (begins within five sec. of student in chair)	
Instruction is appropriately intense – participants are actively responding most of the time	
Staff carries out instruction with professionalism (see "Professional Considerations" in handbook)	
Skill data are collected and graphed when appropriate	

Area Two: Instructional Delivery

Instructional control is established (child is facing instructor or materials and responds to instruction, no inappropriate behaviors – see BIP)	
Group size is appropriate, given learner skills	
Session focuses on skills or extension of skills within the learner's current program	
Learner has pre-requisite skills for group instruction within his or her repertoire	
Learning trials are kept relatively discrete (S^D– Response – Consequence. .little variation)	
Instructional delivery is natural (no exaggerated inflection)	
Instructional delivery enthusiastic when appropriate	
Content is interspersed appropriately, including verbal operants	
Response requirement is interspersed appropriately	
Effective prompting strategies are selected	
Prompt fading is implemented when appropriate	

Pace of instruction is appropriate	
S^D topography is varied when appropriate	

Area Three: Error Correction

Appropriately selects error correction procedures	
If using N-N-P, remains faithful to sequence	
Allows no more than two cycles of NNP before return to errorless procedures	
Fades prompting if NNP was reverted to	
Refrains from backing up to easier tasks after S^D delivery, unless topographically related to shaping/successive approximations	
Re-presents instructional target at an adequate ratio	
Repeats target after prompted trial of NNP until independent, conducts distractor trials, and quickly returns to target at an adequate ratio (expanding or collapsing model)	

Area Four: Reinforcement

Delivers reinforcers quickly	
Teacher controls access to reinforcers	
Schedule of reinforcement is appropriate	
Reinforcement is differentiated	
Effort is made to make S^{r+} compete with S^{r-}	
Social reinforcement is paired with tangibles reinforcement	
Reinforcement type is varied to reflect MO	

Area Five: Behavior Management

Extinction procedures are implemented	
Composure is maintained during problem behavior (no change in inflection or affect)	
Agreed-upon intervention is implemented when problem behaviors occur	
Behavior data are recorded when behavior occurs	

Total "+" : _____

Number of areas evaluated (do not count "N/A"): _____
% of criteria met: _____
Graph % on performance graph

Avg.: ________
Rate (per minute): ________

Teaching Samples:
Opportunities to respond – 30 second timing:
1. ______________________________ total: ________
2. ______________________________ total: ________
3. ______________________________ total: ________

Correct responses per minute – 1 minute timing:
Correct: ________________ Incorrect: ________________

Strengths:

Targets / Constructive Suggestions / Suggested Timelines:

Signature of observer: ______________________________ Date: ____________

Signature of Staff: ______________________________ Date: ____________

Prior to employment as the director of this particular program, the first author had interfaced with many organizations which were also providers of BHRS services, and had met with those responsible for releasing funds to pay for treatment (such as administrators, executives, and medical directors of managed care organizations contracted by county governments to ensure fiscally responsible applications of funds designated for BHRS). A common issue that frequently found its way into conversations was that treatment plans that were being submitted for approval (and subsequent reimbursement for services delivered based upon them) were lacking in their 1) adherence to procedural policies and 2) development of measurable goals and objectives. As the first author moved into this leadership role at a provider organization, the same was noted; the treatment plans were often missing essential demographic information and associated paperwork; and client behaviors targeted for treatment were defined in subjective terms (e.g. "Miguel will display appropriate coping skills," "Ramona will improve her attitude," etc.) that defied measurement because they did not define any particular behavior(s) that could be counted or otherwise objectively observed and quantified. Because of this last issue in particular, it was impossible to present any data (displayed graphically or otherwise) that documented actual behavioral progress, thereby making it difficult to make an argument to the payers that such services were efficacious or continued to be justified. Additionally, the regional climate regarding the administration of such programs had (until recently) been marked by a "laissez-faire" managerial approach, as treatment plans had historically been approved and services paid for regardless of the procedural and clinical integrity of the documents. Things changed, however, when many of the counties in the region had shifted from county administration of such programs to a "for-hire" administration of the programs via non-local managed care organizations. These organizations were contracted by the counties to curb what seemed like a hemorrhage of spending for services for which there was no evidence of their efficacy. At the same time they were charged with ensuring that every county resident who demonstrated a legitimate need for services would get the best level of care possible.

Once this transition occurred, the managed care organizations issued polite, but clear, cautionary memos indicating that services and treatment plans would be more closely scrutinized prior to authorization for payment. With this shift, many organizations found themselves unprepared to revise their approaches, for they had no background in the development of behaviorally-based definitions of client outcomes, as much of the work in which they had been immersed involved vague descriptions of feelings, beliefs, and attitudes. The key to surviving this transition was to find a way to operationalize client behaviors in measurable terms, develop treatment plans that would produce progress and outcomes data that could drive changes in treatment and justification for service continuation, and to demonstrate to the taxpayers that public funding was being well-spent.

Applying the concepts described in previous pages, the first author developed a data-based performance monitoring and feedback system to train staff, monitor their exhibition of trained skills, and maintain high levels of performance with regard to the development of treatment plans that were both procedurally and clinically sound.

First, a training session was held for all clinical staff that were responsible for developing treatment plans, in which the trainer discussed the changing attitudes toward measurement of behavioral services and the need for measurable goals and objectives regarding client behaviors. Examples of non-objective goals contained in existing treatment plans were provided, with a lesson on re-writing these in measurable terms. For example, rather than writing "Maura will demonstrate appropriate coping skills," the trainees were asked to produce goals that included statements such as "Maura will ask her teachers for assistance or a brief break when her math work becomes too difficult."

Concurrent with this training experience, the trainer conducted an audit of existing client charts with a chart audit tool in the form of a performance monitoring checklist. Similar to the work referenced by Christie and Yell (2010), above, the monitoring tool consisted of sections that evaluated the procedural soundness of the treatment plan or client chart, as well as the clinical soundness of the treatment plan (e.g. the therapeutic content). Clinical soundness items reflected evidence-based practice in the fields of autism intervention and Applied Behavior Analysis.

The monitoring tool produced a percentage of total required elements as its indictor of performance, which then became the graphable datum. Additionally, the tool allowed for supervisory input regarding recommended action and deadlines for correction of any errors. The monitoring tool is found in Table 4.

Table 4. Performance Monitoring checklist for treatment plan development

Team Leader: ____________________
BSC: ____________________
Reviewer: ____________________
Date: ____________________
Remediation
Learner whose book was reviewed (ID#): ________

Key:
\+ = Satisfactory
\- = Needs

Mark a "+" if target was satisfactory. Mark a "-" if target needs remediation. Write "N/A" if the target was not evaluated or appropriate for evaluation given circumstances. Do not count "N/A" when developing %.

Targets	+/-	Comments	Remediation Due	Remediation Compl.
Area One: General Considerations				
Plan is written professionally, is neat, and is free of typographical errors.				
Sections are distinct and labeled clearly.				
General program information, specific skill-building programs, and Behavior Reduction are represented in discrete sections				
Other:				
Area Two: Clinical Soundness of Plan				
Targets (goals) for acceleration are included in the plan.				
Targets (goals) for deceleration are included in the plan, if applicable.				
Targets/Goals reflect core autism deficits (when applicable).				
Targets/Goals are defined in objective/operational terms.				
Targets/Goals include measurable outcome criteria.				
A written and specific behavior plan is included in the treatment plan and contains clear procedures.				
Functional analysis of problem behaviors has been conducted prior to the selection of intervention methodologies.				
Treatment selection is based on the function of behavior, and appropriately matched to function.				
Initial baseline data are available and represented in the plan.				
Treatment data (from previous and current review periods) are available and summarized.				
Procedures for data-based program monitoring are included and specified within the plan.				
Progress recording is data-based (i.e. above procedures are being implemented).				
Copy of treatment plan is available				
Instructional plans are present				
Data are accurate and current.				
Progress data are graphed at least once per week.				
Graphs are present, accurate, and contain aims.				

Table 4. (Continued)

Program change forms are completed, implemented, and represented on graphs.				
Other:				

Area Three: Procedural Compliance

Notice of Privacy Practices Receipt				
Releases are current				
Consent for Treatment is current				
Parent/Child invitation is present				
Intake information is present				
Psychological Evaluation/Medical Necessity is current				
MA 97 is Current (HIPP)				
ISPT Signature page is complete				
Plan of care matches evaluation				
Treatment plan is consistent with evaluation				
Treatment plan is current and complete				
Authorization is present				
BSC/MT Progress notes are current (within 30 days) and refer to current goals and objectives				
TSS Progress notes are current (within 30 days) and follow current goals and objectives				
Full name on each page				
Monthly review by lead clinician				
Weekly supervision documented				
Encounter forms match (match authorization?)				
Other:				

Total "+" : _____

Number of areas evaluated (do not count "N/A"): _____

% of criteria met: _____

Graph % on performance graph

Targets for remediation / Constructive Suggestions / Suggested Timelines:

Signature of reviewer: ______________________ Date: __________

Signature of Staff: ______________________ Date: __________

After the skills training session for treatment plan development was conducted, the trainees were given a copy of the plan evaluation checklist, and asked to revise the plans for which they were responsible.

After about a month, random charts were selected by the supervisor and reviewed. Additionally, any new treatment plans that were submitted to the managed care organization were first submitted to the supervisor for approval and evaluation according to the checklist. A graph to correspond with the treatment plan checklist was also developed for each clinician, so that his or her performance over time could be documented. In the graph, the dimension of behavior that was being displayed was percentage of checklist items that were scored. The authors contend that this model could easily be adapted from its current context in human services to monitor the integrity of IEP-writing processes in the schools.

This model of performance monitoring and feedback also continues to prove itself valuable to the first author in his role as an autism consultant, where the frequent charge from hiring school districts is to assist in the development of intensive, behaviorally-based school programs.

In this case, the role of the consultant is usually to work with the district's autism specialists or lead special education staff to conduct an "overhaul" of existing autism support services. Typically, this involves many training workshops, where general ideas are discussed with groups, followed by a combination of in-situ classroom consultations with the staff of entire classrooms, or case consultation with individual students.

Table 5. Performance Monitoring checklist for program binder management (Some elements of form layout and content adapted from the clinical work of Vincent Carbone, Ed.D.)

Book Management Evaluation Form

Staff:____________________
Observer:____________________
Date:____________________
Learner whose book was reviewed: ________________

Key:
+ = Satisfactory
- = Needs Remediation

Mark a "+" if target was satisfactory. Mark a "-" if target needs remediation. Write "N/A" if the target was not evaluated or appropriate for evaluation given circumstances. Do not count "N/A" when developing %.

Targets	+/-	Comments	Remediation Due	Remediation Compl.
Area One: General Considerations				
Book is neat and clean				
Dividers are in place between each section and labeled correctly				
General Program Information, NET and DTI programs, and Behavior Reduction are represented in sections				
Other:				
Area Two: Curriculum / Program Management				
Program List is complete, current, and checked off daily				
Program sections match program list				
IEP Goals and Objectives are present				
Assessment summaries from ER are present				
IEP/ER/Progress Report dates and time schedules are present				
Copy of ABLLS grid is present				
Other:				
Area Three: Within-Program Organization				
Skill program graphs are the first page inside section				
Skill program graphs are accurate, neat, and up to date				
Frequency/fluency/percentage aims are established				
Data sheets are present and filled in correctly				
Item lists are up to date and correctly completed				
Item lists and data sheets face one another				
Initials and dates appear on data sheets and graphs				
Program change forms are completed, implemented, and represented on graphs				
Distractor cards are available for target interspersal				
Other:				

Table 5. (Continued)

Area Four: Behavior Reduction

Target behaviors listed and operationally defined				
Functional analysis information present				
Written behavior strategies present				
Data sheets are available				
Data are accurate and current				
Data are graphed at least once per week				
Graphs are present, accurate, and contain aims				
Program change forms are completed, implemented, and represented on graphs				
Other:				

Total "+": ____
Number of areas evaluated (do not count "N/A"): ____
% of criteria met: ____
Graph % on performance graph

Targets for remediation / Constructive Suggestions / Suggested Timelines:

Signature of reviewer: ________________ **Date:** ________

Signature of Staff: ________________ **Date:** ________

The classroom and case consultations almost always involve descriptions of educational and intervention techniques followed by modeling from the consultant, before the skills are transferred to the attending staff according to the methods described elsewhere in this chapter.

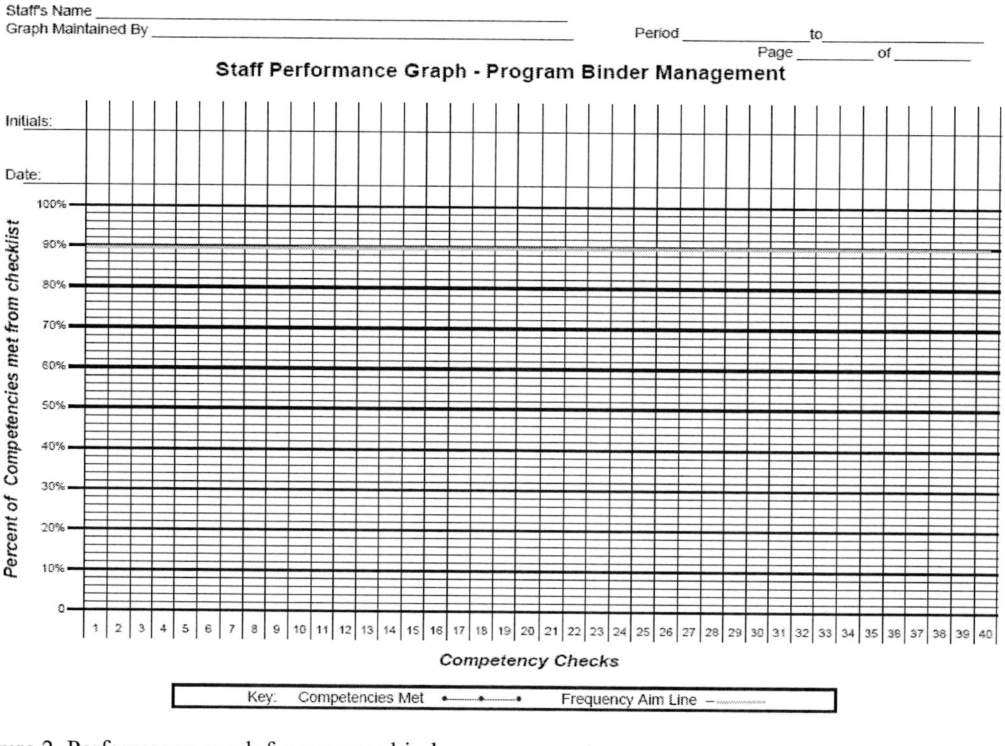

Figure 2. Performance graph for program binder management.

A great challenge, however, is presented when looking at overall program design, and how to monitor staff's implementation of general ideas when the consultant is absent (which is most of the time, given the relatively low frequency of on-site contact inherent to consulting relationships). An efficient skills instruction program for a learner with autism consists of curriculum protocol, analysis, and implementation and program structuring (Lund, 2000).

Curriculum is highly individualized, based on a thorough assessment and IEP goals and objectives, and forms the "what" that teachers and language therapists do during most of their time with learners with autism.

Analysis refers to the data collection and progress monitoring within the curriculum. Implementation and program structuring refer to the organizational infrastructure that the teacher puts in place to make sure that all elements of the program may be incorporated with the greatest degree of efficiency. In a way, it is the program structuring piece that serves as the "glue" to bind together all of the program components into a comprehensive and tenable course of action for the educational interventionist.

To assist toward this end, the first author will recommend that consultees compile a program binder that contains the learner's IEP or treatment plan, behavior intervention plan, relevant assessment data, current and past skill acquisition programs that comprise the individualized curriculum, organizational tools to manage instructional content within each skill acquisition program, and data collection tools (and accompanying graphs) to demonstrate progress in each component of the curriculum. All of these binder components, when viewed individually, could pose a daunting organizational challenge to the person responsible for the learner's programming.

However, with an established system of organization in place, the binder becomes an efficient means to manage and document the learner's progress across all instructional areas, increasing the likelihood that instruction will remain intense, individualized, and guided by data. When training consultees to organize an instructional program for a learner with autism, the first author will again follow the standard training protocol adopted across varying contexts and previously described in the chapter.

First, an explanation is offered, accompanied by a description of what is expected. Sometimes, simultaneously, a video is provided (from Gulick and Kitchen, 2007) that shows the components of the program binder and its organization, so that the video may be reviewed in the absence of the consultant. Second, a sample program binder is presented that has been set up in the desired manner. At this time, a book management performance monitoring checklist is provided to the consultee (Table 5), which lists, in writing, the requirements of a well-managed program binder. In situations where there is supervisory function over those responsible for maintaining the learners' program binders, there is a corresponding performance graph (Figure 2) that is utilized for providing performance feedback, and upon which the delivery of reinforcement or corrective action may be based.

SUMMARY

It would be beyond the scope of a single chapter in a text to demonstrate the possible applications of data-based performance feedback mechanisms within the education and treatment of individuals with intellectual and developmental disabilities. However, a model has been provided by which almost any behavior on the part of either teacher/trainer or learner may be trained, monitored, and improved. Any activity on the part of those providing educational or behavioral services that is deemed beneficial to those under their tutelage is susceptible to measurement, if the observer is provided with sufficient tools. Measurement is the first step toward documentation of progress, and progress is an indicator of behavioral change. School districts are accountable for the outcomes of the educational resources provided to their students. Providers of services that are paid for by third parties, whether by means of government funds or insurance reimbursement, are also increasingly being held accountable for the outcomes of the services being funded. Research has reliably demonstrated that effective intervention techniques exist and will lead to greater student or client outcomes if they are implemented consistently and accurately. Therefore, the burden of accountability should not simply rest on student outcomes measured in a vacuum, but also on degrees to which we can accurately measure and change the performance of those behaviors on the part of implementers that are associated with said outcomes. Simply put, the success of our programming rests largely with our abilities to precisely describe the research-validated activities in which teachers and trainers should be engaging, training them to perform these activities, and finally monitoring their performance of these behaviors in objective terms.

The tasks described above may be subdivided into the following recommended steps for consultants or supervisors:

1. Look for evidence-based solutions to instructional problems.
2. Operationalize procedures by constructing a task analysis, a checklist, or both.
3. Describe the desired staff behaviors.
4. Model the desired staff behaviors.
5. Provide guided practice for the staff with supervisory feedback in real time.
6. Provide a skills checklist for self-monitoring.
7. Observe the staff performing the skill at regular intervals, scoring the performance with the checklist.
8. Graph checklist data.
9. Provide immediate, supportive feedback to the staff.
10. Reinforce desired changes in behavior; Provide error correction for non-desired changes.

Besides the obvious and most socially pertinent benefit of data-based performance management in educational and human service environments, which is improvement on the part of the student or client for whom services are provided, it also offers some assistance to potential human resources dilemmas regarding the objective evaluation of staff performance. Aside from the fundamental issues associated with vague and subjective rating scales (What is the operational difference between "somewhat satisfactory," "satisfactory," "good," or "very good?"), a data-based performance management system based on performance checklists also provides highly-individualized and specific information to each staff member with regard to strengths and deficits in performance. Data-based management also lends itself extremely well to contingencies of reinforcement (positive reinforcers such as small bonuses or negative reinforcers such as a day off of bus duty) for performance at or above expected aims, which provides further motivation for teachers to engage in the most effective teaching behaviors.

The contexts for the applicability of solid, data-based measures of performance are virtually limitless. It has been the intention this chapter's authors to introduce the reader to several applications related specifically to the education and therapeutic treatment of individuals with intellectual and developmental disabilities. Should these and similar procedures become standard practice in human service and educational settings, many of the instructional issues faced by populations with instructional difficulties may be ameliorated, and progress may be hastened. The potential result of such progress would undoubtedly be improvement in the quality of life experienced by individuals with disabilities and better utilization of the public resources that fund service and education programs.

REFERENCES

Arco, L. (1991). Effects of outcome performance feedback on maintenance of client and staff behavior in a residential setting. *Behavioral Residential Treatment, 6,* 231-247.

Auld, R.G., and Belfiore, P.J. (2010). Timing is everything: Using positive behavior supports in student-teaching. In *Progress in education*, R.V. Nata (Ed.), (pp. 159-177). Hauppauge, NY: Nova Science Publishers.

Auld, R.G., Belfiore, P.J., and Scheeler, M.A. (2010). A study of treatment integrity for differential reinforcement of an alternative behavior (DRA) training on pre-service teachers in general education settings. *Journal of Behavioral Education, 19,* 169-183.

Auld, R.G., Belfiore, P.J., and Scheeler, M.A. (2007). Preparing pre-service teachers to use positive behavior supports in general education classrooms. *Pennsylvania Teacher Educator, 6*, 50-57.

Baer, D. M., Wolf, M. M., and Risley, T. D. (1968). Some current dimensions of applied behavior analysis. *Journal of Applied Behavior Analysis, 1*, 91-97.

Balcazar, F., Hopkins, B. L., and Suarez, Y. (1985). A critical, objective review of performance feedback. *Journal of Organizational Behavior Management, 7,* 65-89.

Belfiore, P.J. and Browder, D.M. (1992). The effects of self-monitoring on teacher's data-based decisions and on the progress of adults with severe mental retardation. *Education and Training in Mental Retardation, 27*, 60-67.

Belfiore, P. J., Fritts, K.M., and Herman, B. C. (2008). The role of procedural integrity: Using self-monitoring to enhance discrete trial instruction. *Focus on Autism and Other Developmental Disabilities, 23*, 95-102.

Belfiore, P.J., Lee, D.L., Scheeler, M.C., and Klein, D. (2002). Implications of behavioral momentum and academic achievement for students with behavioral disorders: Theory, application, and practice. *Psychology in the Schools, 39*, 171-179.

Belfiore, P.J., Pulley -Basile, S., and Lee, D.L. (2008). Using a high probability command sequence to increase classroom compliance: The role of behavioral momentum. *The Journal of Behavioral Education, 17*, 160-171.

Barlow, D.H., Nock, M.K., and Hersen, M. (2009). *Single case experimental designs: Strategies for studying behavior change*. NY: Pearson Education.

Cautilli, J. D., and Santilli-Connor, L. (2000) Assisting the Client/Consultee to Do What is Needed: A Functional Analysis of Resistance and other Forms of Avoidance. *The Behavior Analyst Today, 1*, 37-42.

Christie, C. A. and Yell, M.L. (2010). Individualized education programs; legal requirements and research findings. *Exceptionality, 18,* 109-123.

Cooper, J. O., Heron, T. E., and Heward, W. L. (2007). Applied behavior analysis (2nd ed.). Upper Saddle River, NJ: Pearson.

Daniels, A.C. and Daniels, J.E. (2006). *Performance management: changing behavior that drives organizational effectiveness.* Atlanta:Performance Management Publications.

Detrich, R., Keyworth, R., and States, J. (2007). A roadmap to evidence-based education: Building an evidence-bases culture. *Journal of Evidence-based practices for schools, 8*, 26-44.

DiGennaro, F. D., Martens, B. K., and Kleinmann, A. E. (2007). A comparison of performance feedback procedures on teachers' treatment implementation integrity and students' inappropriate behavior in special education classrooms. *Journal of Applied Behavior Analysis, 40,* 447–461.

DiGennaro, F.D., Martens, B.K., and McIntyre, L. L. (2005). Increasing treatment integrity through negative reinforcement: Effects on teacher and student behavior. *School Psychology Review, 34*, 220-231.

Greiner, C.S. and Smith, B. (2009). Analyses of selected specific variables and teacher attrition. *Education,* 129, 579-583.

Gulick, R. and Kitchen, T. (2007) Effective Instruction for Children with Autism: *An Applied Behavior Analytic Approach.* Erie: Dr. Gertrude A. Barber Educational Institute.

Heward, W. L. (2003). Ten faulty notions about teaching and learning that hinder the effectiveness of special education. *The Journal of Special Education*, 36, 186-205.

Horner, R.H., Carr, E.G., Halle, J., McGee G., Odom, S. and Wolery, M. (2005). The use of single-subject research to identify evidence-based practice in special education. *Exceptional Children, 71*, 165-179.

Individuals with Disabilities Education Act, 20 U.S.C. §1401 *et seq*.

Kissel, R. C., Whitman, T. L., and Reid, D. H. (1983). An institutional staff training and self-management program for developing multiple self-care skills in severely/profoundly retarded individuals. *Journal of Applied Behavior Analysis,* 16, 395-415.

Kitchen, T., Belfiore, P.J., and Kitchen H.L. (2009). The necessity of measures of procedural integrity to ensure effective delivery of evidence-based interventions for children with autism spectrum disorders. In *Special Education in the 21st Century*, M.T. Burton (Ed.) (pp. 67-94). Hauppauge, NY: Nova Science Publishers.

Kratochwill, T. R., Hitchcock, J., Horner, R. H., Levin, J. R., Odom, S. L., Rindskopf, D. M and Shadish, W. R. (2010). Single-case designs technical documentation. Retrieved from What Works Clearinghouse website: http://ies.ed.gov/ncee/wwc/pdf/wwc_scd.pdf.

Kratochwill, T.R. and Mace, F.C. (1984). Time series research in psychotherapy. In M. Hersen, L. Michelson, and A Bellick (Eds.) *Issues in Psychotherapy Research*, NY: Plenum.

Lane, K., Bocian, K., MacMillan, D., and Gresham, F. (2004). Treatment integrity: An essential but often forgotten component of school-based interventions. *Preventing School Failure, 48*, 36-43.

Lavie, T, and Sturmey, P., (2002). Training staff to conduct a paired-stimulus preference assessment. *Journal of Applied Behavior Analysis, 35*, 209-211.

Leblanc, M., Ricciardi, J.N., and Luiselli, J.K. (2005). Improving discrete trial instruction by paraprofessional staff through an abbreviated performance feedback intervention. *Education and treatment of Children, 28,* 76-82.

Lee, D.L., Belfiore, P.J., and Budin, S.G. (2008). Riding the wave: Creating a momentum of school success. *Teaching Exceptional Students, 40*, 65-70.

Levin, J.R., O'Donnell, A.M., and Kratochwill, T.R. (2003). Educational/pstchological intervention research. In W. Reynolds and G. Miller (Eds.), *Handbook of Psychology, Vol. 7: Educational Psychology* (pp. 557-581). Hoboken, NJ: Wiley and Sons.

McIntyre, L.L., Gresham, F.M., DiGennaro, F.D., and Reed, D.D. (2007). Treatment integrity of school-based interventions with children in the *Journal of Applied Behavior Analysis* 1991-2005. *Journal of Applied Behavior Analysis, 40*, 659-672.

McWilliams, R., Nietupski, J., and Hamre-Nietupski, S. (1990). Teaching complex activities to students with moderate handicaps through the forward chaining of shorter total cycle response sequences. *Education and Trainin in Mental Retardation and Developmental Disabilities, 25,* 292-298.

Odom, S.L., Brantlinger, E., Gersten, R., Honer, R.H., Thompson, B., and Harris, K.R. (2005). Research in special education: Scientific methods and evidence-based practices. *Exceptional Children, 71*, 137-148.

Odom, S.L., Brown, W.H., Frey T., Karasu, N., Smith-Canter, L.L., and Strain, P.S. (2003). Evidence-based practices for young children with autism: Contributions for single-subject design research. *Focus on Autism and Other Developmental Disabilities, 18,* 166-176.

Peterson, N. (1982). Feedback is not a new principle of behavior. *The Behavior Analyst, 5,* 101-102.

Peterson, L., Homer, A., and Wonderlick, S. (1982). The integrity of independent variables in behavior analysis. *Journal of Applied Behavior Analysis, 15*, 477-492.

Plavnick, J.B., Ferreri, S.J., and Maupin, A.N. (2010). The effects of self-monitoring on the procedural integrity of a behavioral intervention for young children with developmental disabilities. *Journal of Applied Behavior Analysis,* 43, 315-320.

Reid, D. H., and Whitman, T. L. (1983). Behavioral staff management in institutions: A critical review of effectiveness and acceptability. *Analysis and Intervention in Developmental Disabilities, 3*, 131-149.

Repp, A. C., Felce, D., and DeKock, U. (1987). Observational studies of staff working with mentally retarded persons: a review. *Research in Developmental Disabilities, 8,* 331-350.

Resnick, B., Wang, M. C., and Kaplan, J. (1973). Task analysis in curriculum design: A hierarchically sequenced introductory mathematics curriculum. *Journal of Applied Behavior Analysis,* 6, 679-709.

Richman, G. S., Riordan, M. R., Reiss, M. L., Pyles, D. A. M., and Bailey, J. S. (1988). The effects of self-monitoring and supervisor feedback on staff performance in a residential setting. *Journal of Applied Behavior Analysis, 21*, 401-409.

Sarakoff, R.A., and Sturmey, P. (2004). The effects of behavioral skills training on staff implementation of discrete-trial teaching. *Journal of Applied Behavior Analysis, 37*, 353-358.

Schoen, A.A. (2003). What potential does the applied behavior analysis approach have for the treatment of children and youth with autism? *Journal of Instructional Psychology, 30*, 125-131.

Schlosser, R.W. (2009). The role of single-subject experimental designs in evidence-based practice times. *National Center for the Dissemination of Disability Research.*

Schlosser, R.W., and Raghavedra, P. (2004). Evidence-based practice in augmentative and alternative communication. *Augmentative and Alternative Communication, 20*, 1-21.

Seligson-Petscher, E., Bailey, J.S. (2006) Effects of training, prompting, and self-monitoring on staff behavior in a classroom for students with disabilities. *Journal of Applied Behavior Analysis,* 39, 215-226.

Shriver, M.D. (2007). Roles and responsibilities of researchers and practitioners for translating research to practice. *Journal of Evidence-Based Practices for Schools, 8*, 4-25.

Shriver, M.D. and Watson, T.S. (2005). Bridging the great divide: Linking research to practice in scholarly publications. *Journal of Evidence-Based Practices for Schools, 6*, 5-18.

Simek, T.C. and O'Brien, R.M. (1981). *Total golf: a behavioral approach to lowering your score and getting more out of your game.* New York: Doubleday and Co.

Skinner, B. F. (1938). *The behavior of organisms*. Englewood Cliffs, NJ: Prentice Hall.

Skinner, B. F. (1953). *Science and human behavior.* New York: Free Press.

Skinner, B. F. (1974). *About behaviorism*. New York:Knopf.

Smith, D. M. (1995). A system of program evaluation and the use of feedback as a means of improving service delivery. *Behavioral Interventions, 10,* 225-236.

Tillman, T.C. (2000) Generalization Programming and Behavioral Consultation. *The Behavior Analyst Today, 1,* 30-34.

U.S. Department of Education, National Center for Education Statistics (2011). *Digest of Education Statistics, 2010* (NCES 2011-015), Chapter 2. Retrieved from http://nces.ed.gov/fastfacts/display.asp?id=64.

U.S. Department of Education (2010). Fiscal Year 2011 Budget Summary - February 1, 2010. Sec. 3. Part B. Retrieved from http://www2.ed.gov/about/overview/budget/budget11/summary/edlite-section3b.html.

Vollmer, T.R., and Iwata, B. (1992). Differential reinforcement as treatment for behavior disorders: Procedural and functional variations. *Research in Developmental Disabilities,13,* 393-417.

Yell, M.L., Katsiyannis, A., and Hazelkorn, M. (2007). Reflections on the 25th anniversary of the Supreme Court's decision in *Board of Education v. Rowley. Focus on Exceptional Children, 39,* 1-12.

Zhan, S., and Ottenbacher, K.J. (2001). Single subject research designs for disability research. *Disability and Rehabilitation, 23*, 1-8.

This chapter was reviewed 08/29/2011 by: Leanne Roberts, Ph.D.

In: Intellectual Disability
Editors: Domenico F. Mancini and Carlo M. Greco ISBN: 978-1-61942-298-8

Chapter 3

INTELLECTUAL DISABILITY MANAGEMENT, CAUSES AND SOCIAL PERCEPTIONS TOWARDS WELL-DEFINED SITUATIONS

George S. Mouzakitis[*]
Educational Organization e-DEKA,
Korinthos, Greece

ABSTRACT

For decades, psychologists, educationalists, even University faculty used to attach labels to describe persons deviating from what has been attributed to be normal. Yet, from the linguistic, communicative and psychological points of view the majority of these terms do not convey the aimed message. Obviously, this practice has resulted to serious problems of understanding the specific issues and developing the appropriate remedial measures.

Consequently, there is a serious problem faced by all people with disabilities due to a variety of terms attached to such persons, for example handicapped, exceptional, retarded and other. Instead of these terms, the most authentic world organizations refer to persons with disabilities, which is, also, fully accepted by the unions of these persons. The United Nations Organization (UNO) in the convention of the rights for *persons with disabilities* (2006) support that the relative problems result from the interaction between persons with impairments and attitudinal and environmental barriers.

The World Health Organization (WHO), in 2001 defined that *disability* is not something that only happens to a minority of people and recognizes the experience of disability as a universal human experience.

The Council of Europe (2006) supports that the key target of the *Disability Action Plan* is to serve as a practical tool to develop and implement viable strategies to bring about full participation of *people with disabilities* in society. The employment and Social Affairs of EU27 (2010) defines *disability* as a right issue and not a matter of discrimination. The paradox about the terminology used so far is that most of the member-countries of these organizations, though signatory, continue to use terminology

[*] E-mail: geom.@hol.gr

which was adopted many years ago. Additionally, the fact that gifted persons (another wrong term) are classified among the persons "with special needs" is beyond any logic concept. More specifically, the term *"mental retardation"* is not the appropriate one. *Mental* refers to the health or illnesses of the mind. *"retardation"* means reduction or delay of the rate of developing of something. Using this term to describe someone who has not developed mentally as much as most other people of the same age, is considered and really is *offensive*. The alternative term *" developmental disability"* or even *" Intellectual Disability"*, is closer to the accurate description of these persons, since *"developmental"* means a person's (child's) growth and ability to learn things and *"disability"* denotes a condition in which someone *is not able to use a part of the body or mind properly.* On the other hand, intellectual denotes the ability to think in an intelligent way and understand things. This term is used in USA and Canada to describe almost life-long disabilities related to the condition of persons to perform in these areas. A supportive element is the definition of the American Association on Mental Deficiency (1973) relating mental retardation *to deficits manifested during the developmental period.* Based on these concepts, this chapter will discuss issues of management, causes and social perceptions of this disability and criticize the various definitions, the IQ testing, levels of severity, reliability of prevalence, future trends. Finally, recommendations suitable to provide solutions to this situation will be tabled.

INTRODUCTION

It has been identified that the communication process sometimes is ineffective to convey the correct message. This is, almost, due to the use of terms which are either inappropriate or confusing. Even the definition of the term *communication*, as used by many people is *discredited by the experts*. The typical definition most often used is: "The process for transferring thoughts and ideas from one person to another .Yet, Hamilton, C. [1] argues that the definition implies that communication is one way process, which is wrong. He further cross-refers to Berlo, D., who supports that "Communication does not consist of the transmission of meaning. Meanings are not transferable. Only messages are transferable, and meanings are not in the message, they are in the message user [2]. It is obvious that both Hamilton and Baro are right as much as according to the *oxford English Dictionary* [3] the root of the term is the Latin *communicare* which means " to make common to many, to share". Therefore, communication is the process of people sharing thoughts, ideas, and feelings with each other in commonly understandable ways.(figure 1)

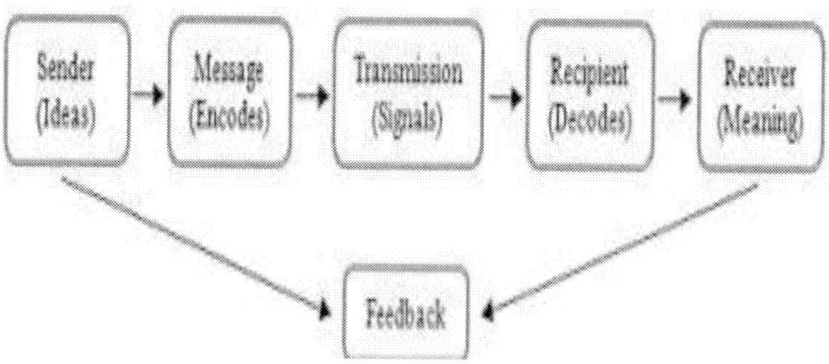

Figure 1. Communication mechanism.

The mechanism of communication develops in five stages plus one, the confirmation one, not always followed.

Stage one: The idea is formed in the mind of sender.
Stage two: The message is encoded.
Stage three: Transmission- Sender speaks.
Stage four: Recipient decodes the message.
Stage five: Receiver understands the message.
Stage six: Feedback process, which means the message has been received and understood.

This whole procedure matches with Scott Maclean's definition [4] : "You only communicate when the message you send out has been received and sent back to you, so you know that it has been properly understood". In our everyday activities we communicate with other people. Our thoughts ideas, proposals or information are conveyed by means of linguistic systems or symbols, or else words The system requires a receiver and a sender operating (tuned) in the same wave band. Linguistically, the wave band is the word. In case communication process uses words of confusing or unknown meaning there is no communication and hence understanding. Let us take as example a Greek person who does not know foreign languages. A message in his mobile: "This is a free invitation for two persons to a wine festival at Nemea" means nothing. It can be concluded, therefore, that effective communication is a process where a message is received and understood by the receiver in the manner that the sender intended it to be. The confusion and misunderstanding of messages are directly affected by the following factors:

- Language unknown to the receiver.
- Different system of logic between sender and receiver.
- Terms unknown to the receiver.
- Different background of sender and receiver.
- Cultural differences.
- Different points of view.

A highly illustrative example is mentioned in Cheryl Hamilton' s book: "Communicating for Results" (page 9):

"A college professor was a member of a particular credit union. Needing a quick loan one day, she filled out all necessary application forms and waited while the employee typed the request into the computer terminal. When the answer was received, the employee told the professor:

- I am very sorry, but we cannot give you a loan.
- Why not?
- I don't know why, but the computer says we can't.
- What does the computer say?
- The computer typed out the words: *No loan this member.*

Urged by the professor, the employee referred the matter to the manager only to learn that the message of the computer meant that the professor did not have a loan. If she had already had a loan with the credit union, the computer would have responded with *one loan this member"*.

Unfortunately, this negative phenomenon happens in the area of persons with disabilities, as well. Even the general term of "Special Education" is confusing and misleading. The term "special" is used to characterize persons with inferiority status in social, educational and professional sectors.

Yet, "special" means distinguished, better than normal. Vocational Schools offer many special courses, say for nurses, electricians or other professionals. All these people are not necessarily disabled Misused terms and terms recommended as appropriate are cited here below . But first, the definition of certain terms used to describe persons with disabilities, is considered very important in order to facilitate communication with these persons, recognition of the specific problems, degree of severity of the relative problems.

- Deficiency : Lack of something required by the body
- Disability : Lack of ability to use a part of body or brain properly.
- Disorder: Illness or medical condition.
- Disturbance: The case when someone's mind or body develops a problem and stops operating in the usual way.
- Handicap: Physical or mental injury or illness which is severe and permanent.
- Impairment: The case when a part of the body is unable to perform an activity fully.
- Discrepancy: A difference between things which should be the same,

It is surprising that, for decades, this part of education for persons with disabilities follows the terms which have been originally used. The use of terms not easily understood or creating confusion may have serious impacts on the lives of persons It is interesting to note that important organizations worldwide have decided to change the terms which are not appropriate any more, to new ones scientifically supported:

To begin with, the term PERSONS WITH SPECIAL NEEDS is not anymore accepted even by the disabled persons themselves. Instead, the term *PERSONS WITH DISABILITIES* has been introduced:

a) The United Nations Organization (UNO) in the Convention of the Rights for persons with *Disabilities* (2006) support that they result from the interaction between persons with impairments and attitudinal and environmental barriers.
b) The World Health Organization (WHO, 2001) defines that *disability* is not something that only happens to a minority of humanity and recognizes the experience of *disability* as a universal human experience.
c) The Council of Europe (2006) supports that the key target of the *Disability* Action Plan is to serve as a practical tool to develop and implement viable strategies to bring about full participation of *people with disabilities* in society.
d) The Employment and Social Affairs of EU27 (2010) defines *disability* as a right issue and not a matter of discrimination.

It is advisable that definitions used to describe persons of any sort of disabilities should be universally accepted to ensure clear understanding. In science, there is not a matter of *traditional pursuit,* but a purely scientific discourse. Tradition is a long-established way of defining the various terms related to persons with disabilities. On the other hand, scientific ways of defining terms conform with the principles or methods used in describing specific situations. However, apart from the linguistic point of view there is, also, the psychological and sociological dimension. Quite a few terms are considered insulting and are substituted by other terms which are not only scientifically correct but, at the same time, they are sensitive to the problems and feelings of persons with disabilities. Mental retardation (say: *ree*-tar-day-shun) is a term that was once commonly used to describe someone who learns and develops more slowly than other kids. But it is not used as much anymore because it hurts people's feelings. [5]. Instead, you might hear terms like "intellectual disability" or "developmental delay." All these words mean basically the same thing. Someone who has this kind of problem will have trouble learning and functioning in everyday life. But having an intellectual disability doesn't mean a person can't learn. Some kids with autism, Down syndrome, or cerebral palsy may be described as having an intellectual disability, yet they often have a great capacity to learn and become quite capable kids. An interesting development in the process of labeling persons with intellectual disabilities is presented by Raynold, T., [6] and others and I am tempted to transfer it to these pages as an unalterable text:

> QUOTE:"Over the past decade, it has become widely accepted that the diagnostic label "mental retardation" has come to carry and convey a negative social stigma. As a consequence of this realization, steps are underway to replace the label "mental retardation" with an alternative, more neutral and less stigmatizing label which nevertheless preserves clinicians' ability to communicate about the diagnosis. In 2002 the Surgeon General's Office issued the following statement, "The Office of the Surgeon General is aware that there is a controversy around the use of the term "mental retardation" and that advocacy groups and professional associations are currently discussing various alternatives such as "cognitive developmental disabilities" and "intellectual disabilities." Until a consensus is reached, and with the goal of drawing attention to the great health disparities faced by people with what has been traditionally known as mental retardation in mind, the term "mental retardation" will be used in official media information on the Surgeon General's initiative."

In October 2010 President Barrack Obama signed into law a bill known as Rosa's Law that requires the terms "mental retardation" and" mentally retarded" to be stripped from federal health, education, and labor policy and replaced with the terms "intellectual disability" and "individual with an intellectual disability." Meanwhile, progress has continued on the much anticipated release of a new Diagnostic and Statistical Manual of Mental Disorders (DSM-5). Although it may be several years before the new DSM-5 is released, it is expected that this new DSM will replace the term "mental retardation" with the term "intellectual developmental disorder." However, professional organizations such as the American Association on Intellectual and Developmental Disabilities (AAIDD at www.aaaidd.org) and advocacy groups such as The Arc have applied it UNQUOTE. [6].

To this point supporting evidence and opinions could be mentioned:

- *According to Jack Hourcade [7]:* " The term *mental retardation* has been the term of choice for individuals with significant limitations in intellectual functioning and adaptive behavior for many decades now. However, as was the case for its predecessor term *mental deficiency,* over the past few years the term *mental retardation* has lost much professional acceptance. In 2002 the Council for Exceptional Children's Division of Mental Retardation and Developmental Disabilities voted overwhelmingly to change its name to the Division on Developmental Disabilities. In deciding to remove the term *mental retardation* from their name, they concluded that the term *was offensive, excluded many individuals with cognitive and intellectual disabilities, including those with autism.*
- Additionally, according to the NICHCY Disability Fact Sheet 8 [8] " Until Rosa's Law was signed into law by President Obama in October 2010, **I**ndividuals with **D**isabilities **E**ducation **A**ct **(IDEA)** used the term"*mental retardation"* instead of "*intellectual disability"*.

Just like other health problems, an intellectual disability can be mild (smaller) or major (bigger). The bigger the disability the more trouble someone will have learning and becoming an independent person. During school, a child with intellectual disability will probably need help. Some children have aids who stay with them during the school day. They may be in special classes or get other services to help them learn and develop. During the early years in the history of "Special Education" various scientists, mainly psychologists, classified people into groups according to their disabilities. As a result of this movement, the following categories have been registered:

- Learning Disabilities
- Emotional Disturbance
- Speech and Language Disorders
- Hearing Impairment
- Visual Impairment
- Physical Handicaps
- Mental Retardation
- Behavior Disorders

The lack of linguists in the process of defining the various impairments is obvious and has resulted to the creation of misunderstandings among everybody concerned with special education. The following recommendations are tabled for concern and discussion

Existing Terms Of Persons In Need	Recommended Changes
Mental Retardation	Intellectual Disability Developmental Disability
Learning Disabilities	Learning Discrepancies
Emotional Disturbance	Emotional Disturbance
Speech And Language Disorders	Speech And Language Deficiacy
Hearing Impairment	Hearing Impairment
Visual Impairment	Visual Impairment
Physical Handicaps	Physical Deficiency
Multiple Handicaps	Multiple Disabilities

DEFINITIONS: THE UNSCIENTIFIC GAME

It is a frequent phenomenon various sources defining terms related to health, psychology, sociology or other sectors to use idiomatic expressions not considered, examined or tested according to methods which scientists think necessary. In the case of defining *developmental disabilities* there is a host of entries cited both in general and medical dictionaries. It might be claimed that *pluralistic varieties* contribute to a better understanding, and assimilation of ideas.

General English Dictionaries

- *Babylon English:* Mental retardation is a condition in which the intellect does not develop normally. [9]
- *iMedix:* Mental retardation is a developmental disability that first appears in children under the age of 18. [10]
- *WordNet 2.0* : It is lack of normal development of intellectual capacities.[11]
- *Answers . com:* It is an abnormal intellectual development as a result of congenital causes, or disease and characterized by any of various cognitive deficiencies.[12]
- *Merriam Webster:* It is a sub-average intellectual ability equivalent or less than an IQ of 70 that is accompanied by significant deficits in abilities necessary for independent daily living.[13]
- *Dictionary.com:* It is a developmental disorder characterized by a subnormal ability to learn and a substantially low IQ.[14]

Scientific Dictionaries

- *Medical Dictionary:* Mental retardation is a developmental disability that first appears in children under the age of 18. It is defined as an Intellectual functioning level that is well below average and significant limitations in daily life skills. [15]
- *Webster's New World Medical Dictionary:* Mental retardation is a term used when a person has certain limitations in mental functioning and in skills such as communicating , taking care of him/herself, and social skills. [16]
- *Psychological Dictionary:* Mental retardation is a term technically used in Britain and North America for describing people who score less that 70 IQ.[17]
- *Oxford Dictionary of Sociology:* Mental retardation is a mental sub-normality, one of the clusters of terms used, such as mental deficiency, mental impairment , mental retardation and mental handicap which refer to states of arrested or incomplete development of intellectual capacities, where intelligence is considerably below normal [18]
- *Dictionary of Education:* A term referring to that group of conditions characterized by (a) slow rate of retardation, (b) reduced learning capacity, and (c) inadequate social adjustment. [19].
- *The Massachusetts Regulatory Definition* of mental retardation confirms that mental retardation before the age of 18 and is manifested by significantly sub-average intellectual functioning existing concurrently with related limitations in two or more of the following applicable adaptive skills areas:[20]

- Communication
- Self-care
- Home living
- Social skills
- Community use
- Self-.direction
- Health and safety
- Financial academics
- Leisure and work

The American Association on Mental Retardation (AAMR) [21] supports that mental retardation is not a medical disorder, nor a mental disorder. It is a particular state of functioning that begins in childhood and is characterized by limitation in both intelligence and adaptive skills.

A careful tracing among or between the lines of all the above definitions about *developmental disabilities* concludes that the basic core of the definitions coincide closely with each other , for example:

- Intellect does not develop.
- Developmental disability.
- Lack of normal development.
- Abnormal intellectual development.
- Sub-average intellectual ability.
- Developmental disorder.
- Limitations of mental functions.
- IQ score less than 70.
- Mental sub-normality.
- Reduced learning capacity.

A prominent query that has been unanswered so far is why the existing terminology has not been substituted by any of the converging terms of the definitions listed above, such as *developmental, intellectual, mental sub-normality etc.* Ordinary, normal people are not used to tracing the most appropriate meanings of terms by looking up the words to dictionaries in order to find the particular piece of information.

The use of terms not easily understood or creating confusion may have serious impacts on the lives of persons with disabilities. For example, the use of the terms handicapped, exceptional, retarded and other similar ones, result to confusion.

A typical example of the confusion created by the variety of definitions concerning the various disabilities among the EU27 countries is the decision of the European Union to assign to the Brunel University [22] to perform a comparative analysis of the definitions of disability used in the social security and employment area across the European Union member states.

To validate the notion about the communication problems created by the terms used, which people do not understand, we carried an empirical research with a sample of 68 persons randomly selected, aged 25 to 45 years. The problem statement was:

"Your son has low achievement score at school. His teacher informed you that your son is an underachiever. What do you understand is the case?

We distributed two answer sheets of four options each. Sheet A(Table 1) included the term "Mental Retardation" which was substituted by the term " His mind has not developed yet" in Sheet B.(Table 2) Of course, the research was conducted in the Greek language with strict authentic translation of the English terms. Interviewees were asked to tick only one option from each sheet. The results have been unexpectedly clear.

In sheet "A" they did not know the term mental retardation, whereas in sheet "B" the term: "his mind has not developed yet" was understood.

Table 1. Sheet A

Sheet "A"	Persons	%
Mental retardation	6	8.82
He goes to school late	30	44.12
He does not read well	16	23.53
I do not understand	16	23.53

Table 2. Sheet B

Sheet "B"	Persons	%
His mind has not developed yet	40	58.82
He goes to school late	8	11.76
He does not read well	10	14.71
I do not understand	10	14.71

From the comparison of the findings of the two question sheets it is concluded that the use of terms which are universally understood is quite important for the planning, implementation, monitoring and evaluation of the effectiveness ot the treatment applied to the persons with disabilities.

MEASUREMENT OF INTELLIGENCE

Though the intelligence measurement is often disputed as to the decisive role it plays in the diagnosis of the various types of disabilities, yet the IQ score is a useful tool for predicting but, also, categorizing the various degrees of disability. (figure 2). Two most reliable and commonly used scales are the *Wechsler IQ scale* and the *Stanford-Binet scale.* As seen in figure 2 Standard Deviations and cumulative percentage are the same. The difference is in the extremes, lower 40 and highest 160 in the first scale and lower 36 and highest 164 in the second scale. On the basis of the above figure, the classification of intelligence according to Wechsler IQ scale is the following. (Table 3)

According to Stanford Binet scale, the classification of Intelligence presents some differences. The classification of Wechsler is more general as concerns the top score (>=130) as well as the lowest score (below 70) as compared with the Stanford-Binet scale which facilitates more accurate measurements of IQ. (Table 4)

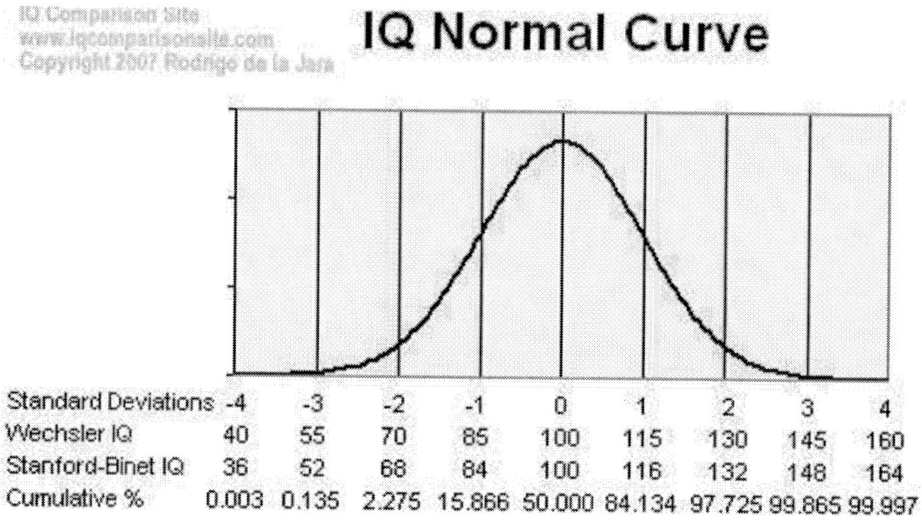

Figure 2. Scales of intelligence measuring.

Table 3. IQ Classification

Wechsler's	Classification
IQ Range	Intelligence Classification
>= 130	Very Superior
120-129	Superior
110-119	Bright normal
90-109	Normal
80-89	Dull normal
70-79	Borderline
Below 70	Mentally retarded

Table 4. IQ classification

Stanford-Binet	Classification
IQ Range	Intelligence Classification
164 and over	Genious and near genious
148-163	Very superior intelligence
132-147	Superior intelligence
116-131	Above average intelligence
84-115	Normal or average
68.- 83	Duliness
52- 67	Borderline deficiency
Below 52	Mental deficiency

The following figures show the normal distribution of IQ scores:

- 50% of IQ scores fall between 90 and 110
- 70% of IQ scores fall between 85 and 115
- 95% of IQ scores fall between 70 and 130
- 99.5% of IQ scores fall between 60 and 140

With reference to the specific categories and the classification of *persons with Intellectuall disabilities* the following IQ Chart reflects IQ scores of people who suffer from Intellecrtual Disability problems. The boarderline of Intellectual Disability starts at an IQ score of 70 and continues through profound mental retardation in which scores are 19 and lower.

- *IQ of 50 - 69* - Mild Intellectual Disability represents 85% of the population of mental retardation
- *IQ of 35 - 49* - Moderate Intellectual Disability represents 10% of the population of mental retardation
- *IQ of 20 - 34* – Severe Intellectual Disabilityn represents 4% of the population of mental retardation
- *IQ under 20* - Profound Intellectual Disability represents 1% of the population of mental retardation

According to the World Health Organization (WHO), the characteristics of the above categories are: [34]:

- *Mild Intellectual Disability:* Intellectual Disabled children acquire language with some delay, but most achieve the ability to use speech in everyday purposes, to hold conversations, and to engage in the clinical interview. Most of them, also, achieve full independence in self-care (eating, washing, dressing) even if the rate of development is considerably slower than normal.
- *Moderate Intellectual Disability:* Individuals in this category are slow in developing comprehension and use of language, and their eventual achievement in this area is limited. Achievement in self-care and motor skills is, also, retarded and some need supervision throughout life. Progress in school work is limited. However, a proportion of these individuals learn the basic skills needed for reading, writing and counting.
- *Severe Intellectual Disability:* Achievement and behavioral are, almost, identical with moderate level. Yet, most people in this category suffer from a marked degree of motor impairment or other associated deficits reveling the existence of clinically serious damage to the central nervous system.
- *Profound Intellectual Disability:* The IQ in this category is under 20, which practically means that individuals are of severe inability to understand or comply with requests or instructions. They are unable or restricted in mobility Comprehension and use of language is limited to understanding basic commands and making simple requests.

Evidently, these problems necessitate a global understanding and care for a population which represents, by majority, a dormant workforce. This is for the benefit of people and the economic development of countries. Unfortunately, bureaucratic procedures matched with deferred policies, result to much more expenditure through unemployment benefits instead of the payment of salaries in return of people performing at the highest of their capability. [22].

Indeed, market research has shown that persons with disabilities constitute a very useful tool for offering their services in a variety of jobs and will contribute to the welfare of societies.

To this effect, the verse of the Chilean poet Gabriela Mistral is self-explanatory:

- Many things can wait.
- This child cannot.
- Now is the time.
- His blood is being formed.
- His bones are being made,
- His mind is being developed.
- To him, we cannot say tomorrow,
- His name is today

Educationalists classify persons with Intellectuall Disabilities into four groups with different IQ score range. According to this classification, GROUP I includes persons whose IQ ranges from 70 to 84. GROUP II includes persons who can acquire minimum functional literacy with IQ range 50-69. GROUP III includes persons who though they may be trained to perform some personally and socially useful functions, they cannot acquire functional literacy, IQ range 30-49. In GROUP IV the persons are unable to profit from education and training, since their IQ is below 30.

What Causes Developmental (Intellectual) Disabilities (Ex Mental Retardation)

As explained in a preceding page of this chapter, American Association on Mental Retardation (AAMR) considers that Developmental (Intellectual) Disabilities are not considered to be a medical disorder nor a mental disorder. This fact explains why there are hundreds of causes supported by medical and/or educational sources. However, most analysts agree to six crucial reasons which, in fact, cover the majority of instances.

a) *Genetic conditions:* In about 5% of persons with Intellectual Disabilities the reason is attributed to hereditary factors. Intellectuall Disability may be caused by an inherited abnormality in the genes [15]
b) *Problems during pregnancy:* An Intellectual Disability can result when the baby does not develop inside the mother properly. [8]
c) *Problems at birth:* If a baby has problems during labor and birth, such as not getting enough oxygen, he/she may have an Intellectual Disability.[15]

d) *Problems after birth:* Childhood diseases, such as chicken pox or measles can damage the brain. [8]
e) *Health problems:* Diseases like meningitis can cause Intellectual Disabilities. They can, also, be caused by not eating right, not getting enough medical care. [8]
f) *Environmental factors:* Neglected infants who are not provided the mental and physical stimulation.[15]

It is supported that "a diagnosis of Intellectual Disability carries with it certain unique treatment needs which must be understood and addressed. Unfortunately, most psychiatrists are ill-equipped to handle this situation, having received little or no formal training in this area. [24]

However, classification of Intellectual Disabilities according to causes is very difficult. In fact, of the cases related to the identification of the causes of developmental disabilities, it is estimated that only 5 t0 6 percent of the persons with intellectual disabilities can be identified from causes with some degree of certainty [23] Never the less, the AAMD identifies nine general causal groupings for developmental disabilities:

- Infections and intoxications
- Trauma or physical agent
- Metabolism or nutrition
- Gross brain disease
- Unknown prenatal influence
- Chromosomal abnormality
- Gestational disorders
- Retardation following psychiatric disorder
- Environmental influence

New trends in the identification of causes of intellectual disabilities divide them into two categories – brain damage and cultural familial. Yet, the AAMD has substituted in their terminology the phrase *cultural-familial* with the term *psychosocial disadvantage.* In the following lines, each of the above terms wil be discussed briefly, though by no means all the identified syndromes can be included:

Analytically, the causes mentioned by AAMD can be defined as follows: [15]

1. *Congenital infections* affect babies as the result of infection of the mother during pregnancy. Infection of the infant can occur before the infant is born or during the birth process. For example, syphilis can cause retardation in the unborn fetus .Intoxication is the acute state of physical and cognitive impairment caused by drinking alcohol or being exposed to a psychoactive drug *Examples: Congenital rubella, Encephalitis, Meningitis*
2. *Trauma:* Any injury, whether physically or emotionally inflicted. "Trauma" has both a medical and a psychiatric definition. Medically, "trauma" refers to a serious or critical bodily injury, wound, or shock. This definition is often associated with trauma medicine practiced in emergency rooms and represents a popular view of the term. In psychiatry, "trauma" has assumed a different meaning and refers to an

experience that is emotionally painful, distressful, or shocking, which often results in lasting mental and physical effects. "Trauma" is the Greek word for a "wound" and for "damage or defeat" *Examples: Intracranial hemorrhage, before and after birth, lack of oxygen to the brain before, during or after birth, severe head injury.*

3. *Metabolism:* The whole range of biochemical processes that occur within an organism. Metabolism consists both of anabolism and catabolism (the buildup and breakdown of substances, respectively). The biochemical reactions are known as metabolic pathways and involve enzymes that transform one substance into another substance, either breaking down a substance or building a new chemical substance. The term is commonly used to refer specifically to the breakdown of food and its transformation into energy. *Example: Malnutrition.*

Most of the foods and drinks people ingest are complex materials that the body must break down into simpler substances. This process may involve several steps. The simplest substances are then used as building blocks , which are assembled into the materials the body needs to sustain life.. The process of creating those materials may, also, require several steps. The major building blocks are:

- Carbohydrates
- Amino acids
- Fats (lipids)

This complicated process of breaking down and converting the substances ingested is called metabolism.

Metabolism is carried out by chemical substances called enzymes, which are made by the body. If a genetic abnormality affects the function of an enzyme or causes it to be deficient or missing altogether, various disorders can occur. Some hereditary disorders of metabolism (such as lipidoses) can be diagnosed in the fetus by using a blood test or examination of a tissue sample to determine whether a specific enzyme is deficient or missing. [29]

4. *Gross brain diseases:* The following diseases are considered crucial in the appropriate function of the brain

- Encephalopathy
- Encephalopathy means brain disease, damage, or malfunction. Causes of encephalopathy are varied and numerous.
- Low Blood Pressure

It includes light-headedness, dizziness, or even fainting if not enough blood is getting to the brain. Diseases and medications can result to pressure which increases the risk of developing: heart disease, kidney dysfunctions etc.

- Transient Ischemic Attack (TIA, Mini-Stroke) When a portion of the brain loses blood supply, through a blood clot or embolus, a transient ischemic attack (TIA, mini-stroke) consisting of small blood clots can be formed and travel to the brain to cause damages

- Multiple sclerosis (MS) is a disease which progressively injures the nerves of the brain and spinal cord, reflected by alterations resulting to multiple sclerosis.
- Behcet's Syndrome Behcet's syndrome is a disease characterized by three symptoms: genital ulcers, recurring mouth ulcers, and inflammation.
- MELAS Syndrome

The genetic material (DNA) in the mitochondria cause MELAS syndrome. Symptoms of MELAS include ***brain*** dysfunction (encephalopathy).

- Narcolepsy

Narcolepsy, a chronic disease of the central nervous system causes have not been fully determined....

- Drug Abuse

Drug addiction is a chronic disease that causes drug-seeking behavior

5. Unknown prenatal influence

It refers to dysfunctions caused to the embryo (fetus) during the pregnancy period for unidentified reasons. *Prenatal:* Occurring or existing before birth. The term as is defined makes no sense. What is probably unknown is the cause of the prenatal effect. Therefore, the term should be : *"Prenatal influence due to unknown reasons".*

Prenatal care is the regular health care women should receive during pregnancy from an obstetrician or midwife.

Prenatal development is the growth and development of a single-celled zygote which is formed by the combination of a sperm and an egg into a baby.

Prenatal diagnosis is diagnosis before birth by techniques such as ultrasound, chorionic villus sampling (CVS), and amniocentesis.

The word "prenatal" comes from the Latin "pre-," before + "(g)natus," birth = before birth. "Antenatal" is often used in lieu of "prenatal" in the UK, Australia, etc.

With increasingly sophisticated technology, the fetus has been studied and is considered to be an active agent in its own development. Many scientists believe that anything that affects the environment of the fetus can have an effect upon development beginning at conception and not at birth.

Environment does indeed begin to influence the individual as soon as he or she is conceived. As the zygote undergoes mitosis (cell division), the new cells themselves become part of the mother's environment, and through their particular physical and chemical influence they guide and control the development of further new cells.. Meanwhile, the lump of cells is surrounded by the larger environment of the mother's uterus, and this environment is surrounded by the mother and the world in which she lives.

The great majority of women have uncomplicated pregnancies and give birth to healthy babies, and for many years it was believed that the baby in the uterus was completely insulated from outside influences. Scientists now know that this is not entirely true.

Environmental influences ranging from radioactivity and stress in the outside world to drugs, chemicals, hormones, and viruses in the mother's bloodstream can affect prenatal development.

Such threats affect the health of the fetus in several ways. This is because the body organs and parts develop at different speeds and go through definite phases. First they go through a phase of rapid multiplication in the number of cells. Then there is an increase in both the number of cells and in cell size. In the third and final phase of development, cell size continues to increase rapidly, but cell division slows down.

When a body part or organ system is growing most rapidly both in cell number and size, this is known as a critical period. If an environmental factor, such as a chemical or virus, interferes with growth during the critical period, development of that organ system will be permanently affected. [30].

6. Chromosomal abnormality

Chromosome: A visible carrier of the genetic information.

*Examples: chromosomal transformations, defects in the chromosomal inheritance, errors of chromosome numbers (Down syndrome)*The 3 billion bp (base pairs) in the human genome are organized into 24 distinct, physically separate microscopic units called chromosomes. All genes are arranged linearly along the chromosomes. The nucleus of most human cells contains two sets of chromosomes, one set given by each parent. Each set has 23 single chromosomes--22 autosomes and an X or Y sex chromosome. (A normal female will have a pair of X chromosomes; a male will have an X and Y pair.) Chromosomes contain roughly equal parts of protein and DNA; chromosomal DNA contains an average of 150 million bases. DNA molecules are among the largest molecules now known.

Chromosomes can be seen under a light microscope and, when stained with certain dyes, reveal a pattern of light and dark bands reflecting regional variations in the amounts of A and T vs G and C. Differences in size and banding pattern allow the 24 chromosomes to be distinguished from each other, an analysis called a karyotype. A few types of major chromosomal abnormalities, including missing or extra copies or gross breaks and rejoinings (translocations), can be detected by microscopic examination; Down's syndrome, in which an individual's cells contain a third copy of chromosome 21, is diagnosed by karyotype analysis.

Most changes in DNA, however, are too subtle to be detected by this technique and require molecular analysis. These subtle DNA abnormalities (mutations) are responsible for many inherited diseases such as cystic fibrosis and sickle cell anemia or may predispose an individual to cancer, major psychiatric illnesses, and other complex diseases.

7. Gestational disorders:

These disorders refer to the period of time from conception to birth. [23]. Usually , they refer to an abnormal length of pregnancy, either too short (premature) or too long (post maturity) According to Robinson, N.M. and Robinson H.R. [25] post maturity is not as likely to cause retardation as the prematurity, although the fetus is possible to suffer from under nutrition if it is long overdue.

An invention revealed that sex hormone binding globulin (SHBG) and/or placental growth factor (P1GF) can be used as early indicators for the risk of developing any of the pregnancy complications preeclampsia, gestational diabetes, and gestational hypertension The assays for SHBG and P1GF are simple and inexpensive, can be reformed during the first trimester as early as 5 weeks after conception, and do not require any preparation on the part of the woman (for example, the tests can be done under fasting or non-fasting conditions). Thus, the invention provides methods for utilizing insulin resistance biomarkers, and cytokines and angiogenic biomarkers,, as indicators of the risk for developing various pregnancy complications.

In general, the invention features methods of determining a woman's risk of developing a gestational disorder, during pregnancy, by obtaining a biological sample, such as blood or serum, from a pregnant woman during the first or second trimester of pregnancy [31].

8. Retardation following psychiatric disorder [23]

Psychiatric: Pertaining to or within the purview of psychiatry, the medical specialty concerned with the prevention, diagnosis and treatment of mental illness. It is a considerable difficulty in distinguishing between a retarded and an emotionally disturbed individual. It is even more difficult to determine whether emotional disturbance causes mental retardation or vice versa.

Maternal stress may influence the fetal development by reduction of the vascular transport of oxygen and nutrition to the fetus or by influence of the hormonal environment transferred to the fetus. A decreased blood supply may restrict the supply of oxygen and nutrition and cause damages to the developing brain. Still, the brain sparing mechanism seems to favor the brain except in extreme situations, and protect from damage. A decreased blood supply is therefore not the most likely way that the maternal stress response is transferred to the fetus, but a compromised supply to other organ systems may result in a hormonal stress response that may accelerate brain maturation resulting in slightly poorer cognitive outcomes.

9. Environmental influence

Environment: The sum of the total of the element, , factors and conditions in the surroundings which may have an impact on the development action or survival of an organism or group of organisms. By far the most commonly assumed etiological category is that environmental influence is estimated to be at least 80 percent of all mentally retarded individuals. *Example: Deprivation syndrome.*

Development of an individual obviously depends on both its genes and its environment, but the precise character of the interplay between the developing individual and its environment is critical. At each phase of development the organism may be sensitive to particular environmental cues with the effects of its responses impacting on subsequent stages of development.

In sheep, the nutritional status of the mother at around conception can influence how the late gestation foetus responds to subsequent maternal nutritional stress (Harding 1997). The setting of the hypothalamic pituitary adrenal axis may also respond in parallel and, hence, lead to changes in the postnatal responses to external stressors [33]

Signs and Symptoms

Intellectuall Disability, in simple terms means sub-average general intellectual functioning, existing concurrently with deficits in adaptive behavior appearing during the developmental period, affecting a child's educational performance. It is divided in five groups according to the specific sector, *intellectual, academic, behavior, communication and physical.*

Specifically, *intellectual sector* includes (a) difficulty applying abstract processes like *conceptualization, generalization, transfer.* (b) limited intellectual functioning in areas such *memory, imagination, creativity.*

Academic factor includes (a) sub-average performance in basic academic skills, (b) oral communication skills normally exceed written communication skills, (c) problems in reading and listening comprehension such as *following complex directions, dealing with problem situations, generalizing from rules and principles.*

Behavioral sector includes: (a) social skills irrelevant to age, (b) difficulty in comprehending social situations, (c) poor self-concept phenomena, (d) easily influenced by socks.

Communication sector includes (a) below average for age in language skills, (b) limited vocabulary, (c) delayed speech and language, (d) articulation disorders, (e) limited written communication skills.

Physical sector includes (a) acute chronic health problems, (b) development proceeding at a slower rate such as *sitting, walking etc.*

It is claimed that the signs and symptoms of developmental disabilities are all behavioral. Most people with such disabilities do not look like they have any type of intellectual disability, especially if the disability is caused by environmental factors.

Children with mental retardation may learn to sit up, to crawl, or to walk later than other children, or they may learn to talk later. Both adults and children with mental retardation may also exhibit some or all of the following characteristics[26]

- Delays in oral language development
- Deficits in memory skills
- Difficulty learning social rules
- Difficulty with problem solving skills
- Delays in the development of adaptive behaviors such as self-help or self-care skills
- Lack of social inhibitors

Children with mental retardation learn more slowly than a typical child. Children make longer to learn language, develop social skills, and take care of their personal needs, such as dressing or eating. Learning will take them longer, require more repetition, and skills may need to be adapted to their learning level. Nevertheless, virtually every child is able to learn, develop and become a participating member of the community. Following are some additional characteristics of persons with developmental disabilities.[8].

- Language difficulty, often not able to communicate at age appropriate levels.
- Short attention span.

- May have poor muscle tone, comprehension and balance below normal.
- Find it hard to remember things.
- Do not understand how to pay things.
- Have trouble understanding social roles.
- Have trouble seeing the consequences of their actions.
- Have trouble solving problems.
- Have trouble thinking logically.
- Typically do not look different from their non-disabled peers.
- Often have only mild or moderate development delays, except in academics.

NUMEROUS DISPUTANDUM

Prevalence in the sectors of disabilities in no way can be considered a reliable indicator. Determining the number of persons with disabilities with accuracy is not feasible. Parents are reluctant to have their children identified as having disabilities and tend to consider such classification as a family stigma. Moreover, in most cases they are unaware of such situations. Besides, the various definitions which are used erroneously create confusion resulting to misconceptions. Therefore, the problem is problem of communication, sociological, psychological, educational and professional dimension.

According to estimates, developmental disabilities are:

- Ten times more prevalent than cerebral palsy.
- Twenty times more prevalent than spina bifida.
- Twenty five times more prevalent than total blindness.
- Fifty times more prevalent than total deafness.

At the moment, the estimated population with disabilities in EU27 is 42.9 million or the 8.56% of the total population. The respective figure of the Euro Area 16 is 24.42 million or 7,41%.

Some key indicators include:

1. Globally, only 5% of children with physical or mental disorders complete primary school as compared to nearly 9% of non-disabled peers.
2. In developing countries 98% of children with disabilities are not enrolled in school and 99% of girls with disabilities are illiterate. Individuals with mental illness are unemployed by 90%
3. In developed and developing countries 5-15% children aged 3-15 suffer from mental handicaps, as much as 30 million are severely retarded, 8 million mildly or moderately mentally retarded globally. [38].
4. Asphyxia and birth trauma are two leading causes of mental handicaps in developing countries where over 1.2 million newborns die each year from moderate and severe brain damage.

In the United States

5. Intellectual Disability affects about 1-3% of the population. There are many causes of this disability. , but doctors find a specific reason in only 25% of cases [40]
6. The prevalence of intellectual disability in the non-institutionalized population of the United States is estimated to be 7.8 people per thousand [37]
7. Intellectual Disability is on the rise in the United States. The rate of children born with fetal alcohol syndrome has increased from 1 per 10,000 births in 1979 to 6.7 per 10,000 births in 1993. [41]
8. According to the U.S. Department of Education,1% of school aged children presently are receiving special education services under the category "mental retardation [41]
9. Intellectual disability is the most common developmental disability[40]
10. Approximately 6.5 million people in the United States have an intellectual disability.[42]
11. More than 545,000 children 9ages 6-21) have some level of intellectual disability and receive special education services in public school under this category in IDEA. [41] [12] In fact, in every 10 children who need special education have some form of intellectual disability.

World Health Organization

As the WHO announced, among others [34]

12. Of all the world's premature deaths and years of life with disabilities, 14% is attributed to mental neurological and substance abuse reasons.
13. *Women's mental health: The Facts:*

- Depressive disorders account for close to 41.9% of the disability from neuropsychiatric disorders among women compared to 29.39% among men, which affects the health of fetus.
- Mental health problems of the elderly depression are organic brain syndromes The majority are women.

[15] According to the World Health Organization [34] approximately 160 million eople or 3 percent of the world's population have problems of Intellectual Disabilities . (Table 5)

Table 5. Prevalence of people with Intellectual Disabilities

Africa	20,310,000
Australia	5,250,000
Asia	97,710,000
Europe	15,390,000
Latin America	13,800,000
North America	8,610,00.0

The United Nations Organization (UNO) presents data through Fact Sheet 1 (2010) on people with disabilities in almost every country. Data provided by media and reports reveal an “anecdotal” picture of he current situation.

Globally, in developing countries 80% to 90% of persons with disabilities of working age are unemployed, whereas in industrialized countries the relative figure is below 50% to 70% (The Washington Post, 2005) In most developed countries the official rate of unemployment for persons with disabilities is at least twice that for those who do not have any disability (Employer’s Forum on Disability, 2010).

16. Employment for persons with disabilities

The World Health Organization estimates that five of the ten leading causes of disability worldwide are mental problems. The document, prepared by Dr Gaston Hamois (WHO) and Phyllis Gabriel (International Labor Office) indicate that, through national surveys , the persons with mental illness who are employed ranges from 44% to 72%.

Table 6. Intellectual disability categorization

Category	IQ range	% of MR/ID	Educational level Adaptive skills	Support required	% of total population
Mild	50-55 to 70	85%	Up to 6th grade	Intermittent Under stress	0.9-2.7%
Moderate	35-40 to50-55	10%	2nd grade, supervised	Limited, supervised	0.3-0.4%
Severe	20-25 to 35-40	4%	May learn words, elementary self-care skills	Extensive supervision, family home	0.3-04%
Profound	< 20-25	1%	Little to no self skills	Constant aid and supervision	0.3-0.4%

In parallel, persons with schizophrenia and related conditions are associated with the lowest rate of employment ranging from 22% to 40%.

- On the basis of the degree of impairment, Intellectual Disability is classified in four categories(Table 6) which require specific support and treatment according to the relative educational level and adaptive skills. To facilitate researchers, educationalist and medical practitioners in their studies, the table includes data related to :
- Required support according to their educational level and adaptive skills
- Percentage of disabled individuals as of the total population.
- The most reliable IQ range per category of impairment.

Myths and Misconceptions about Intellectual Disability

It has been debated in the preceding pages of this chapter and strongly supported that certain definitions related to persons with disabilities are crucial and dangerous both for the health of this category of individuals and their erroneous exclusion from normal education and professional sectors. The same notions have been tabled in my presentations in international conferences and articles in international journals.

One reason for this dangerous situation is the usage of linguistically inappropriate definition of terms within the disability environment. An equally important factor is the prevailing mythology as to what Intellectual Disability or Developmental Disability (instead of the wrong Mental Retardation) means.

Mental illness often generates misunderstanding, prejudice, confusion and fear. Some people with mental illness report that the stigma can at times be worse than the illness itself. There are many myths about mental illness which further add to stigma and discrimination. [43].

According to the National Institute of Mental Health, mental ailments affect more than a quarter of the adult population in the United States and about 6 percent are classified as serious mental disorders. This article focuses on the top ten myths that are prevalent about mental illness.[45].

Public perceptions of attention- deficit hyperactivity disorder (ADHA) are replete with myths, misconceptions and misinformation about the nature, course and treatment of the disorder.[46]

Misconceptions about mental illness are pervasive, and the lack of understanding can have serious consequences for millions of people who have a psychiatric illness, according to the National Alliance for Research on Schizophrenia and Depression (NARSAD).[47] Despite the changing perceptions, many myths and misconceptions about mental retardation persist among large sections of the population in several countries.[32]

Often people are afraid to talk about mental health because there are many misconceptions about mental illnesses. It is important to learn the facts to stop discrimination and to begin treating people with mental illnesses with respect and dignity. [48]

Practice has shown that researchers and other scientists who participate in a round table discussions and international conferences find it difficult to understand scientific terms used by speakers. Besides, it is not an easy task to look up the terms in dictionaries, even claiming to be of the specific cognitive area, since quite often either the definition of the term is not included in the entries or the definition is confusing and unrelated to the specific scientific sector. It seems that there is a universal demand on the importance of common understanding of the various terms in as much as communication is effected in various language due to the advent of globalization in our lives. On the other hand, there is a need that the terms used in the scientific communication intercourse in different phases and by different people should have the same meaning for all participants. As science and technology grows, some definitions and terms have to be clear to all persons concerned, particularly if they originate from different languages.As World Health Organization supports, definitions of terms are socially constructed and therefore vary by language, culture, environment and time. For example, disability is no longer determined by how a person looks and acts. Disability, according to new definition can be determined only by assessment of individual performance. I would add that the appropriate definition is not the only measure for creating the necessary environment for the inclusion of persons with disabilities in all community activities. There are some myths and misconceptions which hinder any proper communication for medical, educational, social and professional reasons. These discrepancies should be waved.An interesting and promising development in renaming the erroneous terms is illustrated in a study of Schalock, R. et.al. [50] published in a journal under name "Intellectual and Developmental Disabilities. supporting that the term intellectual disability is increasingly being used instead of mental retardation. Indeed, it seems there is an emerging consensus that the term in tellectual disability is preferable for 1+4 reasons:

- It is because Barrack Obama signed into law a bill that requires the terms " Mental Retardation" and "Mentally Retarded" to be replaced by the terms "Intellectual Disability" and "Individuals with Intellectual Disability".
- The term reflects the change construct of disability, described also by World Health Organization.
- The term aligns better with current professional practices which focus on functional behavior and contextual factors.
- The term, also, provides a logical basis for individualized support, and finally
- It is less offensive.

Four broad approaches have been used for purposes of definition and classification, i.e. *social, clinical, intellectual and dual-criterion.*

- *Social approach:* In the past, individuals were defined and identified as having mental retardation because they failed to adapt socially to their environment.
- *Clinical approach:* With the use of the medical method the definitional focus shifted to one's symptom complex and clinical syndrome. This criterion gradually shifted to a more medical model.
- *Intellectual approach:* With the emergence of intelligence as a viable construct and the use of mental testing movement, the approach changed to an emphasis in intellectual functioning as measured by an IQ test and reflected in an IQ score.
- *Dual criterion approach:* An attempt to systematically use both intellectual functioning and adaptive behavior to define the class decided in 1995 by the American Association of Mental Deficiency (AAMD), in which mental retardation was referras a sub-average general intellectual functions

Myths and Realities about Intellectual Disabilities (Ex Mental Retardation)

There are lots of myths about intellectual disabilities which make treatment difficult if not dangerous. Some key symbols in the tables which follow and which will not follow the numbers of the tables related to the content of this chapter: ADHD = Attention- Deficit Hyperactivity Disorder. M.R. =Mental Retardation. THE TERMS IN THE TABLES ARE THOSE OF THE SOURCES.

TABLE A

SOURCE: Hunter Institute of Mental Health, 20111 [44]	
Mental illness is a life sentence	Mental illness is not a life sentence
Mental illnesses are all the same	There are many types of mental illnesses
People who are mentally ill are violent	No ,if they receive treatment
Some cultural groups experience mental illness easier than others	No, anyone can develop mental illness
SOURCE: Healthmad: , 2008 [46]	
Only weak people suffer from mental illness	The biggest mistake
People with mental disorders are lazy	Yes, but it is the cause and not the result that makes them lazy.
Only old people suffer from mental sickness(depression)	NO, the majority of people who have depression are 18-29 years

SOURCE: Daniel P. Hallahan and James M. Kauffman (1978), [23].

A person's low IQ score means subnormal adaptive skills	It is possible for a person with low IQ to have adequate adaptive skills.
Children moderately retarded need different curriculum than those mildly retarded.	This generalization is not always true.
The retarded go through different learning stages than normal individuals.	Retarded people go through the same stages but at a slower rate.
Most mentally retarded children look different from normal children.	Most mildly retarded children are not different from normal children.
In most cases , a cause for the retardation can be identified.	In most cases the cause cannot be identified, but simply guessed.
SOURCE: Thyroid Newsroom (2001) [48]	
Psychiatric disorders are not true medical illnesses	Brain disorders , like heart disease are medical illnesses
Depression results from a personality weakness.	Depression has nothing to do with being weak or lazy.
Schizophrenia means split personality.	Schizophrenia is often confused with multiple personality disorder. In fact, it is a brain disorder.
SOURCE: SAMHSA, (2011), [49]	
There is no hope for people with mental illness	Wrong. People with mental illnesses lead active, productive lives.
I can't do anything for someone with mental health needs.	People can do a lot to treat people with mental needs.
Mental illness cannot affect me.	Mental illnesses do not discriminate.
People with mental illness never recover	Studies show that most people with mental illnesses get better, and many recover completely.

TABLE C

Myths about Intellectual Disabilities	Reallity about intellectual disabilities
SOURCE: Phyllis Anne Teeter Ellison, Ed.D.[47]	
ADHD is not a real disorder	WRONG it is a chronic disorder
ADHD is a disorder of childhood	NO, it is a lifelong disorder
ADHD is over diagnosed	It is difficult to prove it.
Children with ADHD are over-medicated	NO, inceased use is due to other reasons
Poor parenting causes ADHD	It is a misconception

Minority children are over-diagnosed and over medicated	Diagnosis and treatment vary according to race, gender and social status
Girls have lower rates and less severe ADHD than boys.	In fact, conduct problems are lower in girls than in boys.
SOURCE:World Health Organization (2010), [34]	
Mental retardation is a hereditary problem	NO, only a few cases are hereditary.
Bad deeds in previous life of parents cause Mental Retardation.	Completely false, even if you believe in repeated cycles of life.
Mental retardation is caused by pregnant women not following food restrictions	Pregnant women must maintain good nutrition for themselves and the fetus
Mental retardation is infectious	This is completely false.
SOURCE: HealthMed, (2008), [46)	
People get better by taking their medication	It is difficult to determine, since medication is an individual's matter.
People can get rid of MR if they want it	Will power is not enough.
Several mental disorders are incurable	Nothing could be more faulty
People are responsible for their mental issues	WRONG. No one chooses to be ill.
Electroconvulsive therapy is an uncivilized way to treat people.	NO. It is less painful than a dentist's visit
With time it will go away by itself.	NO. The longer is left untreated the worse it gets.

It might be unexpected and unbelievable , but it is not, that religious misconceptions are, also, involved in the process of defining intellectual disabilities.

As expressed by Elder Alexander B. Morrison [44], " in the book of Mormon (2 Nephi 5:27) we read that the Nephites, obedient to God's laws," lived after the manners of happiness" Furthermore, the author explains that if we are obedient and follow God's commandments, we will be happy regardless of our circumstances.

In this cause-and-effect relationship people have to decide which they prefer, to live on earth with all pros and cons this might mean or to anticipate the Eden of the after-death life. A re-noun Greek poet, Costas Varnalis urgued that even if this procedure exists he would like to have the right of choice himself and not to be biased to follow the decisions of third parties in lieu.

Back to the myths and misconceptions about the causes of mental illnesses as claimed to be by fanatical over religious individuals: [44].

1. All mental Illness is Caused by Sin.
2. Someone is to blame for Mental Illness.
3. All That People with Mental Illness Need is a Priesthood Blessing.
4. Mentally Ill Persons Just Lack Will-Power.
5. Mentally-Ill Persons are Dangerous and Should be Locked up.
6. Mental Illness Does not Strike Children and Young People.
7. Whatever the cause, Mental Illness is Untreatable.

Under any scientific point of view, these arguments cannot be debated because of lack of scientific authority. The truth is that *the vast majority of people with mental illness are not violent.* Nobody can refuse that over the last 40 years effective medications for mental illnesses have been available. Besides, it cannot be denied that six million young people in USA suffer from a mental health disorder.

Management (The What? How? Initiatives)

In contemporary language usage the term management is defined by various processes of meaning determinations. From the educational point of view it denotes a distinct process consisting of planning, organizing, actuating and controlling the work of individuals , performed to accomplish objectives.[15].

From the linguistic point of view management means the technique, practice , administration or control of an activity.[52]

From the management point of view management denotes the organization and co-ordination of the activities of an enterprise in accordance with certain policies and in achievement of defined objectives. [51].

With regards to the case of individuals with intellectual disabilities a blend of paraphrase of social management and of treatment policies is considered to be more effective in coping with the current demands of disabled persons. What is "Social Management?" It is a social risk management (SRM) designed by the World Bank in the framework of a social policy, under which individuals, households and communities are assisted to elevate living standard . The system consists of three strategies, i.e. prevention, mitigation and coping. which means obstruction from doing undesirable activities, reduction of the harmful effects of activities, and finalization of an activity. With a broad interpretation of the three notion these strategies can be applied to the management of any situations referring to individuals with intellectual disabilities. Managing the persons with these disabilities is a broad three-phase sectors, workplace, school setting and social concern.

The International Labor Office [53] drafted the objective of a code in order to provide practical guidance on the management of disability issues in the workplace with a view to:

a) ensuring that people with disabilities have equal opportunities in the workplace. (b) improving employment prospects for persons with disabilities by facilitating, recruitment, return to work, job retention and opportunities for advancement.
b) (c) promoting a safe, accessible and healthy workplace.
c) (d) assuring that employer costs associated with disability among employees are minimized
d) including health care and insurance payments, in some instances
e) (e) maximizing the contribution which workers with disabilities can make to the enterprise.

Managing Disabilities at School Settings

A UK legislation operational from December 2006, provides that all public authorities including higher education institutions promotes equality of opportunity for people with disabilities. Universities have a number initiatives in place to develop good practice in this area.

Social Concern

The greatest problem of having a disability is society's negative attitudes towards people with disabilities .People with disabilities face many different obstacles in their lives. The span of 3511 years (from the ancient era of 1500 B.C. to our contemporary era ,the history of people with disabilities is a history of absolute shame, beasty attitude, criminal activities, inhuman actions coupled with educational initiatives, which started in about 1700 with special schools for treatment of children with disabilities, actually deaf children, though this activity in no way can compensate the cruelties towards individuals with disabilities.

The origin of inhumane, cruel and brutal behavior is traced as early in history as the before Christ period when the "brave" Spartans abandoned "deformed and sickly infants". In ancient Greece, persons with disabilities were called "terata" (monsters) and in ancient Rome the equivalent term was "monstra"

In ancient Athens, Plato (427-.347) supported that "the offspring of the inferior or of the better when they chance to be deformed shall be put away", whereas Aristotle insisted that " Let there be a law that no deformed child shall live"

The birth of a disabled child was regarded by the Romans as a great misfortune. A high percentage of disabled children were abandoned outdoors immediately after birth and left to die because many Romans felt it was pointless to prolong lives that could prove to be a practical and financial burden on the rest of the family. Dionysios of Halikarnassos wrote about the founder of Rome: "Romulus demanded that all the city's residents should raise all their male children and the first born of the girls and not kill any child under three unless the child was disabled"

Roman religion also encouraged parents to 'expose' their offspring. Just as physical fitness and health were believed to be signs of the gods' favour, so disability was a mark of the gods' displeasure. [55]

The parade of shame started in 1907 when Indiana became the first of 29 states to pass compulsory *sterilization laws* directed at people with genetic illnesses or conditions. The chain development is well on the way: The commonwealth of Virginia (1924), the Supreme court decision that forced sterilization of people with disabilities was not a violation of their constitutional rights (1927), Denmark (1929), Nazi sterilization progamme (1933), Norway (1934), Sweden (1935), Finland (1935), Estonia (1936), Czechoslovakia, Yugoslavia, Lithuania, Latvia, Hungary, Turkey (1936)

All these examples illustrate a strong discrimination against a category of people who in return of a humane attitude on the part of individuals without disabilities are in a position to contribute in the welfare of the societies in which they live.

Nazi Germany is the undisputable example of the extreme discrimination. Hitler believed that the pure German people, the Aryans, were the master race. He believed that one of the reasons that Germany lost the First World War was that the German race had been weakened through Aryans marrying non-Aryans. Therefore, if Germany was to become strong again, the Nazis had to ensure the purity of the Aryan race This view of Germans as the master race was encouraged by the use of healthy, "pure" Aryans in Nazi propaganda posters.

Before getting in power, he declared that none but members of the nation may be citizens of the State unless they are Germans in blood. The result of this belief is the campaign he launched against the Jews which culminated in the Holocaust.

Unfortunately, broad prejudice against persons with disabilities survives even at the first years of the 21st century.

In spite of the efforts of scientists, researchers and educationalists to shift from the old terminology related to the cases of individuals with disabilities to the contemporary reliable and authentic as to the characteristics of the disabilities terms, ordinary people, the man in the street, still use terms which constitute language of the past times. Consequently, terms as : *inferior, idiot, fool, crippled, mute,feeble-minded, unteachable idiots.*

However, as a coin has two sides, the history of disability has the positive developments , as well.

- The first residential institution for people with mental retardation was founded by Samuel Gridley Howe at the Perkins Institution in Boston (1848).
- A major reform in public mental health services, the movement of "community mental health" started in the mid 1950s.
- President Kennedy appointed a special President's Panel on Mental Retardation to investigate the status of people with mental retardation and develop programs and reforms for its improvement. (1961)
- President Barrack Obama signed into law a bill known as Rosa's law which requires that the terms "mental retardation" and "mentally retarded" to be replaced with the terms " intellectual disability" and "individuals with an intellectual disability" (2010)

What Can Management Offer?

The managerial duties associated with individuals with intellectual disabilities consist of organization, coordination, cooperation and control of the team responsible for the care and treatment of such individuals:

- *Families i*n which at least a member has intellectual disabilities. Apart from having first hand information about the behavior of their member, very probably they will need the assistance of an expert.
- *Support workers* who are expected to be a reliable source of information, and are trained and experts for dealing with his kind of individuals.
- *Health care professionals* who are responsible for caring about the health conditions of the persons in need.
- *Additionally, manager's review* should be drafted at specific intervals ina way that it will ensure that the whole procedure achieves the anticipated outcomes.

How the Manager Will Perform?

A well qualified manager will have to follow two stages in order to diagnose the symptoms of the disability of the individual (characteristics of the impairment and degree of severity) and then to identify the reasons, so that to be able to recommend the adequate treatment.

The screening phase focus on three parameters:

- *Activities: Can he/she write, read, tell the tme?*
- *Remember: Can he/she remember significant things about his/her environment?*
- *Life experience: Does he/she attend a special school?*

Factors which contribute to mental health problems in people with intellectual disability (Table 7)

Table 7. Factors contributing to mental health problems

Biological	Psychological	Sociological
Brain damage	Self-worth	Expectations of others
Sensory impairments	Self-image	Family
Genetic conditions	Poor coping mechanisms	Economic disadvantage
Medication	Bereavement and loss	Transitions
Epilepsy	History and expectation of failing	Discrimination
	Dependence on others	Legal disadvantage
		Inappropriate environments
		Exposure to adverse life events
		Reduced social networks

FUTURE TRENDS IN INTELLECTUAL DISABILITIES

Major future trends as concerns individuals with Disabilities refer to Education, Health and Employment,

- *Education:* The concern about education in early 21st century for Intellectual Disabilities is (a) What should be taught and where should be taught, i.e. inclusive settings together with normal peers or in special settings. As to the curriculum, it should consist of teaching, reading, functional daily living skills. There is still a problem among educators and analysts as to whether inclusion or direct systematic instruction is the most effective means of instruction. However, it is anticipated that emphasis will be given on the implementation of educational programmes in order to enhance the qualifications of the persons with intellectual disabilities. [56].
- *World Health Organization* is seeking to find ways to collect essential information about needs and services and assure service quality for individuals for Intellectual Disabilities

In summary, effective information systems need to:

- collect information that is central to the concerns of key stakeholders;
- be methodologically sound in that the information needs to be reliable and “fit for purpose to:

- collect, analyse and disseminate information in a timely manner;
- disseminate information in a manner that makes it accessible to key stakeholders
- be cost-effective and robust over time.

In almost all instances, it will be more cost-effective to build on existing information systems rather than the Development of new systems. The first step, therefore, should be to review the current adequacy and future potential of existing information systems (e.g. national and local surveys, administrative record systems) with regard to providing credible and accessible information on:

- the number of children with intellectual disability in need of support (nationally and within local administrative areas.
- the health status and needs of children with intellectual disability (nationally and within local areas of administration);
- inequalities in the extent and nature of need by family circumstances (e.g. ethnic group, single-parent status, socioeconomic position); and
- change over time in the population's level. [34]
- Employment

International Labor Office reconfirms the human rights of individuals with intellectual disabilities, in view of future trends concerning their employment prospects:

Persons with disabilities suffer from discrimination based on society's prejudice and ignorance. In addition, they often do not enjoy the same opportunities as other people because of the lack of access to essential services.

International human rights law determines that every person has:

1. The right of equality before law
2. The right to non discrimination
3. The right to equal opportunity
4. The right to independent living
5. The right to full integration
6. The right to security

Policy regarding disabilities is often dominated by the notion of "equalization of opportunities", which means that society must employ its resources in such a way that every individual, including persons with disabilities, has an equal opportunity to participate in society.

Conclusion

The use of inappropriate or confusing terms, quite often, creates problems of ineffective communication since the encoding and decoding of messages fail to convey the required meaning of the message. In the case of persons with disabilities a misunderstanding and confusion may result even to death if a treatment is based on wrong understanding related to the type and degree of illness.

It is on the basis of this concept that by decision of world organizations the term "persons with disabilities" has replaced any previously used term.

It has been tabled by the author of this chapter in most World Conferences the opinion that the term "mental retardation" should be replaced with the term "intellectual disorders", which denotes exactly the kind of this disability. A quite positive development is that President Barrack Obama signed into law a bill requiring that the term "intellectual disability" should be in lieu.

Intellectual Disability is defined in various ways, based, also, in the IQ score of persons with intellectual disabilities. Though the causes of Intellectual Disabilities are not quite identified, a common core including genetic conditions, pregnancy problems and other constitute a basic factor.Due to the negative attitude of parents of children with intellectual disabilities and the confusion created by the erroneous use of the term , prevalence figures are disputed. However, persons with disabilities, globally, face problems in the educational, social, employment and psychological sector. Research has shown that certain opinions about persons with intellectual disabilities are myths and it is very important that the situation is clarified.

RECOMMENDATIONS

It is a very positive development that by decision of the President Barrack Obama the term of "mental retardation" and "mentally retarded" will be replaced with 'intellectual disability" and "individuals with intellectual disabity" It is strongly recommended that:

1. Through a round table discussions with the participation of researchers, policy makers and educationalists, but, also, official representatives of associations of persons with disabilities to conclude to replace all terms referring to persons with disabilities, which are inappropriate , with new ones which will denote and describe the real situation of these persons.
2. International Labor Office (ILO) should undertake initiatives to ensure the employability rates of the persons with disabilities, in general, and individuals with intellectual disabilities particularly, since there are quite a lot of jobs available .
3. World Health Organization, should, also, provide support to these persons to improve the quality of health services provided to them.
4. Parents of associations of persons with disabilities should cooperate with responsible authorities to secure that prevalence figures are as close to real ones as possible.
5. OECD and Eurostat services should make readily and easily available updated indicators referring to all categories of persons with disabilities.
6. With the co-operation of all media available ,the truth about disabilities should be explained to as many persons as possible.

References

[1] Hamilton Cheryl and Cordell Parker (2001): "Communicating for Results" *Widsworth Series*, a division of Thomson Learning, Inc.

[2] Berlo, D. (1960): "The Process of Communication", New York, Holt, Rinchart and Winston.

[3] *Oxford English Dictionary* (2010), [http://www.oed.com].

[4] McLean, S.(2010) "*What is Communication, Overview" Business Communication for Success,* flatworld knowledge.

[5] Gavin, M.L. (2010): "*Mental retardation*", Problem Learning and Functioning, Kidshealth, NEMOUN.

[6] Reynold, T. et.al.(2011) "Opening Remarks Regarding Intellectual Disabilities , *Diagnostic Label and Terminology*" MentalHelp.net.

[7] Hourcade, J (2002) "*Mental Retardation*" ERIC Digest.

[8] NICHCY Disability Fact Sheet 8 (2011) " Intellectual Disability" [http://nichcy.org/disability/specific/intellectual]

[9] Babylon English (2011) Babylon English, English Babylon Ltd.

[10] iMedix: Health Information (2007) "*What is Mental Retardation*".

[11] WordNet 2.0 (2011) On line Lexical database for English. [http://wordnet.princeton.edu/]

[12] Answers.com (2011) [http://www.answers.com/main/

[13] Merrian Webster On line (2011) An Encyclopaedia Britannica Company [http://www.merrian.webster.com]

[14] Dictionary.com (2011), [http://dictionary.reference.com]

[15] Medical Dictionary, [http://medical-dictionary.thefreedictionary.com/mentally+retarded]

[16] Webster's New World Medical Dictionary (2011)

[17] *Psychological Dictionary* (2010), About.com.Psychology.

[18] Oxford Dictionary of Sociology (2011): [http://www.enotes.com/oxsoc-encyclopedia.

[19] *Dictionary of Education* (1973), McGraw-Hill.Inc

[20] Recent Massachusetts Regulatory Definition of Mental Retardation, [http://www.psychiatry.com/mr/definition.html]

[21] American Association on Mental Retardation (2002), Introduction to Mental Retardation"

[22] Mablett, D..(2009), " Disability Categories in European Social Policy".

[23] Hallahan, D.R., Kauffman, J.M.,(1978), "*Exceptional Children", Prentice Hall Series in Special Education, pp 71-77*

[24] MedicineNet (2011), "*Brain Diseases*."

[25] Robinson, N.M., and Robinson, H.B., (1979) "The Mentally Retarded Child: A Psychological Approach" (2nd ed.) McGraw-Hill, New York

[26] Wikipedia:"Signs and Symptoms".

[27] Sanders, Lee M, (2011), "Overview of Hereditary Metabolic Disoroders", *The Marck Manual Home Health Handbook.*

[28] Sebastian, C. Simon (2008), "*Mental Retardation: What it is and What it is Not*", Pedriatic Mental Retardation.

[29] Snaders, Lee,M., (2009)"Overview of Hereditary Metabolic Disorder", The Marck Manual, Home Health Handbook.

[30] Scientific Team (2011), "Prenatal Development, Prenatal Environmental influence", Net industries.

[31] Ravi I. Thadhani, S. Ananth Karumanchi « Screening for gestational disorders » Fish and Richardson pc, Minneapolis, MN,US

[32] Carsten Obd, "*Strees during pregnancy and fatal development*"

[33] Gluckman, P.D., Hanson, M.A., Spencer, H.G., and Bateson, P. (2005) "Environmental Influences during development and their consequences for health and disease: implications for the interpretation of empirical studies. Proceedings in the Royal Society.

[34] World Health Organization (WHO): "ICD-10 Guide for Mental Retardation", Geneva/

[35] Zeldin, A.S. (2010) "*Mental Retardation*"

[36] Volkmar, F., Lewis, M. (1996) "*Mental Retardation: Child and Adolescent Psychiatric Clinics of North America*, WB Sounders Co.

[37] Larson, S.A. (2001) "Prevalence of Mental Retardation and Developmental Disabilities", American Journal on Mental Retardation.

[38] Shah, P.M.,(2010) "*Prevention of mental handicaps in children in primary health care*" World Health Organization.

[39] [39a] Eisenberg, Leon (2005) "*Child and Adolescent Mental Health Resources*" Global Concern, Implications for the future, WHO.[39]Shapiro, B.K., Batshaw, M.L. (2007) "Mental Retardation (Intellectual Disability) , Nelson book of Pedriatics, Philadelphia, Pa.

[40] The Arc (2009) "*Introduction to Intellectual Disabilities*" [http://www.cdc.gov/ncbddd/dd/mr3.htm]

[41] US Department of Education (2000) : " Special Education Services"

[42] The Arc (2009): "*Introduction to Intellectual Disabilities*: [www.theorc.org/NetCommunity/Page aspx? pid=2131]

[43] Hunter Institute of Mental Health (2011) " Myths about Mental Illness"[http://www.responsseability.org/site/index.cfm?display=134566

[44] Morrison, Elder-Alexander, B., (2011), "*Myths about Mental Illness*", Presented to pioneer welfare region Leaders in Salt Lake City,UT.

[45] US Department of Education (2008), 29th annual report to congress on the implementation of the individuals with Disabilities Education Act, 2007 Washington D.C.

[46] HealthMed (2008): Article on " A list of false impressions that we have about mental disorders and people who suffer them".

[47] Phyllis Anne Ellison (2009) " *Myths and Misconceptions About ADHD*: Science over Cynicism.

[48] Shomon, M.,(2001) "*Top 10 Myths About Mental Illness",* Thyroid Newroom"

[49] SAMHSA's Resource Center to Promote Acceptance with Mental Health (ADS Center)

[50] Schalock, R., et.al. (2010) "The renaming of Mental Retardation: Understanding the Change to the term Intellectual Disability"

[51] Business Dictionary.com (2011)

[52] The Collins English Dictionary (1967)

[53] International Labor Office (2002), "M*anaging Disability in the workplace*", ingenta connect.

[54] Goode, Jackie (2007), "Managing disability: early expences of University students with disabilities" *Disability and Society*, vol.22, number 1.

[55] Brignell, V., (2008) "*Ancient World*", NewStateman.

[56] Kauffman, James Ma, Hung Li Yub (2009) "Special education for intellectual disability: Current trends and prospective" *Current Opinion in Psychiatry,* vol.22, issue 5.

[57] WHO (2010) "*Better Health, Better Lives: Children and young people with Intellectual Disabilities and their families*" Conference at Budapest, Ro.

In: Intellectual Disability
Editors: Domenico F. Mancini and Carlo M. Greco
ISBN: 978-1-61942-298-8

Chapter 4

Psychosocial and Psychopharmacological Treatment of Comorbid Aggression in Pediatric Mental Retardation and Other Pervasive Developmental Disorders

Robert M. Nevels,[1] Jessica L. Spofford,[1] Michelle L. Smith[1] and Samuel T. Gontkovsky[2]
[1]Jackson State University, Jackson, Mississippi
[2]Methodist Rehabilitation Center, Jackson, Mississippi

Introduction

Children with mental retardation and other pervasive developmental disorders are at increased risk of displaying aggressive behaviors (Brosnan & Healy, 2011; Matson & Rivet, 2008; Nevels, Dehon, Alexander, & Gontkovsky, 2010). Several clinical disorders occur comorbidly with aggression during childhood and adolescence. Attention-deficit hyperactivity disorder (ADHD), mood disorders (in particular bipolar disorders/pediatric mania), mental retardation (MR), schizophrenia, oppositional defiant disorder (ODD), conduct disorder (CD), and autism spectrum disorders (ASDs) most notably are characterized by aggressive behaviors (Barkley, 2003). Approximately 10 to 20% of individuals with intellectual disabilities, including ASDs and mental retardation, display behavior such as self-injury and aggression (McClintock, Hall, & Oliver, 2003). Aggressive behaviors related to ASDs and MR often are compounded by higher rates of comorbid mood disorders, behavioral disorders, psychoses, or other intellectual disabilities. Pervasive developmental disorders (PDDs) and other clinical disorders frequently present with comorbid aggression, which is clinically challenging (Nevels et al., 2010). Pediatric aggression can be serious and costly, and while many children and adolescents display some form of aggression, aggressive displays do not necessarily indicate a psychiatric disorder. Aggressive children and adolescents, however, tend to exhibit hyperactive and impulsive traits as well as lower IQs when compared to their peers (Tremblay et al., 2004). Most children and adolescents who present for therapeutic intervention have some type of behavior problem, and approximately 5 to 14% of preschoolers engage in moderate to severe problem behaviors (Singh et al., 2006).

Disruptive behavior among children in pre-school and kindergarten through sixth grade, characterized by aggression, noncompliance, and negative emotionality, may persist into adolescence and even adulthood. Early diagnosis and intervention, ideally before school entry, therefore is critical to obviating later, more serious problems. Children who fail to learn socially acceptable ways of coping with and expressing feelings of aggression are more receptive to violent and antisocial behaviors as adolescents and adults (Tremblay et al., 2004). Breitenstein, Hill, and Gross (2009) recommend early assessments across domains of behavioral symptoms, developmental functioning, parent – child relationships, and broader family context. According to these researchers, evaluations assessing for aggressive behaviors should include examination of stressors, psychopathology, exposure to violence, and other sociodemographic risk factors. Further, Breitenstein et al. propose that the most effective treatment strategies are structured, goal-oriented, and developmentally attainable and address problems as they occur.

Both psychopharmacological and psychosocial interventions, including behavioral therapies, are used to treat this comorbid aggression with the course of treatment depending upon the severity of the presenting symptom (Scahill, 2008). Ameliorating aggressive symptoms associated with pediatric developmental disorders, specifically MR and ASDs, has been the goal of numerous treatments. Presented here are brief overviews of theories of aggression and also psychosocial and pharmacotherapeutic approaches that have proven useful, and have some empirical support, in treating general pediatric aggression as well as aggression associated with mental retardation, autism spectrum disorders, and other pervasive developmental disorders. The latter sections will focus on psychopharmacological agents that have been used as aggressolytics in pediatric MR and other PDDs. Such psychopharmacy includes psychostimulants, lithium, anticonvulsant mood stabilizers, alpha-2 agonists, beta blockers, atypical antipsychotics, traditional antipsychotics, selective serotonin reuptake inhibitors, and combinations of agents; to a lesser extent, opioid antagonists, memantine, modafinil, bupropion, and other agents will be discussed (see Table 1).

Table 1. Medications Used in the Treatment of Mental Retardation and Other Pervasive Developmental Disorders with Comorbid Aggression

Brand Name	Generic Name	FDA Approved Age
Combination Antipsychotic and Antidepressant Medication		
Symbyax (Prozac & Zyprexa)	fluoxetine & olanzapine	18 and older
Antipsychotic Medications		
Abilify	aripiprazole	10 and older for bipolar disorder, manic or mixed episodes; 13 to 17 for schizophrenia and bipolar;

Brand Name	Generic Name	FDA Approved Age
Antipsychotic Medications (continued)		
Clozaril	clozapine	18 and older
Fanapt	iloperidone	18 and older
fluphenazine (generic only)	fluphenazine	18 and older
Geodon	ziprasidone	18 and older
Haldol	haloperidol	3 and older
Invega	paliperidone	18 and older
Loxitane	loxapine	18 and older
Moban	molindone	18 and older
Navane	thiothixene	18 and older
Orap (for Tourette's syndrome)	pimozide	12 and older
perphenazine (generic only)	perphenazine	18 and older
Risperdal	risperidone	13 and older for schizophrenia; 10 and older for bipolar mania and mixed episodes; 5 to 16 for irritability associated with autism
Seroquel	quetiapine	13 and older for schizophrenia; 18 and older for bipolar disorder; 10-17 for treatment of manic and mixed episodes of bipolar disorder.
Stelazine	trifluoperazine	18 and older
thioridazine (generic only)	thioridazine	2 and older
Thorazine	chlorpromazine	18 and older
Zyprexa	olanzapine	18 and older; ages 13-17 as second line treatment for manic or mixed episodes of bipolar disorder and schizophrenia.
Antidepressant Medications (also used for anxiety disorders)		
Anafranil (tricyclic)	clomipramine	10 and older (for OCD only)
Asendin	amoxapine	18 and older
Aventyl (tricyclic)	nortriptyline	18 and older
Celexa (SSRI)	citalopram	18 and older

Table 1. (Continued)

Brand Name	Generic Name	FDA Approved Age
Antidepressant Medications (also used for anxiety disorders) (continued)		
Cymbalta (SNRI)	duloxetine	18 and older
Desyrel	trazodone	18 and older
Effexor (SNRI)	venlafaxine	18 and older
Elavil (tricyclic)	amitriptyline	18 and older
Emsam	selegiline	18 and older
Lexapro (SSRI)	escitalopram	18 and older; 12 - 17 (for major depressive disorder)
Ludiomil (tricyclic)	maprotiline	18 and older
Luvox (SSRI)	fluvoxamine	8 and older (for OCD only)
Marplan (MAOI)	isocarboxazid	18 and older
Nardil (MAOI)	phenelzine	18 and older
Norpramin (tricyclic)	desipramine	18 and older
Pamelor (tricyclic)	nortriptyline	18 and older
Parnate (MAOI)	tranylcypromine	18 and older
Paxil (SSRI)	paroxetine	18 and older
Pexeva (SSRI)	paroxetine-mesylate	18 and older
Pristiq	desvenlafaxine (SNRI)	18 and older
Prozac (SSRI)	fluoxetine	8 and older
Remeron (SNDI)	mirtazapine	18 and older
Sarafem (SSRI)	fluoxetine	18 and older for premenstrual dysphoric disorder (PMDD)
Sinequan (tricyclic)	doxepin	12 and older
Surmontil (tricyclic)	trimipramine	18 and older
Tofranil (tricyclic)	imipramine	6 and older (for bedwetting)
Tofranil-PM (tricyclic)	imipramine pamoate	18 and older
Vivactil (tricyclic)	protriptyline	18 and older
Wellbutrin	bupropion	18 and older
Zoloft (SSRI)	sertraline	6 and older (for OCD only); 18 and older

Brand Name	Generic Name	FDA Approved Age
Mood Stabilizing and Anticonvulsant Medications		
Depakote	divalproex sodium (valproic acid)	2 and older (for seizures)
Eskalith	lithium carbonate	12 and older
Lamictal	lamotrigine	18 and older
lithium citrate (generic only)	lithium citrate	12 and older
Lithobid	lithium carbonate	12 and older
Neurontin	gabapentin	18 and older
Tegretol	carbamazepine	any age (for seizures)
Topamax	topiramate	18 and older
Trileptal	oxcarbazepine	4 and older

Brand Name	Generic Name	FDA Approved Age
Anti-anxiety Medications *(All of these anti-anxiety medications are benzodiazepines, except BuSpar)*		
Ativan	lorazepam	18 and older
BuSpar	buspirone	18 and older
Klonopin	clonazepam	18 and older
Librium	chlordiazepoxide	18 and older
oxazepam (generic only)	oxazepam	18 and older
Tranxene	clorazepate	18 and older
Valium	diazepam	18 and older
Xanax	alprazolam	18 and older

Brand Name	Generic Name	FDA Approved Age
ADHD Medications *(All of these ADHD medications are stimulants, except Intuniv, Kapvay, and Straterra)*		
Adderall	amphetamine	3 and older
Adderall XR	amphetamine (extended release)	6 and older
Concerta	methylphenidate (long acting)	6 and older
Daytrana	methylphenidate patch	6 and older
Desoxyn	methamphetamine	6 and older
Dexedrine	dextroamphetamine	3 and older
Dextrostat	dextroamphetamine	3 and older
Focalin	dexmethylphenidate	6 and older
Focalin XR	dexmethylphenidate (extended release)	6 and older
Intuniv	guanfacine	6 and older

Table 1. (Continued)

Brand Name	Generic Name	FDA Approved Age
ADHD Medications		
(All of these ADHD medications are stimulants, except Intuniv, Kapvay, and Straterra)		
Kapvay	clonidine	6 to17 for ADHD
Metadate ER	methylphenidate (extended release)	6 and older
Metadate CD	methylphenidate (extended release)	6 and older
Methylin	methylphenidate (oral solution and chewable tablets)	6 and older
Ritalin	methylphenidate	6 and older
Ritalin SR	methylphenidate (extended release)	6 and older
Ritalin LA	methylphenidate (long-acting)	6 and older
Strattera	Atomoxetine	6 and older
Vyvanse	lisdexamfetamine dimesylate	6 and older
	Newer Agents	

Brand Name	Generic Name	FDA Approved Age
Antipsychotic Medications		
Fanapt	iloperidone	18 and older
Saphris	asenapine	18 and older
Latuda	lurasidone	18 and older
Antidepressants		
(Also possibly pancolytic/ anxiolytic/aggressolytic)		
Viibryd	vilazodone	18 and older
Anticonvulsant Mood-stabilizers		
Gabitril	tiagabine	18 and older

Note--Table 1 was adapted from National Institute of Mental Health (NIMH) Table which appears online at www.nimh.nih.gov

THEORIES OF AGGRESSION

Neurobiological Theory

Neurobiological perspectives of aggression and violence propose that various physiological processes contribute to the overt manifestation of aggressive behaviors. The precise means by which internal variables function independently, collectively, and in conjunction with environmental factors to elicit violent responses, however, remain elusive. Several mechanisms have been demonstrated linking brain dysfunction to aggressive behavior, including an association between the dopaminergic system and aggression (Ferrari, Van Erp, Tornatzky, & Miczek, 2003; Höglund et al., 2005; Retz et al., 2003). Animal models of self-injury suggest dysregulation of presynaptic dopamine release or dopamine receptor hypersensitivity as etiological factors (Rothenberger, 1993). Dopamine dysregulation also has been implicated in self-injurious patients with autism (Shea et al., 2004). Antipsychotic medications, as dopamine antagonists, appear to prevent the onset and maintenance of aggression and self-injurious behaviors (King, 2000). The atypical antipsychotic, risperidone, is the only medication approved by the Food and Drug Administration (FDA), which is indicated for the treatment of irritability, including aggression and self-injury, in children with autism. Psychostimulant medications (e.g., methylphenidate and amphetamines) are potent dopamine agonists and have been used in the treatment of aggressive behaviors in children with both autism and MR. The fact that both dopamine agonists and antagonists have demonstrated success in the treatment of aggressive behavior in ASDs and MR children seems paradoxical but likely involves differential availabilities of striatal, prefrontal, and mesolimbic dopamine (Berridge et al., 2006; Stahl, 2008), which results in improved inhibitory control. Both classes of medications, despite differing mechanisms of action, may produce a final common effect in reducing aggression and impulsivity.

Central nervous system serotonin regulation has been implicated in aggressive behavior, specifically serotonin depletion associated with aggression in both humans (Halperin et al., 2006) and animals (Johansson et al., 1999). Similarly, adrenergic regulation may play an etiological role in aggression. Patients with ASDs often experience hyper-arousal in response to ambient stimuli (Toichi & Kamio, 2003), and ASDs children possibly engage in self-injury in an effort to reduce environmental stimulation (King, 2000). Other researchers also have proposed neurobiological mechanisms for aggression in pediatric ASDs, MR, and other PDDs (see Golden, Jackson, Peterson-Rohne, & Gontkovsky, 1996; Gontkovsky, 2005). Beta-endorphin and GABA-mediated mechanisms have been implicated, especially in self-injurious behavior in ASDs (Sandman Hetrick, Taylor, & Marion, 2000); and deficiencies in omega-3 fatty acids also have been implicated in both self-injury and other directed ASDs aggression (Amminger et al., 2007).

Autism spectrum disorders seem to play hide-and-seek genetics in families with at least one child clinically affected by an ASD and at least one full biological sibling who does not meet the criteria for ASDs or another PDDs. In many of these families, the undiagnosed siblings frequently display language delays, social interaction problems, and other mild symptoms. These quantitative characterizations involved 2,920 children from 1,235 families participating in a national volunteer register (Constantino, Zhang, Frazier, Abbacchi, & Law, 2010). In the most comprehensive DNA-autism study to date, an international consortium of researchers scanned the genomes of 996 individuals with autism spectrum disorders and 1,287 healthy controls looking for large deletions or duplications (copy number variants) in the gene sequence. This study revealed that people with autism have 20% more interruptions in stretches of DNA coding for proteins than unaffected individuals. Additionally, these variants were prevalent in areas where genes implicated in autism spectrum disorders and learning disabilities occur (Pinto et al., 2010). Interestingly, recent research has found a genetic link between ASDs and ADHD, both of which involve easy distractibility and aggression (Lionel et. al., 2011).

Pediatric aggression in developmentally normal or developmentally disordered children has two prominent manifestations, both usually readily understood by lay persons (e.g., parents and teachers), proactive aggression, reactive aggression, or both. In proactive aggression, the child or adolescent aggressively acts out in hopes of receiving some type of compensation; reactive aggression is more impulsive, out of control, and overt in nature (Washburn, McMahon, King, Reinecke, & Silver, 2004). Each manifestation can be conceptualized as having individually considered differing degrees of biological and psychoenvironosocial components, or biogeneticopsychoenvironosocial (Nevels, 2011).

Social Information Processing and Other Models

Aggressive behavior can be learned and reinforced in the environment. Barkley (2003) proposes that during the processes of socialization, children and adolescents learn what behaviors are considered socially acceptable. According to this premise, children whose antagonistic behaviors are reinforced and/or those children who fail to learn appropriate ways of responding in social situations often will maintain aggressive behaviors throughout the lifespan, into adolescence and adulthood. The social information processing (SIP) model suggests that children use a three step process when interpreting information from their environment, namely encoding social information, checking schemas to choose an appropriate behavioral response, and engaging in this perceived most appropriate action. SIP posits that aggressive children and adolescents either believe aggression to be an appropriate response in social situations more apt to be encoded as provoking and thereby warranting a defensive response, or may have difficulty controlling their hostile emotions long enough to effectively navigate through the information processing steps (Werner & Nixon, 2005).

Numerous psychosocial variables (e.g., the quality of peer and friend relationships) appear to moderate pediatric aggressive behavior. Aggressive children and adolescents harbor feelings of anger, blame others for social conflicts, and respond to others with more hostility (Barkley & Benton, 1998; Barkley, 2003). Environmental factors can moderate these behaviors, however. Burgess, Rose-Krasnor, Wojslawowicz, Rubin, and Booth-LaForce (2006) found that friendship and close peer relations tended to ameliorate hostile behaviors in aggressive children. Specifically, these researchers found that in emotionally upsetting situations, aggressive children are less likely to respond antagonistically to their friends.

Much research on pediatric aggression has focused on the prevention and consequences of adolescent aggression, which may be related to delayed diagnosis of pre-existing aggression (Nevels et al., 2010). Hostility in youth may manifest before the age of 5 years, and early problematic parent–child relationships correlate with aggressive tendencies by the time children reach this age. Physical aggression has been observed in children as young as 17 months, and the presence of an older sibling in the home increases the likelihood of hostility in young children below the age of 30 months (Gauthier, 2003). Children who fail to learn socially acceptable ways of coping with and expressing feelings of aggression are more receptive to violent and antisocial behaviors as adolescents and adults. Adults reported to be relentlessly hostile as children have been known to exhibit more alcohol and drug related problems, demonstrate a predisposition to accidents, and more frequently engage in criminal behavior, attempt suicide, and perpetrate domestic and family violence (Tremblay et al., 2004).

Traditional Psychosocial Treatments

Traditional psychosocial interventions, such as behavior therapy and applied behavioral analysis (ABA), commonly are used to treat comorbid aggression associated with MR and ASDs. Behavior management techniques, including time-out, response cost, overcorrection, shaping, and extinction help reinforce positive behaviors and decrease maladaptive behaviors (Clark, Tuesday-Heathfield, Olympia, & Jenson, 2006). Because aggressive behaviors can be environmentally learned or reinforced, behavioral modification techniques are particularly effective when treating aggression comorbid with ASDs, MR and other PDDs. A study by Sallows and Graupner (2005) of the Wisconsin Early Autism Project found that 48% of children with autistic disorder given intensive behavioral treatment achieved average outcome scores and succeeded in regular education classrooms. Some children received clinic-based treatment while others received treatment by parents supervised by experts. Both groups showed similar outcomes.

A meta-analysis of behavioral interventions used to treat ASDs found that some behavioral interventions may be preferred to psychopharmacological interventions (Matson, 2009). Similarly, Erikson, Stigler, Posey, & McDougle (2011) reported behavioral interventions as the preferred course of treatment for comorbid aggressive behavior in ASDs, with psychopharmacology being a secondary form of treatment. Behavioral interventions and psychoeducation, including parent skills training, are recommended prior to initiation of aggressolytic pharmacotherapy in all but the most severe cases of MR/ASDs/PDDs comorbid aggression (Nevels et al., 2010). Additionally, behavioral interventions coupled with parent skills training has been found effective in reducing comorbid aggression and problem behaviors in children with ASDSs (Singh et al., 2006).

Other Approaches

Other approaches with little, some, or no research support have included megavitamin and orthomolecular supplement therapies, dietary therapies, herbal therapies, chelation therapies, and possibly effective biofeedback (Haber, 2003; Stahl, 2008; Nevels, et al., 2010). Novel treatment approaches such as electroconvulsive shock therapy (ECT), animal therapy, and the use of micronutrients have been found effective in reducing self-injurious and aggressive behavior in some MR/PDD patients resistant to psychotropic and traditional psychosocial therapies.

ECT originally was designed to treat patients with treatment resistant major depressive disorder and who were manifesting psychotic symptoms (Lally, Meyers, & Sangiorgio, 1990; Preston, O'Neal, & Talaga, 2010). Recently, however, ECT has been used to improve behavior and functioning in children and adolescents with ASDs and MR. ECT improved the behavior and functioning in two adolescent females with ASDs and MR with comorbid catatonic features and aggression (Ghaziuddin, Gih, Barbosa, Maixner, & Ghaziuddin, 2010). This intervention also was found to be effective in reducing self-injurious and aggressive behavior as well as stabilizing the mood of a preadolescent male with ASDs who previously was resistant to psychotropic medications (Wachtel, Jaffe, & Kellner, 2011).

Mehl-Madrona, Leung, Kennedy, Paul, and Kaplan (2010) reported results of a controlled case study in which the use of micronutrients (i.e., combination of vitamins and minerals) to treat comorbid aggression, tantrums, and self-injurious behavior in children with ASDs was comparable and in some ways superior to use of psychopharmacology (micronutrient group; medication group). The Childhood Autism Rating Scale (CARS), Children's Psychiatric Rating Scale (CPRS), Clinical Global Impression Rating Scale (CGI) and the Self-Injurious Behaviors Scale (SIB) were used in this case-controlled study of 124 patients in one psychiatrist's practice. On the CARS, both groups improved significantly and there was no difference between groups except that the micronutrient group improved more in terms of Activity Level ($p = 0.001$). On the CPRS, both groups improved significantly with no differences between them. The micronutrient group, however, improved more on scales of withdrawal, angry affect, and unspontaneous relation to the examiner ($p < 0.0001$). There was no difference in the changes in frequency of SIB for the two groups from start to end. SIB intensity, while similar for the two groups at baseline, was lower in the micronutrient group at the end of the study ($p = 0.005$). Clinician CGI scores decreased from 3.84 to 2.48 for the micronutrient group and did not change for the medication group. The improvement on the CGI was significantly greater for the micronutrient group ($p = 0.0029$). As impressive as this study appears to be, it was taken from the work of one psychiatrist and is subject to various methodological critiques. Nevertheless, micronutrients may offer help for a variety of mental illnesses in both adult and pediatric patients, including those with ASDs and MR.

PHARMACOTHERAPY

There is no established algorithm for the pharmacological treatment of children and adolescents diagnosed with ASDs and MR, and children and adolescents with PDDs have a wider variation of responses to medications than normally developing children (Exkorn, 2005; Preston et al., 2011). Medications have been shown to be beneficial in the treatment and/or control of associated symptoms of these disorders, however, including aggressive behaviors (Julien, Advokat, & Comaty, 2011; Stahl, 2008; Stigler & McDougle, 2008). Specifically, psychotropic medications have demonstrated aggressolytic effects in the treatment of aggression in MR and ASDs (Fukuda, Sugie, Ito, & Sugie, 2001; McDougle et al., 1996; Posey, Stigler, Erickson, & McDougle, 2008). Research variably supports pharmacotherapy with psychostimulants, lithium and other mood-stabilizers, alpha-2 agonists, beta blockers, atypical antipsychotics, traditional antipsychotics, modafinil, and selective serotonin reuptake inhibitors as mono- and combination/augmentation therapy in treating pediatric aggression in MR/PDDs (Cohen, Tsiouris, & Pfadt, 1991; Exkorn, 2005; Preston, O'Neal, & Talaga, 2010) [See Table 1]. The high comorbidity (85% in some studies) of ASDs with MR and other PDDs often necessitates conjoint diagnostic conceptualization of the psychopharmacy used in treating such patients (Exkorn, 2005; Nevels et al., 2010). Often "rational polypharmacy" (Preskorn & Flockhart, 2009) is required to treat symptoms and behaviors associated with comorbid ASDs with MR based on these high comorbidity rates. Such thoughtful, carefully considered polypharmacy should reflect the latest research recommendations and a thorough understanding of dynamics and kinetics, including, of course, drug interactions. Medications typically used to treat symptoms and behaviors in children and adolescents with ASDs and MR include selective serotonin reuptake inhibitors (SSRIs), typical antipsychotics, lithium and older mood stabilizers, newer mood stabilizers, psychostimulants, and atypical antipsychotics, particularly Risperdal (risperidone).

SSRIs have been used to lessen obsessive behaviors, stereotypy, aggression, self-injurious behaviors, and stabilize mood in children and adolescents with ASDs (Fukuda et al., 2001; McDougle et al., 1996). In contrast, King et al. (2009) found citalopram to have no influence on children and adolescents with severe stereotypy as a symptom of ASDs. A recent review of the literature by Williams and associates (2010) found that, based on the research to date, SSRIs cannot be recommended for treating autism or associated manifestations (e.g., aggression) either in children or adults. The analysis found no evidence that SSRIs are effective in children with autism and may even be harmful. Decisions, however, about treating conditions that might accompany autism spectrum disorders, such as obsessive-compulsive disorder or depression, should be made on an individual basis. Williams et al. also indicated that trying to balance benefit and harm, even in consideration of this finding, clinicians, families, and patients still whenever possible must consider the severity of the problem, the associated manifestations, including aggression and self-injury, and the potential risks of SSRI therapy. It is important to note that none of the studies evaluated other drugs often used in clinical practice to treat comorbidities associated with ASDs (e.g., sertraline, paroxetine, or escitalopram). Nevertheless, SSRIs still commonly are recommended and used in children and adolescents with ASDs and MR for the treatment of aggression, stereotypy, self-injurious behavior, and mood instability.

Lithium and other mood stabilizers, including Depakote (valproic acid) and Tegretol (carbamazepine), as well as newer anticonvulsants, such as Lamictal (lamotrigine) and Trileptal (oxcarbazepine), are the mainstay of pediatric bipolar treatment but also have been used to treat aggression and other maladaptive behaviors associated with pervasive developmental disorders. Lithium has been approved by the FDA for use in children 12 to 18 years of age. Lithium treats not only mania but also bipolar depression and may well prevent relapse (Stahl, 2005; 2008). A recent observational cohort study of 4,268 participants in Denmark indicated that lithium was superior to valproate in the number of hospitalizations for bipolar illness and had higher rates of switching to other agents because of ineffectiveness (Kessing, Helmund, Geddes, Goodwin, & Anderson, 2011). There are multiple-hypothesized mechanisms of lithium's mood-stabilizing action, including its inhibition of GSK-3 and its glutamate antagonism at NMDA receptors, both of which potentially make lithium neuroprotective (Wada, Yokoo, Yanagita, & Kobayashi, 2005). Response effectiveness ranges from 50 to 80% in nonrapid cycling bipolar disorder. Lithium-level-monitoring requirements in conjunction with doses and dosing schedules, side effects, and serum chemistry unfortunately often limit its use in pediatric patients. Indeed, lithium has a narrow therapeutic index, can easily become toxic, and has side effects ranging from increased thirst, weight gain, and a worsening of acne to changes in kidney functioning, cardiac conduction abnormalities, and leukocytosis (Preston et al., 2011; Stahl, 2005, 2008). Nevertheless, lithium has aggressolytic properties and generally ameliorates aggressiveness, irritability, and acting out associated with both the manic and depressive phases of pediatric bipolar illness (Julien et al., 2011; Preston et al., 2011).

The anticonvulsants divalproex and carbamazepine both have shown efficacy in the treatment of bipolar disorder in adults and are approved for the acute and maintenance phases of treatment. These and other anticonvulsants appear to be effective in treating both bipolar and seizure disorders through the stabilization of cell membrane ion channels, particularly voltage sensitive sodium channels (VSSC), acting on second messengers intracellularly, potentiating GABA inhibitory neurotransmission, and inhibiting excitatory glutamate transmission (Stahl, 2008). These agents also appear to be neuroprotective. Lamictal (lamotrigine) is approved for treating bipolar depression in adults and may even be a better antidepressant than a mood stabilizer. Its use in treating pediatric bipolar disorder is complicated by one of its side effects, Stevens–Johnson Syndrome, a potentially life-threatening rash that occurs more frequently in children than adults treated with lamotrigine. It is, at best, a second- or third-line agent and generally utilized as augmentation to another mood-stabilizer or an atypical antipsychotic. Any rash should be reported immediately to the child's health care provider, as even indistinguishable benign rashes are more common with Lamictal. Carbamazepine has been shown to be clinically and statistically effective in treating children hospitalized for aggression in some small open-label trials; concordant results have not consistently been found, however, in double-blind, placebo-controlled studies targeted at reducing aggression in similar participants. Lithium repeatedly has shown efficacy in treating aggressive behavior in adolescents and children as has the typical antipsychotic haloperidol. Lithium's efficacy has not only been demonstrated in pediatric bipolar disorder but also in many other conditions presenting with aggressive features (e.g., PDDs and CD). A reported difference between lithium and Haldol is that the latter results in children being more manageable while the former may evoke positive behaviors in children (Campbell et al., 1984). Haldol also is associated with more serious side effects (Findling, 2003).

Haloperidol and other typical antipsychotics, including chlorpromazine, thioridazine, and molindone, have been found effective in reducing pediatric aggression, such as that associated with intermittent explosive disorder (Jensen, Vitiello, Leonard, & Laughren, 1994). These medications, other than haloperidol (usually in psychiatric emergencies), are rarely used anymore due to the revolution in the use of the atypical antipsychotics. Considering findings from recent studies (see below) and with costs increasingly a concern, however, typical antipsychotics such as perphenazine, at lower doses than traditionally recommended, more frequently may be prescribed.

The use of typical antipsychotics has been limited to patients who are resistant to atypical antipsychotics, intolerant to their adverse effects, or require injections or depot preparations (risperidone now is available in depot form, Risperdal Consta, and all of the atypicals are available in fast-acting IM formulations, which may further obviate the use of typical agents). Additional double-blind, placebo-controlled trials and long-term safety assessments are needed before definitive conclusions can be reached about the place of atypical antipsychotics in the therapeutic armamentarium of childhood-onset schizophrenia and especially the treatment of associated aggression. The CATIE (Clinical Antipsychotic Trials of Intervention Effectiveness) and CUtLASS (Cost Utility of the Latest Antipsychotic Drugs in Schizophrenia Study) studies found older typical antipsychotics, especially perphenazine, dosed at lower than usual levels to be just as effective at treating adult schizophrenia as newer atypical agents and this likely will affect clinicians' prescribing patterns for children and adolescents (Tandon, Carpenter, & Davis, 2007). CATIE findings indicate that atypical antipsychotics were no more effective in reducing violent behavior in schizophrenia patients than was the first generation typical antipsychotic perphenazine. Perphenazine was superior to quietiapine in reducing violence in patients who completed 6 months of treatment on assigned medications. The authors suggested that quetiapine's anticholinergic and sedating properties might be disinhibiting, especially when combined with mood-altering substances that also are disinhibitory (e.g., alcohol, benzodiazepines, opioid analgesics, etc.). This seems unlikely as quetiapine is antagonistic at D2 and 5HT2A receptors which independently should decrease aggression.

Stimulants have been used with ASDs and MR patients to treat attention and concentration difficulties as well as hyperactivity. Specifically, methyphenidate (e.g., Ritalin, Concerta, Metadate, Methylin, other formulations; see Table 1) has been proven effective in treating aggression in ASDs. Research has demonstrated that use of methyphenidate to treat hyperactivity, attention and concentration problems, impulsive behavior, and aggression was effective for both children with ASDs and comorbid ASDs/ADHD (Santosh, Baird, Pityaratstian, Tavare, & Gringras, 2006).

Pappadopulos et al. (2006) conducted a meta-analytic review of the literature from 1980 to November of 2005 that yielded 45 randomized, placebo-controlled trials, including a number that looked at MR and PDDs, that addressed the treatment of aggression as either a primary or secondary outcome variable. Effect sizes, as assessed by Cohen's *d*, were calculated for studies that met inclusion criteria treatment, revealing psychotropic agents to have a moderate effect size (ES = 0.56) on symptoms of aggression. The largest effects were found with methylphenidate for ADHD, with comorbid disruptive behavior problems (ES = 0.90) and risperidone for CD and subaverage IQ (ES = 0.90); treatment with mood stabilizers, SNRIs, antidepressants, alpha-2 agonists revealed low to moderate effect sizes (ES = 0.30 - 0.50). These authors concluded that a growing literature supports the use of certain medications for managing pediatric aggression, including pediatric patients with sub-average IQs, MR, and other PDDs, and that future studies should distinguish between impulsive and predatory aggression as well as examine the efficacy of agents over longer treatment periods.

Children and adolescents diagnosed with autism and related PDDs often exhibit irritability, including aggression, self-injurious behavior, and tantrums. Research to date supports the use of the atypical antipsychotics as a first-line pharmacologic treatment for this target symptom domain in PDDs (Stigler & McDougle, 2008). These atypical agents include risperidone, ziprasidone, olanzapine, aripiprazole, lurasidone, iloperidone, asenaprine, and quetiapine (see Table 1). As of March 2010, aripiprazole, olanzapine, quetiapine, and risperidone have FDA-approved pediatric indications for bipolar mania (age 10-17 years; olanzapine, 13-17 years) and for schizophrenia (age 13-17 years). In addition, aripiprazole and risperidone also are indicated for irritability and aggression associated with autistic disorder (age 6-17 years), and controlled trial data exist for disruptive behavior disorders (mostly with risperidone) and tic disorders (Clinicaltrials.gov, 2010). Risperidone orally disintegrating tablets have FDA approval for treatment of the irritability associated with ASDSs. These agents also may be efficacious for hyperactivity and stereotyped behavior but can give rise to significant adverse events including "metabolic syndrome" (i.e., weight gain, hyperlpidemia, insulin resistance, hyperglycemia, and diabetes), cardiac problems including prolonged cardiac conduction times (QTc prolongation), extrapyramidal side effects (e.g., dyskinesias/dystonias), hyperprolactinemia, and neuroleptic malignant syndrome (Posey et al., 2008). Despite adverse side effects, Risperdal (risperidone) is commonly prescribed to treat aggression in children with both MR and/or ASDs, and especially is effective in reducing disruptive behaviors in children with MR (Croonenberghs et al., 2005; Findling et al., 2004). Additionally, Abilify (aripiprazole), another commonly prescribed antipsychotic for children with both MR and ASDs, may have fewer adverse side effects compared to risperidone (Exkorn, 2005). A small study using aripiprazole in the treatment of children with autism, bipolar disorder, and psychosis reported that only four of 16 patients demonstrated improvement in aggressive behavior, however, without significant adverse effects. The most common side effect was increased aggression and lability (Ruginvo & Janvier, 2005). The heterogeneity of disorders in this study limits the conclusiveness of its findings.

Investigations also have looked at combination therapies. One study (Pavuluri et al., 2004) compared the combinations divalproex sodium plus risperidone (DVPX + Risp) and lithium plus risperidone (Li + Risp). Results revealed that both combinations are equally effective and safe for treatment of mania and mixed episodes in children with Bipolar I Disorder. In practice, combinations of psychotropic agents are common in the treatment of comorbid aggression in MR and other PDDs.

In addition to using antipsychotics to treat aggression in children with ASDs and disruptive behavior in children with MR, antipsychotics, particularly risperidone, has been found to advance development of social skills as well as cognitive functioning. Long-term studies have contributed to confidence in the use of risperidone with children in its safety and minimal adverse effects. Most adverse effects included an increase in weight over the initial 6 months of treatment that leveled-off following that time frame; other common side effects included drowsiness, headaches, and rhinitis (Pandina, Aman, & Findling, 2006; Panina, Bossie, Youssef, Zhu, & Dunbar, 2007).

Aggression comorbid with MR/ASDs/PDDs plus psychosis calls for treatment with antipsychotic agents, especially if schizophrenic illness is comorbid with MR or ASDs. The early onset schizophrenia spectrum disorders also share features with other disorders, including PDDs. Often these pediatric patients have been prescribed multiple medications and therefore require a comprehensive evaluation by a clinician well-versed in early onset schizophrenia. In an investigation of 119 children and adolescents with schizophrenia, schizophreniform, or schizoaffective disorder, Frazier and colleagues (2007) found that schizophrenia onset prior to the age of 18 years occurs in approximately 0.5% of cases and very early onset prior to the age of 13 years occurs in approximately 0.002% of cases. Evidence concerning the efficacy and safety of the atypical antipsychotics in children and adolescents with schizophrenia is limited. A recent review by Toren, Ratner, Laor and Weizman (2004) assessed the published data on the use of atypical antipsychotics in children and adolescents with schizophrenia alone and with comorbid disorders to establish formal benefit-risk guidelines for clinicians. Notably, risperidone, olanzapine, and clozapine were found to be effective in the treatment of aggression and mania. Findings suggest that risperidone, and possibly also olanzapine, may be the drugs of choice in children with comorbid tic disorders. Ziprasidone was noted to possess some monoamine reuptake inhibition properties and may be administered as an augmenting agent in children and adolescents with schizophrenia and comorbid anxiety and mood disorders. Compared with the typical antipsychotics, the atypical drugs were found to be more effective as well as better tolerated and lead to better patient adherence. Again, metabolic syndrome is a major side effect.

Less optimistic results come from the TEOSS (Treatment of Early-Onset Schizophrenia Spectrum) study and are far less sanguine regarding long term treatment of early schizophrenia (Findling et al., 2010). Pediatric participants in this study were randomized in a double-blind fashion and received flexible optimized doses of one of three different medications. Two were atypical antipsychotics, olanzapine and risperidone, and the other treatment arm consisted of molindone. All patients treated with molindone also received prophylactic benztropine to minimize risk for extrapyramidal side effects. The results of the acute study phase showed roughly half of 116 young patients with schizophrenia spectrum disorders responded to one of the treatments. Symptomatic responses in all three treatment arms were not significantly different during the first 8 weeks. There were safety concern differences, as treatment with risperidone or olanzapine was associated with greater weight gain, and molindone-treated patients, despite treatment with prophylactic (Cogentin) benztropine, still had higher rates of akathisia. Out of these 116 participants, 54 were accepted into a 44-week extension phase, but *only 14* completed the study. The most common discontinuation reasons were side effects and poor efficacy. There were no outcome differences among the three treatment arms, analogous to acute treatment phase results. Further, despite weight gain during the acute phase, all extension study treatment groups experienced statistically significant additional weight gain. Unlike the acute study where there were weight gain differences between medicines, there were no between-group differences in the magnitude of weight gain seen among the three treatment arms during the extension study. This has significant implications as weight gain was the side effect most associated with discontinuation in this maintenance phase. Extrapyramidal side effects still were a concern for molindone, specifically akathisia-induced pacing and restlessness.

TEOSS was the first trial in which children and adolescents suffering from a psychotic disorder received double-blind treatment for up to a year. This is a unique long-term treatment pediatric patient group who were treated in a methodologically rigorous fashion. Again, only 12% who enrolled in TEOSS completed 12 months of treatment with their original medication. Considering how few participants maintained their course of therapy over the 12 months, and considering that the most common reasons for discontinuation were lack of efficacy and difficulties with tolerability, TEOSS results indicate further the need to find better, safer and more tolerable treatments for vulnerable children and adolescents with psychotic illnesses.

After weight gain and EPS, another major disadvantage of atypical antipsychotics, specifically risperidone, is agent-induced hyperprolactinemia. Also true of typical antipsychotics, hyperprolactinemia can lead to osteoporosis, galactorrhea, gynecomastia, irregular menstruation, and sexual dysfunction. Of the atypicals, olanzapine and ziprasidone are reported to be prolactin-sparing in adults but still may be hyperprolactinemic in children and adolescents. Prolactin levels routinely should be monitored in antipsychotic treated pediatric patients. Children and adolescents with hyperprolactinemia-related effects can be switched to a prolactin-sparing (or more prolactin-sparing) agent, such as quetiapine. All atypical antipsychotics may induce sedation, and *can* produce extrapyramidal symptoms (especially risperidone). Clozapine now rarely is used except in severely refractory cases because of the possibility of agranulocytosis (requires frequent serum monitoring), and extreme metabolic syndrome (Nevels et al., 2010).

Some literature points toward the use of beta blockers (e.g., atenolol and propanolol) and alpha-2 agonists (e.g., clonidine and guanfacine) for treating symptoms of ASDs, such as stereotypy and repetitive movements (Cohen et al., 1991; Preston et al., 2011). INTUNIV, a time-release version of guanfacine, is FDA-approved for the treatment of ADHD in children and adolescents. In a randomized placebo-controlled, flexible-dose study, INTUNIV demonstrated significant ADHD symptom improvement in patients with oppositional symptoms and also overall clinical improvement and reduction of symptoms including anger, defiance, arguing with adults, and loss of temper (Sallee et al., 2009).

Restlessness, agitation, and inattention have been treated with opioid antagonists (naltrexone and naloxone) in individuals with ASDs; however, inconsistent effectiveness is reported in the literature (Campbell et al., 1993; Kolmen, Feldman, Handen, & Janosky, 1995; Williams et al., 2010). Additionally, idiosyncratic drug-induced liver injury can occur in children treated with both lamotrigine and atomoxetine (Molleston et al., 2011).

Erickson and colleagues (2007) reported using an NMDA glutamate receptor antagonist usually used to treat Alzheimer's disease (Namenda) to effectively treat symptoms of ASDs in children. Approximately 30% of subjects, however, experienced adverse side effects, such as seizures. Due to lack of large and numbered trials, the drug's safety and effectiveness with use in children with ASDs cannot be determined. Both modafinil and bupropion, as stimulus stand-in agents, also have been found useful in small studies in treating ADHD and its comorbid aggression, though results were not nearly as robust as those using methylphenidate and amphetamines. Additionally, atomoxetine, though found effective in some studies, also does not appear to have the success rates of traditional stimulant medications (Nevels et al., 2010).

More research is needed on how these psychotropic medications affect children and adolescents, especially preschoolers who would be likely to be diagnosed with PDDs. NIMH has funded some studies on this topic, such as the Preschoolers with ADHD Treatment Study. This investigation involved 300 preschoolers 3 to 5 years old diagnosed with ADHD and found that low doses of the stimulant methylphenidate are safe and effective for preschoolers. Children of this age, however, are more sensitive to the side effects of stimulants, including slower growth rates. Children with diagnoses from ADHD to MR/ASDs, especially with multiple diagnoses, taking methylphenidate should be monitored closely (Greenhill et al., 2006; Swanson et al., 2006; Wigal et al., 2006). A recent, well-designed epidemiological study evaluated a large cohort of children aged 3 to 17 and found that the rate of cardiovascular events and death in children taking medications for ADHD, including stimulants and atomoxetine, was no greater than in children not taking such medications (Schelleman et al., 2011). Additionally, the FDA, in a joint study with the Agency for Healthcare Research and Quality (Multicenter Observational Cohort Study to Assess the Cardiovascular Risks of Medications Prescribed for ADHD), is evaluating such events across 1,500,000 pediatric participants.

COMBINATION: PSYCHOSOCIAL AND PSYCHO-PHARMACOLOGICAL TREATMENTS

In recent years, psychopharmacological treatments have been used in conjunction with psychosocial therapies for children and adolescents with PDDs, comorbid aggression, and ASDs or MR. Even though psychopharmacological treatments have been used as monotherapy to treat children with ASDs, MR and other PDDs and comorbid aggression (Floyd & McIntosh, 2009; Robb, 2010), best practice consists of a combination of psychosocial and psychopharmacological treatment (Nevels et al., 2010).

Frazier et al. (2010) used antipsychotic medication coupled with an intensive behavioral intervention to treat children and adolescents with ASDs and comorbid aggression and found statistically significant decreases in aggressive behavior after the behavioral intervention was introduced. When aggressolytic pharmacotherapy is initiated, behavioral management, from environmental stimulus control to family and/or residential staff behavioral modification training/psychoeducation, is essential (Nevels et al., 2010).

Aggression is a relatively common problem in children and adults with fragile X syndrome (FXS). It is related to problems with impulsivity, over-reactivity to stimuli and mood instability, which are part of the behavioral phenotype in FXS (Hagerman, 1999). In childhood, impulsive hitting when the child becomes angry, upset, or overwhelmed occurs in approximately 405 of cases. Usually behavioral interventions, including a negative verbal response with subsequent timing out and then positive reinforcement for not hitting, will extinguish such behavior (Braden, 1997). If problems persist, then work with a behavioral psychologist on a weekly basis is warranted.

More significant aggression occurs in approximately 20 – 30% of children or adolescents with FXS (Hagerman, 1996). In puberty, hormonal changes can sometimes exacerbate aggressive outbursts, particularly in males. The increased size and strength of the adolescent compared to the child may also cause difficulty in handling an aggressive outburst. Typically an adolescent can become agitated or fearful with a change in activity or a new situation. A rapid change in mood can lead to hitting, throwing objects, or destructive behavior. It is important to prepare an individual for changes with both verbal and visual input, such as using a series of pictures to visualize a transition (Braden, 1997; Scharfenaker et al., 1996). Physical calming techniques, such as brushing, joint compression, or a deep pressure massage also can be helpful in diverting a physical outburst. Occupational therapists trained in sensory integration can teach these techniques to families (Scharfenaker et al., 1996).

Sexual frustration is not uncommon among adolescents and adults with FXS, and it can be exacerbated by obsessional thinking. Interaction with a female with whom an adult male is infatuated may precipitate aggression. Psychological counseling is useful in many ways. It can help the adolescent or adult with FXS recognize an escalation in mood and can help the individual institute self-calming techniques (Braden, 1997). A discussion of individual needs, sex education, and guidance regarding appropriate responses and useful alternatives is beneficial (Braden, 1997; Craft, 1994; Fegan et al., 1993).

If the above interventions do not alleviate aggression, psychotropic medication can be a helpful component to treatment. A synergistic effect often is seen with the concomitant use of behavior modification through counseling and psychotropic medication. Newer anticonvulsants, such as gabapentin (Neurontin) or topiramate (Topamax), can be beneficial, but further trials are needed in pediatric patients with FXS.

TREATMENT GUIDELINES

Efficiency and toxicity of medication should be frequently monitored due to significant variation in medication response in children with ASDs and MR (Exhorn, 2005). Due to the high comorbidity with other medical complications seen in pediatric ASDs and MR, all treatment personnel should made aware of treatment plans and changes in regimens. Additionally, it is recommended that parents record all medications and reactions to medications. Further, parents should record child behaviors, listing frequency, duration, and any patterns, such as with self-injury, tantrums, aggressive behavior, distractibility, and sleep behavior; such records can be used in treatment planning. Detailed records of behavior, particularly aggression and stereotypy, and medication regimens, including start, titration, and discontinuation dates, are important components of efficient psychosocial treatment (Haber, 2003; Julien et al., 2011). The cost of these medicines is increasingly a concern. Since 2010, pharmaceutical companies, in anticipation of less use of new-to-the-market medications, have begun increasing the prices of generic medications. Thus, another reason pharmacotherapy should be accompanied by psychotherapy is to maximize treatment outcomes for cost effectiveness.

The choice of medication for the treatment of aggression in children and adolescents generally depends on the underlying symptoms (Preston et al., 2011; Stahl, 2008). If the child or adolescent has ADHD, for example, and the aggression stems from impulsivity, the use of psychostimulants (e.g., amphetamines or their mixed salts, Adderall, Adderall XR; methylphenidate in its various formulations, preferably time-released; or the newer prodrug, lisdexfetamine [Vyvanse]) can be helpful. If the aggression is marked by hyperarousal to environmental stimuli, treatment with alpha-2 agonists (e.g., clonidine [Catapres] or guanfacine [Tenex or INTUNIV, time-release version]) or beta blockers (e.g., atenolol or propranolol, which decrease norepinephrine levels or block norepinephrine, lower blood pressure and have an overall calming effect) could be useful. Clonidine comes in a transdermal patch that can be changed every 3 to 5 days for maintenance of steady serum levels. Initially, sedation occurs in the majority of children treated with alpha-2 agonists and beta blockers. An EKG also should be done in follow-up treatment, because these medications may prolong cardiac conduction (Hagerman, 1996; Hagerman, 1999; Hagerman, Fulton, Laeman, Riddle, & Sobesky, 1994).

Medications most frequently used for children with ASDs (see Table 1) include SSRIs, typical antipsychotics (e.g., Haldol), older mood-stabilizers (e.g., Depakote and Tegretol) or newer mood-stabilizers (e.g., Trileptal and Gabitril), and psychostimulants (e.g., Ritalin). The atypical antipsychotics, particularly Risperdal, may be used as well. Abilify frequently is being prescribed for children with ASDs because of its more benign appearing side effects profile. Lithium still is prominent in the treatment of agitation and aggression in ASDs and other PDDs, but its use is complicated by its narrow therapeutic index and potential adverse events profile, including toxicity due to dehydration, cardiotoxicity, decreased renal functioning, weight gain, polyuria, polydipsia, intentional tremors, hypothyroidism in addition to the necessity for frequent serum levels monitoring.

Sedative-hypnotics, such as Ambien and Rozerem, sometimes are used in rare situations for occasional sleep problems (Exkorn, 2005). Research shows that SSRIs can decrease obsessive preoccupations, stereotypy, self-injury and aggression as well as anxiety and depressed mood seen in ASDs (Fukuda et al., 2001; McDougle et al., 1996). Citalopram, however, was found to have no effect on stereotypy in subjects with autism and with severe repetitive movements (King et al., 2009). A small, largely imperfect literature suggests that beta blockers, such as atenolol and alpha-2 agonists, including clonidine and guanfacine, also may have some role for treating such symptoms (Cohen et al., 1991; Preston et al., 2010). Opioid antagonists, such as naltrexone and naloxone, also have been utilized in this population and have shown some ability to reduce restlessness and improve attention, but results have been inconsistent (Campbell et al., 1993; Kolmen et al., 1995). More research is needed on the management of all of these target symptoms, including aggression, both for newer agents (e.g., atomoxetine, lurasidone, vilazodone) and for established psychoactive medicines.

Parikh, Kolevzon, and Hollander (2008) searched the PubMed database for English language biomedical articles on clinical trials with medication for treatment of aggression in autism spectrum disorders. Studies were selected based on the following inclusion criteria: (1) randomized placebo-controlled trials; (2) a sample population that included children and adolescents; (3) at least one standardized assessment of aggression as a primary outcome measure of the study. Twenty-one trials with 12 medications were identified. Five medications produced significant improvement as compared to placebo, namely tianeptine, methylphenidate, risperidone, clonidine, and naltrexone. Only risperidone and methylphenidate, however, demonstrated results that had been replicated across at least two studies. These researchers concluded that although many medications had been studied under placebo-controlled conditions for their aggressolytic effects in ASDs, few had produced significant improvement and that more placebo-controlled trials were needed to increase the pharmacotherapeutic options available in the treatment of aggression in ASDs.

Stimulants have demonstrated positive effects on attention, concentration, and decreased hyperactivity in ASDs and MR, as they do with patients with ADHD. Recently, a number of small trials suggested that methylphenidate does have a role in the management of hyperactivity in children with ASDs. Santosh et al. (2006) retrospectively and prospectively studied children with comorbid ASDs and ADHD as well as children with ADHD but without ASDs who received standard treatment with methylphenidate from a specialist center. A combination of standardized and novel outcome tools was used to allow both an exploratory retrospective study of 174 children followed by a prospective study of an additional 52 children. After treatment with methylphenidate, the participants in both groups showed statistically significant improvements in target symptoms of hyperactivity, impulsivity, inattention, oppositionality, aggression, and intermittent explosive rage. The Clinical Global Impression-Improvement and Efficacy index (Guy, 1976) measures also improved in each group. In both the retrospective and the prospective components, there was no statistically significant difference in the degree of improvements between each group. More importantly, neither tics nor repetitive behaviors worsened in either group. Children in the ADHD-only group who were prescribed stimulants experienced significant nausea, giddiness, headaches, and sleep difficulties, whereas sleep difficulties were the only side effect that emerged in children in the comorbid ASDs/ADHD group. Results supported findings from smaller studies demonstrating that children with autism and ADHD can respond as well to stimulants as children with ADHD alone. Research is still sparse in this area, however, and it should be noted that, in addition to their other well-noted side effects, these agents can increase anxiety and agitation in children with ASDs and those with MR (Jepson, 2007; Preston et al., 2011).

As noted, pediatric patients with ASDs and MR have a wider variation of responses to medications than normally developing children, making regular monitoring of treatment plans for assessment of a medication's effectiveness and toxicity (always important) even more necessary. Furthermore, as children and adolescents with these disorders often present with other medical comorbidities (e.g., asthma, diabetes, hyperlipidemia, etc.), all physicians/prescribers involved in the care of these individuals must be informed of any modifications to their medication regimens. Parents should keep written records of all of their children's medications as well as their reactions to these agents. In addition, objective records of their children's behaviors (e.g., frequency of self-injuries, temper tantrums per day, aggressive acts toward others, sleep patterns, ability to focus/concentrate, etc.) are extraordinarily useful in facilitating successful intervention. Properly monitored and flexible prescribing of medications improve the success of behavioral and psychosocial interventions (Haber, 2003; Julien et al., 2011).

Aggression in children with MR and other pervasive developmental disorders, when uncontrolled, frequently results in admission to highly restrictive environments, such as state psychiatric facilities (Benson & Aman, 1999). The medications most frequently used in addressing the aggression of children and adolescents with MR are the atypical antipsychotics, especially risperidone, which was approved by the FDA in October 2006 for the treatment of irritability in children with autism. One long term open-label study of risperidone in children with severe disruptive behaviors and below-average IQ found favorable results (Findling et al., 2004). An investigation by Croonenberghs and colleagues (2005) strengthened previous findings by means of a 1-year open-label study of risperidone in children with disruptive behavior disorders and subaverage IQ. Risperidone was found to substantially reduce severity of disruptive behaviors. Intervention generally was well tolerated; only 9% of participants discontinued treatment due to adverse effects and a high-completion rate (73%) was noted. Risperidone treatment also was associated with improved social skills and cognitive functioning. The most frequently experienced adverse effects were somnolence, rhinitis, and headache. Weight gain was most common in the first few months of treatment, but little change in weight was observed after 6 months. More importantly, this investigation provided evidence for the long-term efficacy and safety of risperidone in the treatment of children.

Several randomized, double-blind, placebo-controlled trials have demonstrated that risperidone is modestly efficacious in reducing aggressive behaviors, hyperactivity, and self-stimulatory behaviors (Pandina et al., 2006; Pandina et al., 2007). A high rate of adverse reactions, including somnolence, headache, weight gain, anxiety, sad mood, dystonias, gynecomastia, and gastrointestinal side effects, also was noted. These detrimental effects are in addition to those reported above for atypical antipsychotics in general.

As noted previously, one small (N = 18) open-label study (Erickson et al., 2007) examined the use of Namenda (memantine), an NMDA glutamate receptor antagonist prescribed in the treatment of Alzheimer's disease, in children with autism. Results revealed modest improvements in the areas of social withdrawal and hyperactivity, including aggressiveness. There were multiple-side effects, including seizures, in over a third of the patients. With the absence of larger trials, no firm conclusions can be drawn concerning either the safety or efficacy of memantine in the treatment of children with ASDSs.

For severe agitation and sleep disturbance, the short-term use of a benzodiazepine such as lorazepam or clonazepam, can be considered. Atypical antipsychotics should be preferred, however, because of the possibility of behavioral disinhibition with the benzodiazepines (Julien et al., 2011; Preston et al., 2011). Again, Buspar (buspirone) might be a long-term option because of its low abuse potential, and again, zolpidem (Ambien), eszopiclone (Lunesta), or other sedative-hypnotics could be considered on a short-term basis for insomnia. If psychosis is comorbid with MR/ASDs/PDDs, of course, atypical antipsychotics are preferred. Atypical antipsychotics would be aggessolytic whether or not the aggression was associated with psychosis.

Psychostimulant treatment of any pediatric patient needs to consider potential cardiotoxicity. On April 22, 2008, the American Heart Association issued a recommendation that children with ADHD receive a careful cardiac evaluation, including an electrocardiogram (EKG), before starting treatment with stimulant drugs (Vetter et al., 2008).

Furthermore, if significant anxiety is present in pediatric patients with MR/PDDs, SSRIs in combination with benzodiazepines may be used with caution in the short term, as the SSRIs and SNRIs (Effexor, Effexor XR, Cymbalta, and now Pristiq [desvenlafaxine, the active, completely renally excreted metabolite of venlafaxine in the OROS time-release formulation]), most of which have been approved to treat various anxiety disorders in adults, all initially may increase anxiety (see Table 1). Buspar (buspirone) also might be a long-term option because of its low abuse potential. Prescribers must remain aware of the possibility for abuse of the benzodiazepines, although the risk appears to be lower than previously thought so long as these drugs are prescribed appropriately, with careful patient monitoring. Overdose precautions are in order for both Effexor and Cymbalta, as some recent anecdotal reports have suggested the therapeutic indexes of these agents may be lower than previously thought.

Min, Fung, Yiming, & Phaik (2010) conducted an electronic literature search of the following sources: MEDLINE, Cochrane Library, PSYARTICLES and PsycINFO with search terms including, but not limited to, "autism", "PDD", "autism spectrum disorder" ("ASDS"), and "pharmacological management". These researchers concluded that while pervasive developmental disorders are associated with emotional and behavioral problems and have no pharmacological cure, comorbidities and dysfunctional behaviors in PDDs can be managed successfully with the range of pharmacological agents mentioned in this chapter. As noted, these drugs help in the management of repetitive stereotyped behaviors, anxiety, aggression/irritability/self-injurious behaviors, hyperactivity/inattention, and sleep disturbances. They conclude, however, that there is a paucity of systemic, well-conducted trials on the use of pharmacological agents in the management of PDDs, and much more research is needed.

All of the mood stabilizing medications and many other psychotropic medications are typically dosed on an mg/kg/day basis in pediatric psychopharmacology. Prescribers must remain aware of and carefully follow these specified parameters. This information is found in all prescribing guides and undergoes continuing revision based on research.

CONCLUSIONS: MULTIMODAL TREATMENT AND FUTURE PHARMACOTHERAPY OF AGGRESSION IN PEDIATRIC PDDS

The current treatment of aggression in children and adolescents with MR/ASDs/PDDs leads to the following conclusions. Firstly, pharmacotherapy, though standard practice in mental retardation and other pervasive developmental disorders, especially the more severe pediatric manifestations with significantly diminished IQ, social comprehension, and severe aggressiveness, should not be monotherapy. Multimodal treatment is required, and psychosocial interventions, including environmental restructuring, behavioral and family therapies (strategic, behavioral, structural, solution-focused) with higher functioning patients with identified PDDs and psychoeducation with lower functioning patients with MR/ASDs/PDDs. These are indispensable elements of successful treatment with this population and should be attempted initially and evaluated carefully prior to initiation of psychopharmacy. Secondly, preventing aggression from developing and becoming consequentially life-changing calls for early diagnosis and intervention, ideally before school entry. Assessments of developmental functioning, parent– child relationships, family context issues, educational access, healthcare and financial systemic stressors, other psychopathology, exposure to violence, and additional risk factors, are needed. Finally, in addition to the need for more long-term safety and efficacy studies of existing medications, newer, safer, and more effective agents with fewer serious side effects are needed for the pharmacotherapy of all childhood disorders, specifically MR and other PDDs with prominent comorbid aggression. Current clinical trials are underway with novel, potentially more effective and less adverse event prone agents. These investigations include GSK-3 inhibitors, "super" triple reuptake inhibitors, glutamate antagonist/agonist anxiolytics and antipsychotics, agents with specific glutamate receptor (AMPA [ampakines], NMDA, aspartate, mGlu, and kainate) and GABA receptor (GABA-A; GABA-B; GAT) targets in the treatment of mood disorders with aggression, nicotinergic antipsychotics, CRF inhibitors, M1 receptor agonists, new monoamine partial agonists, inverse and partial inverse agonists, combinations of existing medications with different pharmacodynamics, agents that more directly increase brain-derived neurotrophic factor, even the antimanic, aggressolytic effects of tamoxifen and other oncology drugs due to their inhibition of PKC. Many of these dynamics co-occur (Julien et al., 2011; Preston et al., 2010; Stahl, 2008). Alternate routes of administration, including transdermal, intravenous, intranasal, sublingual, and inhalation, demonstrate rapid and potentially lasting effects on depression, mania, and associated irritability and aggression. Ketamine and other agents have been used IV to bring about rapid depression relief in adults, and surprisingly, with little evidence of increases in Brain-Derived Neurotrophic Factor (Zarate, 2006). Time-release versions of every class likely will receive approval. The near future pharmacology of aggression in MR, ASDs, and other PDDs hopefully will involve agents and combinations with increased efficacy and safety.

REFERENCES

Amminger, G. P., Berger, G. E., Schafer, M. R., Klier, C., Friedrich, M. H., Feucht, M. (2007). Omega-3 fatty acids supplementation in children with autism: A double-blind randomized, placebo-controlled pilot study. *Biological Psychiatry 61*, 551–553.

Barkley, R. A. (2003). Issues in the diagnosis of attention-deficit/hyperactivity disorder in children. *Brain and Development, 25,* 77–83.

Barkley, R. A., & Benton, C. M. (1998). *Your defiant child: 8 steps to better behavior.* New York, NY: Guilford Press.

Berridge, C. W., Devilbiss, D. M., Andrzejewski, M. E., Arnsten, A. F. T., Kelley, A. E., Schmeichel, B., et al. (2006). Methylphenidate preferentially increases catecholamine neurotransmission within the prefrontal cortex at low doses that enhance cognitive function. *Biological Psychiatry* [Epub ahead of print].

Braden, M. L. (1997). *Fragile, handle with care: Understanding Fragile X Syndrome.* Chapel Hill: Avanta Publishing.

Breitenstein, S. M., Hill, C., & Gross, D. (2009). Understanding disruptive behavior problems in preschool children. *Journal of Pediatric Nursing, 24,* 3–12.

Brosnan, J., & Healy, O. (2011). A review of behavioral interventions for the treatment of aggression in individuals with developmental disabilities. Research in Developmental Disabilities, 32(2), 437-446. doi:10.1016/j.ridd.2010.12.023

Burgess, K. B., Rose-Krasnor, L., Wojslawowicz, J. C., Rubin, K. H., & Booth-LaForce, C. (2006). Social information processing and coping strategies of shy/withdrawn and aggressive children: Does friendship matter? *Child Development, 77,* 371–383.

Campbell, M., Anderson, L. T., Small, A. M., Adams, P., Gonzalez, N. M., & Ernst, M. (1993). Naltrexone in autistic children: Behavioral symptoms and attentional learning. *Journal of the American Academy of Child and Adolescent Psychiatry, 32,* 1283–1291.

Campbell, M., Small, A. M., Green, W. H., et al. (1984). Behavioral efficacy of haloperidol and lithium carbonate: A comparison in hospitalized aggressive children with conduct disorder. *Archives of General Psychiatry, 41*, 650-656.

Clark, E., Tuesday-Heathfield, L., Olympia, D., & Jenson, W.R. (2006). Empirically based interventions for children with autism. J.E. Farmer, J. Donders, & S. Warschausky (eds.) *Treating Neurodevelopmental Disabilities: Clinical Research and Practice.* New York, NY: The Guildford Press.

Clinical Trials.gov. Safety and tolerability of ziprasidone in adolescents with schizophrenia. ClinicalTrials.gov identifier: NCT00265382. Available at: http://clinicaltrials.gov/ct2/show/NCT00265382 Accessed March 9, 2010.

Cohen, I., Tsiouris, J. A., & Pfadt, A. (1991). Effects of longacting propranolol on agonistic and stereotyped behaviors in a man with pervasive developmental disorder and fragile-X syndrome: A double-blind, placebo controlled study. *Journal of Clinical Psychopharmacology, 11,* 398–399.

Constantino, J. N., Zhang, Y., Frazier, T., Abbacchi, A. M., and Law, P. (2010). Sibling Recurrence and the Genetic Epidemiology of Autism. *The American Journal of Psychiatry, 167*, 1349-1356.

Craft, A. (1994). *Practice issues in sexuality and learning disabilities.* London & New York: Routledge.

Croonenberghs, J., Fegert, J. M., Findling, R. L., Smedt, G., VanDongen, S., & the Risperidone Disruptive Behavior Study Group. (2005). Risperidone in children with disruptive behavior disorders and subaverage intelligence: A 1-year, open-label study of 504 patients. *Journal of the American Academy of Child and Adolescent Psychiatry, 44,* 64–72.

Erickson, C. A., Posey, D. J., Stigler, K. A., Mullet, J., Katsche, A. R., & McDougle, C. J. (2007). A retrospective study of memantine in children and adolescents with pervasive developmental disorders. *Psychopharmacology, 191,* 141–147.

Erikson, C. A., Stigler, K. A., Posey, D. J., & McDougle, C. J. (2011). *Antipsychotics*. In E. Hollander & A. Kolevzon (Eds.), *Textbook of autism spectrum disorders*. Arlington, VA: American Psychiatric Association.

Exkorn, K. S. (2005). *The autism sourcebook: Everything you need to know about diagnosis, treatment, coping, and healing*. New York, NY: HarperCollins.

Fegan, L., Rauch, A.. & McCarthy, W. (1993). *Sexuality in people with intellectual disability.* Baltimore: Paul H. Brookes.

Ferrari, P. F., Van Erp, A. M. M., Tornatzky, W., & Miczek, K. A. (2003). Accumbal dopamine and serotonin in anticipation of the next aggressive episode in rats. *European Journal of Neuroscience, 17,* 371–378.

Findling, R. L. (2003). Treatment of aggression in children. Primary care companion. *Journal of Clinical Psychiatry, 5*(Suppl. 6), 5–9.

Findling, R. L., Aman, M. G., Eerdekens, M., Derivan, A., Lyons, B., & the Risperidone Disruptive Behavior Study Group. (2004). Long-term, open-label study of risperidone in children with severe disruptive behaviors and below-average IQ. *American Journal of Psychiatry, 161,* 677–684.

Findling, R. L., Johnson, J. L., McClellan, J., Frazier, J. A., Vitiello, B., Hamer, R. M.,… Sikich, L. (2010). Double-blind maintenance safety and effectiveness findings from the treatment of early-onset schizophrenia spectrum (TEOSS) study. *Journal of the American Academy of Child & Adolescent Psychiatry, 49,* 583-594.

Floyd, E. F., & McIntosh, D. E. (2009). Current practice in psychopharmacology for children and adolescents with autism spectrum disorders. *Psychology in the Schools, 46,* 905-909.

Frazier, J. A., McClellan, J., Findling, R. L., Vitiello, B., Anderson, R., Zablotsky, B., Sikich, L. (2007). Treatment of early-onset schizophrenia spectrum disorders (TEOSS): Demographic and clinical characteristics. *Journal of the American Academy of Child and Adolescent Psychiatry, 46,* 979–988.

Frazier, T. W., Youngstrom, E. A., Haycook, T., Sinoff, A., Dimitriou, Knapp, J., & Sinclair, L. (2010). Effectiveness of medication combined with intensive behavioral intervention for reducing aggression in youth with autism spectrum disorder. *Journal of Child and Adolescent Psychopharmacology, 20,* 167-177.

Fukuda, T., Sugie, H., Ito, M., & Sugie, Y. (2001). Clinical evaluation of treatment with fluvoxamine, a selective serotonin reuptake inhibitor in children with autistic disorder. *No To Hattatsu, 33,* 314–318.

Gauthier, Y. (2003). Infant mental health as we enter the third millennium: Can we prevent aggression? *Infant Mental Health Journal, 24,* 296–308.

Ghaziuddin, N., Gih, D., Barbosa, V., Maixner, D. F., & Ghaziuddin, M. (2010). Onset of catatonia at puberty: Electroconvulsive therapy response in two autistic adolescents. *Journal of ECT, 26*, 274-277.

Golden, C. J., Jackson, M. L., Peterson-Rohne, A., & Gontkovsky, S. T. (1996). Neuropsychological correlates of violence and aggression: A review of the clinical literature. *Aggression and Violent Behavior, 1*, 3–25.

Gontkovsky, S. T. (2005). Neurobiological bases and neuropsychological correlates of aggression and violence. In J. P. Morgan (Ed.), *Psychology of aggression* (pp. 101–116). Hauppauge, NY: Nova Science.

Greenhill, L., Kollins, S., Abikoff, H., McCracken, J., Riddle, M., Swanson, J., McGough, J., ... Cooper, T. (2006). Efficacy and safety of immediate-release methylphenidate treatment for preschoolers with attention-deficit/hyperactivity disorder. *Journal of the Academy of Child and Adolescent Psychiatry, 45(11)*, 1284-1293.

Guy, W. (1976). Assessment manual for psychopharmacology–revised (DHEW Publ No ADM 76-338, pp. 218-222). Rockville, MD: U.S. Department of Health, Education, and Welfare.

Haber, J. S. (2003). *ADHD: The great misdiagnosis.* Lanham, MD: Taylor Trade.

Hagerman, R. J. (1996). Medical follow-up and pharmacotherapy. In R. J. Hagerman & A. Cronister (Eds.), *Fragile X syndrome: Diagnosis, treatment, and research* (2nd ed., pp. 283–331). Baltimore, MD: Johns Hopkins University Press.

Hagerman, R. J. (1999). *Fragile X syndrome.* New York, NY: Oxford University Press.

Hagerman, R. J., Fulton, M. J., Laeman, A., Riddle, J., & Sobesky, W. (1994). *A survey of fluoxetine therapy in fragile X syndrome. Developmental Brain Dysfunction, 7*, 155-164.

Höglund, E., Korzan, W. J., Watt, M. J., Forster, G. L., Summers, T. R., Johannessen, H. F.,Renner, K. J., & Summers, C. H. (2005). Effects of L-DOPA on aggressive behavior and central monoaminergic activity in the lizard *Anolis carolinensis*, using a new method for drug delivery. *Behavior and Brain Research, 156*, 53-64.

Jensen, P. S., Vitiello, B., Leonard, H., & Laughren, T. P. (1994). Design and methodology issues for clinical treatment trials in children and adolescents. Child and adolescent psychopharmacology: Expanding the research base. *Psychopharmacology Bulletin, 30*,3–8.

Julien, R. M., Advokat, C. D., & Comaty, J. E. (2011). *A primer of drug action: A comprehensive guide to the actions, uses, and side effects of psychoactive drugs* (12th ed.). New York, NY: Worth.

Kessing, L. V., Helmund, G., Geddes, J. R., Goodwin, G. M., & Andersen, P. K. (2011). Valproate versus lithium in the treatment of bipolar disorder in clinical practice: An observational study. *British Journal of Psychiatry, 199*, 57-63.

King, B. H. (2000). Pharmacological treatment of mood disturbances, aggression, and self-injury in persons with pervasive developmental disorders. *Journal of Autism Developmental Disorders, (5)*, 439-445.

King, B. H., Hollander, E., Sikich, L., McCracken, J. T., Scahill, L., Bregman, J. D., . . . Ritz, L. (2009). Lack of efficacy of citalopram in children with autism spectrum disorders and high levels of repetitive behavior: Citalopram ineffective in children with autism. *Archives of General Psychiatry, 66*, 583–590.

Kolmen, B. K., Feldman, H. M., Handen, B. L., & Janosky, J. E. (1995). Naltrexone in young autistic children: A double-blind, placebo-controlled crossover study. *Journal of the American Academy of Child and Adolescent Psychiatry, 34,* 223–231.

Lally, S., Meyers, M., & Sangiorgio, M. (1990, January). Dictionary of healing techniques and remedies: Electroconvulsive therapy. *Prevention*, 1990, 135–136.

Lionel, A. C., Crosbie, J., Barbosa, N. T., Goodale N., Thiruvahindrapuram, B., Rickaby, J., Gazzellone, M.,...Scherer, S. W.. Rare Copy Number Variation Discovery and Cross-Disorder Comparisons Identify Risk Genes for ADHD. *Science Translational Medicine*, 2011; 3 (95): 95ra75 DOI: 10.1126/scitranslmed.3002464

Matson, J. (2009). Aggression and tantrums in children with autism: A review of behavioral treatments and maintaining variables. *Journal of Mental Health Research in Intellectual Disabilities, 2*, 169-187.

Matson, J. L. & Rivet, T. T. (2008). The effects of severity of autism and PDD-NOS symptoms on challenging behaviors in adults with intellectual disabilities. *Journal of Developmental and Physical Disabilities, 20*, 41-51.

McClintock, K., Hall, S., & Oliver, C. (2003). Risk markers associated with challenging behaviours in people with intellectual disabilities: A meta-analytic study. *Journal of Intellectual Disability Research, 47,* 405–416.

McDougle, C. J., Naylor, S. T., Cohen, D. J., Volkmar, F. R., Heninger, G. R., & Price, L. H. (1996). A double-blind, placebocontrolled study of fluvoxamine in adults with autistic disorder. *Archives of General Psychiatry, 53,* 1001–1008.

Mehl-Madrona, L., Leung, B., Kennedy, C., Paul, S., & Kaplan, B. J. (2010). Micronutrients versus standard medication management in autism: A naturalistic case-control study. *Journal of Child and Adolescent Psychopharmacology*, *20*, 95-103.

Min, S., Fung, D. S., Yiming, C., & Phaik, Y. (2010). Pharmacological management in children and adolescents with pervasive developmental disorder. *Australian & New Zealand Journal of Psychiatry, 44(5)*, 410-428. doi:10.3109/00048670903493330

Molleston, J. P., Fontana, R. J., Lopez, M. J., Kleiner, D. E., Gu, J., & Chalasani N. (2011). Characteristics of Idiosyncratic Drug-induced Liver Injury in Children: Results from the DILIN Prospective Study for the Drug-Induced Liver Injury Network.

Nevels, R. M. (2011). An even briefer primer for psychopharmacology: The essentials for clinical psychology and other healthcare grad students. Submitted manuscript.

Nevels, R.M., Dehon, E. E., Alexander, K., & Gontkovsky, S. T. (2010). Psychopharmacology of aggression in children and adolescents with primary neuropsychiatric disorders: A review of current and potentially promising treatment options. *Experimental and Clinical Psychopharmacology, 18*(2), 184-201.

Pandina, G. J., Aman, M. G., & Findling, R. L. (2006). Risperidone in the management of disruptive behavioral disorders. *Journal of Child and Adolescent Psychopharmacology, 16,* 379–392.

Pandina, G. J., Bossie, C. A., Youssef, E., Zhu, Y., & Dunbar, F. (2007). Risperidone improves behavioral symptoms in children with autism in a randomized, double-blind, placebo-controlled trial. *Journal of Autism and Developmental Disorders, 37,* 367– 373.

Pappadopulos, E., Woolston, S., Chait, A., Perkins, M., Connor, D. F., & Jensen, P. S. (2006). Pharmacotherapy of aggression in children and adolescents: Efficacy and effect size. *Journal of the Canadian Academy of Child and Adolescent Psychiatry, 15,* 27–39.

Parikh, M. S., Kolevzon, A., & Hollander, E. (2008). Psychopharmacology of aggression in children and adolescents with autism: A critical review of efficacy and tolerability. *Journal of Child and Adolescent Psychopharmacology, 18(2)*, 157-178.

Pavuluri, M. N., Henry, D. B., Carbray, J. A., Sampson, G., Naylor, M. W., & Janicak, P. G. (2004). Open-label prospective trial of risperidone in combination with lithium and divalproex sodium in pediatric mania. *Journal of Affective Disorders, 82,* 103–111.

Pinto, D., Pagnamenta, A. T., Alistair, T., Klei, L., Anney, R., Merico, D., Regan, R.,…Carson, A. R., et al. (2010). Functional impact of global rare copy number variation in autism spectrum disorders. *Nature, 466*, 368-372. doi:10.1038/nature09146

Posey, D. J., Stigler, K. A., Erickson, C. A., & McDougle, C. J. (2008). Antipsychotics in the treatment of autism. *Journal of Clinical Investigations, 118,* 6–14.

Preskorn, S. H., & Flockhart, D. (2009). 2010 Guide to psychiatric drug interactions. *Primary Psychiatry, 16,* 45-74.

Preston, J., O'Neal, J. H., & Talaga, M. C. (2010). *Handbook of clinical psychopharmacology for therapists* (6th ed.). Oakland, CA: New Harbinger.

Preston, J., O'Neal, J. H., & Talaga, M. C. (2011). *Child and adolescent clinical psychopharmacology made simple.* Oakland, CA: New Harbinger.

Retz, W., Rosler, M., Supprian, T., Retz-Junginger, P., & Thome, J. (2003). Dopamine D3 receptor gene polymorphism and violent behavior: relation to impulsiveness and ADHD-related psychopathology. *Journal of Neural Transmission, 110*, 561–572.

Robb, A. S. (2010). Managing irritability and aggression in autism spectrum disorders in children and adolescents. Developmental Disabilities Research Reviews, *16(3),* 258-264. doi:10.1002/ddrr.118

Rothenberger, A. (1993). Psychopharmacological treatment of self-injurious behavior in individuals with autism. *Acta Paedopsychiatrica, 56*, 99-104.

Ruginvo, T. A., & Janvier, Y. M. (2005). Aripiprazole in children and adolescents: Clinical experience. *Journal of Child Neurology, 20,* 603–610.

Sallee, F., McGough, J., Wigal, T., Donahue, J., Lyne, A., & Biederman, J. (2009). Guanfacine extended release in children and adolescents with ADHD: A placebo-controlled trial. *Journal of the American Academy of Child and Adolescent Psychiatry, 48,* 1–11.

Sallows, G.O. & Graupner, T.D. (2005). Intensive behavioral treatment for children with autism: four-year outcome and predictors. *American Journal of Mental Retardation, 110*, 417-438.

Sandman, C. A., Hetrick, W., Taylor, D., & Marion S. (2000). Uncoupling of proopiomelanocortin (POMC) fragments is related to self-injury. *Peptides 21*, 785–791.

Santosh, P. J., Baird, G., Pityaratstian, N., Tavare, E., & Gringras, P. (2006). Impact of comorbid autism spectrum disorders on stimulant response in children with attention deficit hyperactivity disorder: A retrospective and prospective effectiveness study. *Child Care Health Development, 32,* 575–583.

Scahill, L. (2008). How do I decide whether or not to use medication for my child with Autism? Should I try behavior therapy first? *Journal of Autism and Developmental Disorders, 38*, 1197-1198.

Scharfenaker S, O'Connor R, Stackhouse T, Braden M, Hickman L, & Gray K. (1996). An integrated approach to intervention. In: Hagerman, R. J., & Cronister, A. (eds). *Fragile X syndrome: diagnosis, treatment, and research*. Baltimore: The Johns Hopkins University Press, 349–411.

Schelleman, H., Bilker, W. B., Strom, B. L., Kimmel, S. E., Newcomb, C., Guevara, J. P., Daniel, G. W., Cziraky, M. J., & Hennessy, S. (2011). Cardiovascular events and death in children exposed and unexposed to ADHD agents. *Pediatrics.* doi: 10.1542/peds.2010-3371.

Shea, S., Turgay, A., Carroll, A., Schulz, M., Orlik, H., Smith, I., & Dunbar, F. (2004). Risperidone in the treatment of disruptive behavioral symptoms in children with autistic and other pervasive developmental disorders. *Pediatrics, 114(5)*, 634-641.

Singh, N. N., Lancioni, G. E., Winton, A. S. W., Fisher, B. C., Wahler, R. G., McAleavey, K., ... Sabaawi, M. (2006). Mindful parenting decreases aggression, noncompliance, and self-injury in children with autism. *Journal of Emotional and Behavioral Disorders, 14,* 169–177.

Stahl, S.M. (2005). *Essential psychopharmacology: The prescriber's guide.* Cambridge, England: Cambridge University Press.

Stahl, S. M. (2008). *Stahl's essential psychopharmacology: Neuroscientific basis and practical applications* (3rd ed.). Cambridge, England: Cambridge University Press.

Stigler, K. A. & McDougle, C. J. (2008). Pharmacotherapy of irritability in pervasive developmental disorders. *Child & Adolescent Psychiatry Clinics of North America, 17(4)*, 739-52.

Swanson, J., Greenhill, L., Wigal, T., Kollins, S., Stehli, A., Davies,…Wigal, S. (2006). Stimulant-related reductions in growth rates in the PATS. *Journal of the Academy of Child and Adolescent Psychiatry. 45(11)*, 1304-1313.

Tandon, R., Carpenter, W. T., & Davis, J. M. (2007). First- and second-generation antipsychotics: Learning from CUtLASS and CATIE. *Archives of General Psychiatry, 64,* 977–988.

Toren, P., Ratner, S., Laor, N., & Weizman, A. (2004). Benefit-risk assessment of atypical antipsychotics in the treatment of schizophrenia and comorbid disorders in children and adolescents. *Drug Safety, 27,* 1135–1156.

Tremblay, R. E., Nagin, D. S., Seguin, J. R., Zoccolillo, M., Zelazo, P. D., Boivin, M., . . . Japel, C. (2004). Physical aggression during early childhood: Trajectories and predictors. *Pediatrics, 114,* 43–50.

Wachtel, L. E., Jaffe, R. & Kellner, C. H. (2011). Electroconvulsive therapy for psychotropic-refractory bipolar affective disorder and severe self-injury and aggression in an 11-year –old autistic boy. *European Child & Adolescent Psychiatry, 20*, 147-152.

Wada, A., Yokoo, H., Yanagita, T., & Kobayashi, H. (2005). Lithium: Potential therapeutics against acute brain injuries and chronic neurodegenerative diseases. *Journal of Pharmacological Sciences, 99,* 307–321.

Washburn, J. J., McMahon, S. D., King, C. A., Reinecke, M. A., & Silver, C. (2004). Narcissistic features in young adolescents: Relations to aggression and internalizing symptoms. *Journal of Youth and Adolescence, 33,* 247–260.

Werner, N. E., & Nixon, C. L. (2005). Normative beliefs and relational aggression: An investigation of the cognitive bases of adolescent aggressive behavior. *Journal of Youth and Adolescence, 34,* 229–243.

Wigal, T., Greenhill, L., Chuang, S., McGough, J., Vitiello, B., Skrobala, A.,…Stehli, A. (2006). Safety and tolerability of methylphenidate in preschool children with attention-deficit/hyperactivity disorder. *Journal of the Academy of Child and Adolescent Psychiatry, 45(11)*, 1294-1303.

Williams, K., Wheeler, D. M., Silove, N., & Hazell, P. (2010). Selective serotonin reuptake inhibitors (SSRIs) for autism spectrum disorders (ASDS). *Cochrane Database of Systematic Reviews, issue 8*, Published online August 8, 2010. DOI: 10.1002/14651858

Zarate, C. A. (2006). A randomized trial of an *N*-methyl-D-aspartate antagonist in treatment-resistant major depression. *Archives of General Psychiatry*, *63*, 856-864.

In: Intellectual Disability
Editors: Domenico F. Mancini and Carlo M. Greco
ISBN: 978-1-61942-298-8

Chapter 5

Caring for Children with Intellectual Impairments: A Focus on Williams and Smith-Magenis Syndromes

***Laura E. Slosky*[1], *Rebecca H. Foster*[2] *and Sarah H. Elsea*[3, 4*]**
[1]Department of Psychology, Virginia Commonwealth University, Richmond, VA, US
[2]Department of Psychology, St. Jude Children's Research Hospital, Memphis, TN, US
[3]Department of Pediatrics, Virginia Commonwealth University, Richmond, VA, US
[4]Department of Human and Molecular Genetics,
Virginia Commonwealth University, Richmond, VA, US

Abstract

With improved diagnostic techniques, prevalence rates of genetic disorders are increasing steadily, and thus, the number of individuals providing care to affected children is growing. Medical advances have increased survival rates and extended the lifespan of individuals affected by these disorders, which has increased caregiving demands and caregiver burden. While many of these individuals' needs are medical in nature, most also have some degree of intellectual impairment that interferes with their ability to function independently. Specifically, children with Williams syndrome and Smith-Magenis syndrome typically struggle with intellectual disability, in addition to other syndrome complications, such as behavioral problems. As a result, these individuals are typically unable to live independently, which often means that their guardians will assume a caregiver role for the entirety of their lives. Coping with the burden of caring for an individual with such significant needs has been associated with a decline in self-care behaviors, negatively impacting not only the caregiver but also the child and family system as a whole. This chapter examines self-care behaviors among these caregivers and investigates the effects of caregiver well-being on the individuals affected by these syndromes. How these individuals impact an entire family system is also explored.

* Correspondence should be addressed to: Sarah H. Elsea, Ph.D., FACMG, Dept. of Pediatrics, Virginia Commonwealth University School of Medicine, Richmond, VA 23298 USA, Phone: 804-628-0987, Fax: 804-628-1609, Email: selsea@vcu.edu

Finally, current interventions aimed at maximizing adaptive family functioning in these populations are reviewed, and suggestions for future research are discussed.

Keywords: Williams syndrome, Smith-Magenis syndrome, caregivers, intellectual disabilities

INTRODUCTION

Internationally, more than 7.6 million children are born each year with a severe genetic condition (World Health Organization, 2005). These numbers are believed to be an underestimate of actual incidence rates, as a lack of resources in less developed countries leads to many children going undiagnosed. The number of individuals in developed countries affected with such conditions is estimated to be as many as 60 out of every 1000 births (World Health Organization, 2005). These genetic conditions occur when variations in genes or chromosomes result in medical and/or developmental complications. While these genetic variations typically lead to physical differences such as craniofacial abnormalities and significant medical problems, some degree of cognitive impairment is often present. This aspect of genetic disorders is especially salient given that half of all intellectual disabilities are thought to have a genetic basis (Emery and Rimoin, 1990). The current chapter focuses on two such genetic disorders, Williams syndrome and Smith-Magenis syndrome, with a specific emphasis on those who care for individuals with these disorders. Intellectual abilities of individuals with Smith-Magenis or Williams syndromes typically fall into the mild (i.e., intellectual quotient [IQ] of 50-55 to approximately 70 on individually administered validated cognitive assessments) to moderate disability (i.e. IQ of 35-40 to 50-55) range (Greenberg et al., 1996a; Martens, Wilson, and Reutens, 2008; Meyer-Lindenberg, Mervis, and Berman, 2006).

While the intellectual ability of these individuals is heavily influenced by their genetic make-up, current research suggests that the etiology of mild to moderate intellectual disability is both genetic and environmental (Dykens, Hodapp, and Finucane, 2000). With individuals with these syndromes typically falling with in this range of cognitive abilities, they are at much greater risk for environmental deprivation, as they are less likely to be exposed to the same enrichment activities as their typically developing peers due to a preconceived notion that cognitive abilities will be limited (Dykens et al., 2000). This environmental deprivation, compounded by a genetic tendency toward impaired intellectual abilities, places these individuals at greater risk of not developing to their full potential. This makes caregiver intervention early in the child's life especially critical in order to optimize intellectual functioning within these populations (Sameroff and Fiese, 2000).

The caregiving demands placed on primary caregivers of children diagnosed with Williams and Smith-Magenis syndromes are significant, and this role requires a great investment of time and energy simply to meet basic needs (Harrington, Lackey, and Gates, 1996). Going above and beyond this level of care to provide additional enrichment for the child is often more than the caregiver believes that he or she can manage. The overwhelming nature of this role can make it more difficult for the caregivers to care for themselves, which, in turn, often makes it more difficult for the individuals to care for their child. With these challenges in mind, this chapter provides an overview of Williams syndrome and Smith-

Magenis syndrome while offering an overview of the caregiver burden placed upon these caregivers. We then examine self-care behaviors in these individuals and discuss the impact on the child and the family system. Finally, we discuss current interventions aimed at maximizing family functioning in these populations and provide suggestions for future research.

OVERVIEW OF WILLIAMS AND SMITH-MAGENIS SYNDROMES

Williams syndrome

> "If I had to choose a child to raise who had a disability, I would choose [a child with] Williams syndrome. They are amazing kids."
>
> Mother of a child diagnosed with Williams syndrome

Williams syndrome (WS) is a complex neurodevelopmental disorder that results from a deletion of the 7q11.23 region of chromosome 7 (Peoples et al., 2000). This contiguous gene syndrome involves the elastin gene, which is important for normal cardiac development, and several other genes thought to play a role in cognitive functioning. The syndrome affects approximately 1 out of 7,500 individuals worldwide and is a sporadic genetic syndrome, typically not inherited from a parent (Stromme, Bjomstad, and Ramstad, 2002). Individuals are affected equally across genders and racial groups. Moreover, WS is a multi-system disorder characterized by physical, developmental, and behavioral features in addition to medical complications. Common features include intellectual disability, learning difficulties, developmental delay, characteristic craniofacial anomalies, supravalvular aortic stenosis, hypertension, hypercalcemia, low birth weight, feeding problems, hyper sociability, musculoskeletal problems, and hyperacusis (Burn, 1986).

Children are typically first identified by their clinicians as possibly having WS due to their characteristic facial appearance (Burns, 1986). These facial features can range from subtle to striking and, as such, may lead to some variation in time frame required to make a diagnosis. Features include a flat nasal bridge, short upturned nose, long philtrum, delicate chin, periorbital puffiness, full lips, wide mouth, increased interdental spacing, microcephaly, and general hypotonia. Individuals with WS are commonly described as having an "elfin face" due to this combination of features (Burn, 1986, p. 389). The deletion on chromosome 7 is typically too small to be seen on karyotype, so the diagnosis is confirmed via fluorescence in situ hybridization (FISH) testing (Borg, Delhanty, and Baraitser, 1995; Elcioglu, Mackie-Ogilvie, Daker, and Berry, 1998), but until the use of FISH became more commonplace, the diagnosis was often missed. Testing may also be done by comparative genomic hybridization (CGH) microarray.

The presence of these phenotypic abnormalities creates a number of ophthalmological, otolaryngological, and dental problems (Burn, 1986; Pober, 2010). Strabismus and altered visual acuity are common along with narrowed lacrimal ducts. Hyperacusis, high tone hearing loss, and recurrent otitis media are also seen frequently within this population (Pober, 2010). While none of these issues are life threatening, they require frequent doctor visits and can cause discomfort for the individual and added burdens for caregivers.

Along with these phenotypic abnormalities, a number of medical problems characterize the presentation of WS, with the cardiovascular system being most negatively affected (Burn, 1986). Supravalvular aortic stenosis, or abnormal narrowing of medium and large arteries above the aortic valve, is common. When stenosis occurs, the aortic valve fails to fully open and obstructs blood flow out from the heart, causing decreased blood flow and oxygenation to other areas of the body. Therefore, the most common cause of death among individuals with WS is cardiovascular complications, with cardiovascular-related mortality found to be at 25-100 times that of healthy controls (Wessel et. al., 2004).

In addition to cardiovascular involvement, the endocrine system presents with abnormalities in those with a WS diagnosis (Burn, 1986; Pober, 2010). A hallmark symptom of the disorder includes blood calcium abnormalities, or hypercalcemia. While these episodes can be mild, they can also present as moderate to severe, especially in children (Cagle, Waguespack, Buckingham, Shankar, and DiMeglio, 2004; Morris, Clayton, Everitt, Semmence, and Burgess, 1990). Symptoms of a hypercalcemic episode include colic, hypotonia, poor appetite, and constipation. A severe episode is considered to be a medical emergency, as it can result in a comatose state or cardiac arrest (Pober, 2010). Along with these episodes, those with WS often have an impaired glucose tolerance, subclinical hypothyroidism, and early pubertal onset accompanied by an attenuated growth spurt (Cambiaso et. al., 2007; Pober, 2010; Stagi, et. al., 2005). These concerns all require monitoring and the involvement of an endocrinologist in the care of the patient.

While these problems within the cardiovascular and endocrine systems are the most life threatening, problems within the gastrointestinal and genitourinary tracts significantly affect quality of life (Pober, 2010). Both reflux and constipation are prevalent, as well as abnormal weight gain and non-organic abdominal pain. These symptoms are thought to contribute to feeding difficulties, which are often accompanied by problems associated with texture sensitivity. Thus, individuals may be followed by a gastroenterologist or participate in intensive feeding therapy. Many of these children will be labeled as failure to thrive due to their chronic feeding issues. Along with these GI concerns are renal and kidney abnormalities, enuresis, and frequent urinary tract infections, which can require ongoing care from both a nephrologist and urologist.

While not every individual with WS struggles with all of the aforementioned medical issues, most struggle with a significant constellation of these concerns. The number of body systems involved typically corresponds with the severity of syndrome presentation and requires complex medical management by an integrated team of highly trained professionals. While such multidisciplinary teams are largely made up of physicians, families may also benefit from the involvement of a well-integrated psychosocial support team (e.g., psychologists, social workers) and other ancillary services (e.g., physical and occupational therapists).

Along with medical problems and pronounced morphological differences, individuals with WS often experience psychological, developmental, and cognitive challenges. Sleep problems have been reported in the WS population, with individuals typically waking several times each night and exhibiting significant bedtime resistance (Annaz et al., 2010). The development of both gross and fine motor skills is typically delayed along with initial language acquisition (Udwin and Yule, 1991), with language skills typically emerging at approximately three years of age (Mervis et al., 2000). As these individuals grow into adolescence and adulthood, they present with a large and sophisticated vocabulary, but this can be deceiving, as their understanding of these word meanings is often rudimentary (Udwin, 1990). Children with WS display a range of intellectual abilities that typically falls between 40 and 100 on traditional tests of intelligence (Martens et al., 2008). Mean standard scores on these tests have ranged from 50 to 60, which is indicative of a mild to moderate intellectual disability (Martens et al., 2008; Meyer-Lindenberg et al., 2006). Executive functioning is also negatively affected, with planning and problem solving skills falling in the impaired range. This level of functioning makes it difficult for the affected individual to live and function independently as an adult.

While cognitive abilities are typically impaired within this population, the hallmark behavioral symptom of the disorder is a lack of stranger anxiety and a "cocktail party personality" (Pober, 2010, p. 245). Individuals with WS are highly social and empathic, but this lack of stranger anxiety can also cause problems. Such hyper-sociability increases the child's vulnerability and increases their monitoring needs. This heightened level of vigilance places added stress on the caregiver, as they frequently worry that their child's personality may cause them to associate with people who may cause them harm and that the child will fail to know when he or she is in danger. Imaging studies have shown decreased activity in the amygdala when viewing threatening faces but increased activation when viewing non-social threatening stimuli; findings that suggest a unique malfunction within the limbic system (Schumann, Bauman, and Amarai, 2010). Other research has found that despite the overly social personality, many of these individuals become socially isolated as a result of their anticipatory anxiety (Dykens, 2003). The presence of obsessions and hyper-attentiveness in some domains has also been noted and can interfere with social functioning (Davies, Udwin, and Howlin, 1998). Interestingly, one study found that despite the lack of social anxiety, more than 80% of these patients also meet clinical criteria for an anxiety disorder, attention deficit disorder, or, commonly, a combination of both disorders (Leyfer Woodruff-Borden, Klein-Tasman, Fricke, and Mervis, 2006). With these symptoms, the involvement of psychological professionals can be especially beneficial to patients and their families.

Smith-Magenis syndrome

> "Smith-Magenis syndrome is an ongoing 'onion' that has so many complex layers that continually unravel. When one behavior settles down, another one emerges, and you never know what is coming next. There are still so many unknowns with this disorder, and many uncertainties apply."
>
> Mother of a child diagnosed with Smith-Magenis syndrome

Smith-Magenis syndrome (SMS) is also classified as a neurodevelopmental disorder and is a result of a deletion on chromosome 17p11.2 that includes the *RAI1* gene (Elsea and Girirajan, 2008; Smith et al., 2006). Approximately 90% of individuals have a chromosomal deletion, while about 10% have a mutation of the *RAI1* gene. This syndrome affects approximately 1 out of every 15,000 to 25,000 births worldwide and is typically a sporadic syndrome not inherited from a parent (Greenberg et al., 1991). Diagnosis is made by chromosome or DNA analysis, and individuals are affected equally across genders and racial groups (Elsea and Girirajan, 2008). Like WS, SMS is a multisystem disorder characterized by physical, developmental, and behavioral features, along with medical complications. Common features among those diagnosed with SMS include characteristic craniofacial abnormalities, a hoarse voice, feeding problems, hypotonia, developmental delays, decreased sensitivity to pain, chronic sleep disturbances, attention problems, mood lability, and self-injurious behaviors (Elsea and Girirajan, 2008; Smith et al., 2006).

With respect to diagnosis, clinicians may first suspect that a child has SMS based on a phenotypic appearance and behaviors. SMS was not documented in the literature until the early 1980s (Smith, McGavran, Waldstein, and Robinson, 1982), and until the use of FISH testing became more commonplace, the small chromosomal deletion needed for diagnosis was often missed (Dykens et al., 2000). Diagnosis is now commonly made with CGH microarray. Additionally, SMS is often misdiagnosed or underdiagnosed given the overlap of physical characteristics with other genetic syndromes, such as Prader-Willi syndrome (Greenberg et al., 1996b).

Facial features associated with SMS include a flat midface, square-shaped head, broad nasal bridge, bow-shaped upper lip, ear abnormalities, and a deep voice (Smith, et al., 1986). These facial features are often associated with ear infections, hearing impairments, speech problems, feeding difficulties, and vision problems. Along with such phenotypic abnormalities and associated complications, a number of medical problems are also associated with SMS. Congenital heart defects are often seen along with seizure disorders, peripheral neuropathy, scoliosis, ophthalmological problems, and urinary tract abnormalities (Smith, et al., 2006). The complexity of these medical issues, as well as the varied presentation, requires significant medical management by an integrated multidisciplinary team of highly trained professionals. While these teams are largely comprised of physicians, like families coping with WS, families caring for an individual diagnosed with SMS also benefit from psychosocial support teams, including psychologists, social workers, and educational advocates and other ancillary services such as physical therapy.

Individuals with SMS typically display a number of atypical maladaptive behaviors that create additional challenges for their caregivers. Aggression, attention problems, hyperactivity, impulsivity, and self-injurous behaviors are all common (Colley, Leversha, Voullaire, and Rogers, 1990; Stratton et al., 1986). Disobedience, temper tantrums, stubbornness, property destruction, attention-seeking behaviors, and difficulty controlling bowels and bladders have also been documented (Dykens and Smith, 1998). Perhaps one of the most significant issues in individuals with SMS involves the presence of sleep disorders. Individuals with SMS typically struggle with nocturnal wakefulness and associated daytime hypersomnia, shortened sleep cycles, difficulty falling asleep, and deficits in rapid eye movement sleep (Smith, Dykens, and Greenberg, 1998b). These sleep issues are highly problematic for caregivers and contribute greatly to the stress placed on the family system (Hodapp, Fidler, and Smith, 1998). Many of the maladaptive behaviors seen in SMS individuals also become more frequent and increasingly problematic as sleep disturbances increase (Dykens and Smith, 1998).

Compounding these behavioral issues is the level of intellectual functioning typically associated with these individuals. The majority of those affected with SMS fall into the mild to moderate range of intellectual disability. A mean IQ of 47 with a range of 20 to 78 has been documented within this population, indicative of a moderate level of intellectual impairment (Greenberg et al., 1996a). Their cognitive profile includes weaknesses in sequential processing and relative strengths in acquired knowledge, reading, and arithmetic (Dykens, Finucane, and Gayley, 1997). With such significant psychological and intellectual issues, the involvement of psychological professionals can be especially beneficial to patients and their families.

Syndrome Comparison

> "Networking, networking, networking. Any family with a disabled child deals with so many issues - not necessarily the same one, but they do understand what one is going through."
>
> Mother of a child diagnosed with WS

Despite the presence of a similar degree of intellectual disability due to a primarily genetic etiology in both WS and SMS, individuals with these diagnoses present very differently. Behaviorally, these individuals create very different challenges for their caregivers. While the majority of caregivers struggle with their child's inattention, those caring for a child with WS are primarily concerned about internalizing symptoms (e.g., anxiety, depressive symptoms), while those with SMS are more commonly managing externalizing behaviors (e.g., tantrums; Davies et al., 1998; Stratton et al., 1986). While children with externalizing problems may create a more immediate concern for their caretakers, those with internalizing issues place similar stressors on the caretaker, simply in different ways (Brannan and Heflinger, 2001). For example, a caregiver who cannot take his or her child to the grocery store because of the anxiety of being in such a crowded place causes significant stress and frustration. Similarly, caregivers with a child having violent temper tantrums for no apparent reason face significant stress, as they must address these issues in a public setting while also dealing with the comments and stares of others. Despite the differences in presentation of psychological symptoms, the stress placed on the caregiver is significant across syndromes (Brannan and Heflinger, 2001).

In addition to these psychological differences, the two syndromes also present differently in terms of cognitive strengths and weaknesses, medical complications, and support services that are needed. Despite these differences, both sets of caregivers are coping with pervasive disorders in individuals with significant intellectual impairments who require complex management by a multidisciplinary team of professionals. The complexity of these syndromes, the intellectual challenges faced, and the number of people involved in their care creates similar experiences for these caregivers despite the differences in presentation.

Caregiver Burden

> "While it has been challenging, she is a blessing. I love her beyond belief. There are many times when I feel very overwhelmed and very isolated. Many people do not know anything about WS and everything that comes along with it. I wish that her doctor was more

knowledgeable about it. I wish that there was a support group in my town. It is a huge responsibility on my shoulders. I feel that I am responsible to ensure that she becomes all that she can be, and I need to give her all that I can. If I fail to give her the therapies, etc., she may not thrive to what she is capable of. That is a huge weight."

Mother of a child diagnosed with WS

Acting as the primary caregiver for any typically developing child is a demanding task. The average parent of a healthy child takes on the monumental task of caring and providing for that child for at least the better part of two decades in ever-changing capacities. While this alone is a significant financial, time, and emotional commitment, most parents do not plan to incur significant medical bills, provide for exceptional educational needs, or have to provide for their child throughout their adult lives (Davies, Howlin, and Udwin, 1997). In addition to the challenges and responsibilities that a parent of a typically developing child must assume, caregivers of a child diagnosed with WS or SMS must be able to readily adapt to the physical and behavioral features of the disorder as they fit within the typical developmental experiences across the lifespan. These include difficulties with feeding behaviors, adhering to intense medical regimens, handling a child with a difficult temperament, managing chronic sleep deprivation, and coping with the stressors that result from family members, educators, and medical professionals, who may not fully comprehend the child's diagnosis and ongoing care needs (Pober, 2010). As the child ages, developmental delays emerge, and maintaining a number of weekly therapy appointments becomes necessary (e.g., speech and language therapy, physical therapy, psychotherapy). Additionally, caregivers must monitor the mental health needs of their child carefully, as the child may impulsively endanger himself/herself or fail to show typical signs of distress (Dykens and Hodapp, 1997).

Perhaps most challenging for caregivers is balancing personal needs and the needs of one's spouse, other family members, and friends with the needs of the child with SMS or WS (Silver, Westbrook, and Stein, 1998). The cumulative effects of having the primary caretaking responsibility for such a special needs child contributes to a great degree of stress and caregiver burden (Fidler, Bailey, and Smalley, 2000). Adding to this burden is the knowledge that this role will be needed for the duration of the child's life, as individuals with WS or SMS are typically unable to achieve a level of adaptive functioning that allows for independent living (Davies, Howlin, and Udwin, 1998; Udwin, Webber, and Horn, 2001). With both syndromes involving such significant behavioral and intellectual concerns, the barriers against independent living once the individual reaches adulthood are great. Although these levels of impairment are frequently seen, there are many interventional strategies that allow individuals to maximize their own abilities. Further, parents often need to worry about care for their child after they themselves have passed away. This accumulation of stressors has led many in the field to conceptualize having a child with a disability as potentially traumatic (Turnbull and Turnbull, 1986) and to understand that caregivers often need to grieve the loss of the typically developing child they do not have (Seligman, 1985). The allostatic, or cumulative load, of such a caregiving burden has a significant impact on caregivers over time (Clark, Bond, and Hecker, 2007).

The definition of caregiving has been broken down into five categories: 1) anticipatory, 2) preventive, 3) supervisory, 4) protective, and 5) instrumental activities (Bowers, 1987). Much of this work is not as overtly visible and involves activities such as decision making and planning for the child's current and future needs. Over time, the taxing nature of such an intense role can become increasingly burdensome, especially in the case of caring for a child with significant functional impairments such as those often seen in populations with intellectual disabilities (Raina et al., 2004). Caregiver burden involves daily adjustments and changes that could prevent caregivers from attending to their own needs (Graham Ballard, and Sham, 1997; Hasselkus, 1988). Adding to the difficulty of being a caregiver for these individuals is the fact that the intensity of the role is often unexpected (Eicher and Batshaw, 1993) and that training for the role is non-existent prior to having the child. Despite these differences from more traditional occupations, many have come to conceptualize this role as the caregiver career (Lindgren, 1993; Raina et al., 2004). This comparison is a fitting description given the full time nature of the role, although a caregiver's job does not end at any point during the day or, in many cases, in their lifetime. Caregivers also are not granted the rights and benefits that come with more formal career paths, nor are they advanced in their position based on their effort and success in the role. These enduring, challenging tasks in the absence of traditional external rewards lead the care giving career to take a significant toll on individuals over time. This burden often creates feelings of helplessness and ineffectiveness over time and can create the feeling of being trapped (Call, Finch, Huck, and Kane, 1999). These negative feelings, in addition to the cumulative amount of time that must be devoted to these children, are thought to contribute to higher levels of stress and poorer self-care behaviors among primary caregivers.

Caregiver Health and Well-Being

> "Although there are moments when it is difficult to care for my son, I draw from his strength. He has been through so much in his short life, yet he always has a smile for me."
>
> Mother of a child diagnosed with SMS

Empirical research examining the impact of having a child with WS or SMS on caregivers and families is only just beginning to emerge (e.g., Foster et al., 2010; Scallan, Senior and Reilly, 2010). Because of the emerging nature of this area, studies of caregivers of children with other neurodevelopmental and intellectual disabilities have been used as a guiding framework. Stress can affect many different parts of a person's life, including mental and physical health (Lin and Ensel, 1989). A study on the health and well-being of caregivers of children with cerebral palsy showed such results and serves as a proxy for what may be expected among caregivers of individuals with WS or SMS (Raina et al., 2004). Results indicated that the best predictors of caregivers' well-being were child behavior, caregiving demands, and family functioning. Fewer caregiving demands were associated with better psychological and physical health. Other studies have found that social support (Barakat and Linney, 1992), spousal support (Erickson and Upshur, 1989), and marital satisfaction (Friedrich, 1979) were also associated with maternal well-being. With the high levels of caregiving demands that a child with WS or SMS necessitates, it can be presumed that these caregivers would exhibit poorer levels of well-being and likely have a more difficult time caring for themselves and coping effectively. This was supported by recent research that found that maternal well-being was directly related to perceived child health vulnerability, caregiver satisfaction, and benefit finding in the Smith-Magenis community (Foster et al., 2010). Other findings have spoken to an increased need for counseling services among caregivers of children with WS and SMS (Foster et al., 2010; Scallan et al., 2010).

An important part of caregiving is taking care of oneself (Foster et al., 2010). Despite its importance, many caregivers experience difficulty balancing their own needs with those of their child. According to a study performed by Evercare®, a provider of health plans for people who have chronic or advanced illness and the National Alliance for Caregiving (NAC), a leading authority on caregiving, 91% of caregivers surveyed saw a decline in their health as a result of caregiving, and 90% reported that their level of stress increased as a result of caregiving (Washington, 2006). A significant number of caregivers also reported poorer sleep hygiene, poorer eating behaviors, and reduced exercise behaviors. Furthermore, many caregivers indicated that they had not attended to personal medical concerns as often as they should. Reasons for this decline in self-care were attributed to a lack of time and energy among caregivers. Based on these findings, it is believed that caregivers of individuals diagnosed with WS or SMS likely encounter challenges maintaining their own level of well-being. This includes potential challenges with maintaining personal health care behaviors. One study of caregiver well-being in the Smith-Magenis community found increased levels of anxiety and depression among caregivers, disrupted sleep patterns, and difficulty maintaining annual physical examinations (Foster et al., 2010). A similar study of those caring for a child with a developmental disability found that caregivers demonstrated significant difficulties balancing personal needs with the demands of the child (Gowen, Johnson-Martin, Goldman, and Appelbaum, 1989). As caregiver well-being is known to adversely affect children's own level of well-being (Luoma et al., 2001), this presents a significant concern for individuals affected by WS or SMS.

One hypothesis posits that more of the burden of caring for a child with a disability falls on the primary caregiver than in the past. As the average number of children in a family has decreased and the divorce rate has increased, family size has become significantly smaller (Aneshensel, Pearlin, Mullan, Zarit, and Whitlatch, 1995). Concurrently, more children are surviving pregnancy and infancy with significant disabilities due to advances in medical technologies (Dumas, Peron, and Peron, 1992). With larger family units, the care responsibility for individuals with exceptional needs was better distributed among a number of individuals. What was once a responsibility shared by many has now been placed on a few caregivers. With this shift in care, it is more important than ever to intervene with caregivers early in their caregiving career to maximize the quality of life of the caregiver, the child, and the family system as a whole.

Impact of Poor Self-Care on the Family System

> "This is the toughest job I can ever imagine. Sometimes I resent other 'typically developing families' with their insignificant challenges."
>
> Mother of a child diagnosed with SMS

Caregiver adjustment to a child with a disability is often viewed as an adaptational process (Crnic, Friedrich, and Greenburg, 1983). This view encompasses the family system as a whole and can also be used to describe the adaptation of the family to a caregiver whose well-being has declined over time. A popular adaptational model (Crnic et al., 1983) views the child as a stressor, analogous to any other stressor, to which the family must adjust. As such, adjustment is thought to occur within the context of a stress and coping model. This viewpoint has marked a shift away from Freudian perspectives on childrearing that focused on parental pathology (Solnit and Stark, 1961). The more recent adaptational model aimed to account for the full range of outcomes (i.e. both positive and negative) that a caregiver of a child with a disability may experience. The child with special needs or cognitive challenges is perceived as a stressor that triggers a number of challenges within the family system. The system's response to these challenges is mediated by the coping resources of the entire family (Crnic et al., 1983). Crnic and colleagues used Folkman's (1979) conceptualization of coping resources when describing these resources in their adaptational model. These resources include parental mental health, cognitive resources, support resources, socioeconomic status, and religious beliefs as possible mediators of the stress response within the ecological context. The model stresses the inclusion of the ecological context as it is thought to be qualitatively different for families with a child with exceptional challenges than for families of typically developing children (Crnic et al., 1983). One ecological difference these authors cited when comparing families with typically developing children and families with exceptional children was a decreased amount of social interaction and opportunities for support. Because of these significant differences, Crnic and colleagues (1983) postulated that it was important to consider both an ecological and a stress and coping perspective when designing their own adaptational model.

The impact of caregiver well-being on the child is significant. Research in this area has primarily focused on parental depression, which has consistently been described as a significant predictor of both emotional and behavior problems in children (Beck, 1999; Goodman and Gotlib, 1999; Webster-Stratton and Hammond, 1998). Children in these families are at significantly increased risk for psychological, academic, and social problems (Anderson and Hammen, 1993), as these issues can interfere with typical development of the child and place additional stress on the caregiver, as well as other family members. Caregivers who struggle with mood problems are more likely to be irritable, inconsistent, less supportive of their children, and receive less support (Cummings and Davies, 1992). These behaviors increase the stress level in the home environment and impact both the child and the family (Langrock, Compas, Keller, Merchant, and Copeland, 2002). Physical illness or disability in a caregiver can have a similar effect on the family with others needing to compensate for what the caretaker is no longer able to handle, placing additional stress on the system.

Interventions Targeting Family Functioning

"My number one stressor is continuing to move forward as a family. My son, as a person, as a human being, is easy. He is, by far, the most beautiful human being I have ever met. I love my life; however, with that being said: The cost, time, and stress of having a child diagnosed with WS are overwhelming. These factors are only compounded by a lack of education and viable ways to fund a life that statistically costs 3-4 times that of a typical family. How do we survive the cost? How do we survive the divorce rate among parents with children diagnosed with special needs? How do we fund the whole operation?"

Mother of a child diagnosed with WS

Given the importance of the entire family and caregiver well-being in facilitating the optimal development of children with both WS and SMS, it is important to examine and continually improve upon interventions targeting family functioning in these populations. Interventions within these populations have primarily focused on increasing social support, parent management training, and behavioral family interventions (e.g., Gammon and Rose, 1991; Kirkham and Schilling, 1990). The goal of such interventions is to teach caregivers to minimize opportunities for negative behavior while simultaneously responding to behavior in a contingent manner (Roberts, Mazzucchelli, Studman, and Sanders, 2006). Much success has been documented with typically developing children using these interventions and recently similar results have been documented among children with developmental and intellectual disabilities (Feinfield and Baker, 2004; Roberts, Mazzucchelli, Taylor, and Reid, 2003; Webster-Stratton, Reid, and Hammond, 2004).

Parent Child Interaction Therapy (PCIT) is one form of therapy with demonstrated efficacy in promoting adaptive family dynamics (Querido, Berass, and Eyberg, 2002). The goals of PCIT include the establishment of a more positive relationship between parent and child as well as teaching parents strategies for managing their child's behavior (Hanf, 1969). This approach is used to treat behavior problems in children by combining behavioral intervention and relationship improvement techniques (Querido et al., 2002). Play is used as a therapeutic tool and provides a foundation for modeling adaptive parenting techniques. The first phase of treatment is child-directed and focuses on the parent-child relationship, while the second phase is parent-directed and focuses on behavior management skills. Limit setting, discipline, expectations, and responding to negative behavior are all topics covered by this type of intervention. These intervention strategies can be especially useful for parents of children with developmental disabilities, as disruptive behavior problems are typically comorbid (McDiarmid and Bagner, 2005). Modifications to this type of intervention for an intellectual disability population include spending extra time ensuring that the child understands the verbalizations of the parent and using treatment time to increase the child's communication skills, which allows the child to express him or herself more effectively. The use of praise, effective commands, and setting clear behavioral expectations are all key components of this therapy. The effective use of these interventions has been well documented in typically developing populations (e.g., Eyberg and Matarazzo, 1980; McNeil, Capage, Bahl, and Blanc, 1999; Schuhmann, Foote, Eyberg, Boggs, and Algina, 1998), and PCIT's efficacy within populations with developmental disabilities and genetic disorders is beginning to emerge in the literature (McDiarmid and Bagner, 2005).

Other effective family-based interventions aimed at helping parents care for children with significant care needs are grounded in cognitive behavioral theory (CBT; Roberts et al., 2006). These interventions are primarily conducted with parents and focus on building problem solving skills as well as using cognitive restructuring techniques (Beck, 1999). These tools allow parents to better handle daily challenges and reduce parental stress that comes with having a child with significant care needs (Roberts et al., 2006). Cognitive behavioral interventions may also focus on contingently responding to the child's behavior and planning activities in a manner that minimizes opportunities for disruptive behavior (Kazdin, 2005). Such interventions have been found to reduce child behavior problems, harsh parenting styles, and parental stress while also improving positive parenting techniques. These interventions may also be delivered in a group format, which increases cost effectiveness (Gammon and Rose, 1991). The efficacy of such CBT interventions has been well-documented among families with both typically developing children (Kazdin, 2005) and children with developmental and intellectual disabilities, as well as genetic disorders (Gammon and Rose, 1991; Kirkham and Shilling, 1990). These results have also been documented among caregivers of children with Down syndrome and other neurodevelopmental disabilities of a genetic etiology (Plant and Sanders, 2008).

Future Research and Clinical Implications

> "Anything worth doing well is challenging. Cherish this experience. [Few] moms get to take this journey. It makes you realize all the little things we take for granted. [My child] is extremely loving and social. She can make anyone smile. That is my silver lining for all the stress, heartache, worry, etc. She has been able to remind me of the human perspective of life verses money or job titles."
>
> Mother of a child diagnosed with WS

While research on interventions targeting family functioning in populations with intellectual disabilities has advanced significantly, there is still a great need for further research. Much of the research examining the impact of having a child with WS or SMS has been focused on mothers or on family units as a whole (e.g. Erikson and Upshur, 1989; Foster et al., 2010; Friedrich, 1979). Less is known about the psychological impact that these children have on fathers and their caregiving efforts. This is an area that would benefit from further exploration and possible intervention to promote healthy adaptation to caregivng roles. To date, one study investigating caregiver well-being among fathers of children diagnosed with SMS suggested strong relationships among depressive symptoms, benefit-finding, and caregiver well-being (Foster et al., 2010). Such a study serves as a solid foundation for further investigating specific factors that may predict caregiver outcomes or adaptive parenting strategies. Additionally, while many treatment effects have been identified (e.g. fewer child behavior problems, reduced parental stress, and increased use of positive parenting techniques), mediators and moderators of treatment effects are not as well understood and should be further explored within these populations. Dismantling studies aimed at examining aspects of treatment most beneficial to families of children with intellectual disabilities would also serve to advance this field of research.

While specific parenting interventions such as PCIT and other CBT techniques have been examined in other populations with intellectual disabilities (e.g., Down syndrome), they have not been examined in populations diagnosed with WS or SMS specifically. Examining interventions that target these specific populations would represent a significant contribution to the literature. Such interventions would allow for problem solving surrounding unique behaviors present in these children and have the potential to facilitate social support avenues within these communities if delivered in a group format. For example, within families coping with SMS, sleep behaviors and interventions would be an especially salient target for intervention. Among families coping with WS, interventions targeting appropriate social skills and development of social boundaries may be beneficial. Finally, given the importance of early diagnosis and intervention, examining ways to intervene within these families immediately following diagnosis would represent a large clinical contribution. Possible avenues to facilitate this may include genetic counselors and neonatal intensive care unit (NICU) staff who could provide information and referral resources when working with families who have children newly facing these issues.

RESOURCES FOR FAMILIES

"It's been a huge learning curve, and I'm always on the lookout for people and resources that can help me be a better caregiver for my son."

Mother of a child diagnosed with WS

Coping appropriately with the demands of caring for a child with an intellectual disability often requires a large support network that reaches beyond immediate and extended family members. Families will likely benefit from speaking with their pediatrician, family physician, or genetic counselor about referrals to the following people or services:

Person or Service	Services Provided
Psychologists	Developmental, cognitive, and academic assessment Neuropsychological assessment Caregiver, family, and child/adolescent therapy Parent-child interaction therapy, other CBT interventions for behavior management Sleep and feeding behavior intervention Social skills development Assistance with educational or vocational planning Adaptive functioning, independent living skills
Psychiatrists	Pharmacological interventions for children and/or caregivers for emotional of behavioral concerns
Educational Services – School Psychologists and Guidance Counselors	Development of Individualized Education Plans (IEPs) or 504 Plans Psychoeducational assessment
Hospital-Based Educational Advocates	Work with schools to develop IEPs and to determine educational and interventional needs
Occupational Therapy	Sensory integration intervention Feeding therapy Assistive devices and daily living aids
Physical Therapy	Assessment of gross and fine motor skills Therapeutic approaches to development of motor skills Assessment and ongoing evaluation for assisted needs
Speech and Language Therapy	Speech and language evaluations Speech and language therapy Feeding interventions

Person or Service	**Services Provided**
Social Workers	Case management across multiple agencies
Nutritionists	Assessment of nutritional needs Feeding interventions
Sleep Specialists	Assessment of sleep-related disorders Pharmacological interventions

CONCLUSION

Genetic disorders are believed to account for approximately one half of all cases of intellectual disability (Emery and Rimolin, 1990). Smith-Magenis and Williams syndromes are two excellent examples of complex genetic disorders that also result in medical, psychological, and developmental problems. Providing care for individuals affected by these disorders requires a significant investment of time and energy above and beyond that of a caregiver of a typically developing child (Harrington et al., 1996). This creates an increased burden on caregivers, and the impact reaches not only the caregiver and the child, but also the family system as a whole (Fidler et al., 2000).

A number of interventions have been shown to improve family functioning within these populations (e.g. Gammon and Rose, 1991; Kirkham and Schilling, 1990). However, future research in this area is needed to target the most effective components of existing interventions, adapt them to meet the unique needs of these families, and further improve the quality of life of these exceptional individuals.

REFERENCES

Anderson, C. A. and Hammen, C. L. (1993). Psychosocial outcomes of children of unipolar depressed, bipolar, medically ill, and normal women: a longitudinal study. *Journal of Consulting and Clinical Psychology, 61*, 448-454. doi:10.1037//0022-006X.61.3.448.

Aneshensel, C. S., Pearlin, L. I., Mullan, J. T., Zarit, S. H., and Whitlatch, C. J. (1995). *Profiles in caregiving: The unexpected career*. San Diego, CA: Academic Press.

Annaz, D., Remington, A., Milne, E., Coleman, M., Campbell, R., Thomas, M., and Swettenham, J. (2010). *Atypical development of motion processing trajectories in children with autism*. Retrieved from psyc.bbk.ac.uk.

Barakat, L. P., and Linney, J. A. (1992). Children with physical handicaps and their mothers: The interrelation of social support, maternal adjustment, and child adjustment. *Journal of Pediatric Psychology, 17*, 725-739. doi:10.1093/jpepsy/17.6.725.

Beck, C. T. (1999). Maternal depression and child behaviour problems: A meta-analysis. *Journal of Advanced Nursing, 29*, 623-629. doi:10.1046/j.1365-2648.1999.00943.x.

Borg, I., Delhanty, J.D., and Baraitser, M. (1995). Detection of hemizygosity at the elastin locus by FISH analysis as a diagnostic test in both classical and atypical cases of Williams syndrome. *Journal of Medical Genetics, 32*, 692-696. doi:10.1136/jmg.32.9.692.

Bowers, B. (1987). Intergenerational caregiving: Adult caregivers and their aging parents. *Advances in Nursing Science, 9*, 20-31. Retrieved from journals.lww.com/advancesinnursingscience/.

Brannan, A. M., and Heflinger, C. A. (2001). Distinguishing caregiver strain from psychological distress: Modeling the relationships among child, family, and caregiver variables. *Journal of Child and Family Studies, 10*, 405–418. doi:10.1023/A:1016705306848.

Burn, J. (1986). Williams syndrome. *Journal of Medical Genetics*, *23*, 398-395. doi:10.1136/jmg.23.5.389.

Cagle, A.P., Waguespack, S.G., Buckingham, B.A., Shankar, R., and DiMeglio, L.A. (2004). Severe infantile hypercalcemia associated with Williams syndrome successfully treated with intravenously administered pamidronate. *Pediatrics, 114*(4), 1091-1104. doi:10.1542/peds.2003-1146-L.

Call, K., Finch, M., Huck, S., and Kane, R. (1999). Caregiver burden from a social exchange perspective: Caring for older people after hospital discharge. *Journal of Marriage and the Family, 61*, 688–699. doi:10.2307/353570.

Cambiaso, P., Orazi, C., Digilio, M.C., Loche, S., Capolino, R., Tozzi, A.,…,and Cappa M. (2007). Thyroid morphology and subclinical hypothyroidism in children and adolescents with Williams syndrome. *Journal of Pediatrics, 150,* 62–65. doi:10.1016/j.jpeds.2006.10.060.

Clark, M. S., Bond, M. J., and Hecker, J.R. (2007). Environmental stress, psychological stress and allostatic load. Psychology, Health, and Medicine, *12*, 18-30. doi:10.1080/13548500500429338.

Colley, A., Leversha, M., Voullaire, L., and Rogers, J. (1990). Five cases demonstrating the distinctive behavioral features of chromosome deletion 17(p11.2) (Smith-Magenis Syndrome). *Journal of Pediatrics and Child Health, 26*, 17-21. doi:10.1111/j.1440-1754.1990.tb02372.x.

Coping with the stress of parental depression: Parents' reports of children' coping, emotional, and behavioral problems. *Journal of Clinical Child and Adolescent Psychology, 31*, 312-324. doi:10.1207/153744202760082577.

Crnic, K., Friedrich, W., and Greenburg, M. (1983). Adaptaton of families with mentally handicapped children: A model of stress, coping, and family ecology. *American Journal of Mental Deficiency, 88,* 125-138. Retrieved from www.aaiddjournals.org/.

Cummings, E. M., and Davies, P. T. (1992). Parental depression, family functioning, and child development: Risk factors, processes, and pathways. In D. Cicchetti and S. L. Toth (Eds.), *Rochester symposium on developmental psychopathology: Vol.4. A developmental approach to affective disorders* (pp. 283-322). Rochester, NY: University of Rochester Press.

Davies, M., Udwin, O., and Howlin, P. (1998). Adults with Williams syndrome. Preliminary study of social, emotional and behavioural difficulties. *British Journal of Psychiatry*, *172*, 273-276. doi:10.1192/bjp.172.3.273.

Davies, M., Howlin, P., and Udwin, O. (1997). Independence and adaptive behavior in adults with Williams syndrome. *American Journal of Medical Genetics, 70*, 188-195. doi:10.1002/(SICI)1096-8628(19970516)70:2<188::AID-AJMG16>3.0.CO;2-F.

Dumas, D., Peron, J., and Peron, Y. (1992). *Marriage and conjugal life in Canada* (pp. 62). Ottawa: Statistics Canada.

Dykens, E. M. (2003). Anxiety, fears, and phobias in persons with Williams syndrome. *Developmental Neuropsychology, 23*, 291–316. doi:10.1207/S15326942DN231and2_13.

Dykens, E. M., and Hodapp, R. M. (1997). Treatment issues in genetic mental retardation syndromes. *Professional Psychology: Research and Practice*, 28, 263–270. doi:10.1037//0735-7028.28.3.263.

Dykens, E. M., and Smith, A. (1998). Distinctiveness and correlates of maladaptive behavior in children and adolescents with Smith-Magenis syndrome. *Journal of Intellectual Disability Research, 42*, 481-489. doi:10.1046/j.1365-2788.1998.4260481.x.

Dykens, E. M., Finucane, B., and Gayley, C. (1997). Brief report: Cognitive and behavioral profiles in persons with Smith-Magenis syndrome. *Journal of Autism and Developmental Disorders*, 27, 203-211. doi:10.1023/A:1025800126086.

Dykens, E. M., Hodapp, R., and Finucane, B. (2000). *Genetics and Mental Retardation Syndromes. A New Look at Behavior and Interventions.* Baltimore, MD: Paul H. Brooks Publishing Company.

Eicher, P. S., and Batshaw, M. L. (1993). Cerebral palsy. *Pediatric Clinics of North America*, 40, 537-551. Retrieved from www.pediatric.theclinics.com/.

Elcioglu, N., Mackie-Ogilvie, C., Daker, M., and Berry, A. C. (1998). FISH analysis in patients with clinical diagnosis of Williams syndrome. *Acta Paediatrica. 87*, 48– 53. Retrieved from www.wiley.com/bw/journal.asp?ref=0803-5253.

Elsea, S.H., and Girirajan, S. (2008). *Smith-Magenis Syndrome. European Journal of Human Genetics, 16*, 412-21. doi:10.1038/sj.ejhg.5202009.

Emery, A.H,, and Rimoin, D.L, (1996). *Principles and Practice of Medical Genetics*. 3rd ed. New York, NY: Churchill Livingstone; 1996.

Erickson, M. and Upshur, C. (1989). Caretaking burden and social support: A comparison of mothers of children with and without disabilities. *American Journal on Mental Retardation, 94*, 250-258. Retrieved from www.aaiddjournals.org/.

Eyberg, S. M., and Matarazzo, R. G. (1980). Training parents as therapists: A comparison between individual parent-child interaction training and parent group didactic training. *Journal of Clinical Psychology, 36*, 492-499. Retrieved from onlinelibrary.wiley.com/journal/10.1002/(ISSN)1097-4679.

Feinfield, K. A., and Baker, B. L. (2004). Empirical support for a treatment program for families of young children with externalizing problems. *Journal of Clinical Child and Adolescent Psychology, 33*, 182–195. doi:10.1207/S15374424JCCP3301_17.

Fidler, D.J., Bailey, J.N., and Smalley, S.L. (2000). Macrocephaly in autism and other pervasive developmental disorders. *Developmental Medicine and Child Neurology*. 42, 737–740. doi:10.1017/S0012162200001365.

Folkman, S. (1997). Positive psychological states and coping with severe stress. *Social Science and Medicine, 25,* 1207-1221. doi:10.1016/S0277-9536(97)00040-3.

Foster, R., Kozachek, S., Stern, M., and Elsea, S.H. (2010). Caring for the caregivers: An investigation of factors related to well-being among parents caring for a child with Smith-Magenis syndrome. *Journal of Genetic Counseling, 19*, 187-198. doi:10.1007/s10897-009-9273-5.

Friedrich, W. (1979). Predictors of coping behavior of mothers of handicapped children. *Journal of Consulting and Clinical Psychology*, *47*, 1140-1141. doi:10.1037//0022-006X.47.6.1140.

Gammon, E.A., and Rose, S.D. (1991). The coping skills training program for parents of children with developmental disabilities: An experimental evaluation. *Research on Social Work Practice, 1,* 244-256. doi:10.1177/104973159100100302.

Goodman, S. H., and Gotlib, I. H., (1999). Risk for psychopathology in the children of depressed mothers: A developmental model for understanding mechanisms of transmission. *Psychological Review, 106*, 458-490. doi:10.1037//0033-295X.106.3.458.

Gowen, J., Johnson-Martin, N., Goldman, B., and Appelbaum, M. (1989). Feelings of depression and parenting competence of mothers of handicapped and nonhandicapped infants: A longitudinal study. *American Journal on Mental Retardation, 94*, 259-271. doi:10.1016/0193-3973(89)90014-2.

Graham, C., Ballard, C., and Sham, P. (1997). Carers' knowledge of dementia, their coping strategies and morbidity. *International Journal of Geriatric Psychiatry, 12*, 931-936. doi:10.1002/(SICI)1099-1166(199709)12:9<931::AID-GPS666>3.0.CO;2-8.

Greenberg, F., Guzzetta, V., de Oca-Luna, R., Magenis, R., Smith, R., Richter, S., … Lupski, J. (1991).Molecular analysis of Smith-Magenis Syndrome: A possible contiguous-gene syndrome associated with del(17) (p11.2). *American Journal of Human Genetics, 4*, 1207-1218. doi:10.1002/ajmg.1320410219.

Greenberg, F., Lewis, R., Potocki, L., Glaze, D., Parke, J., Killian, J., … Lupiski, J. (1996a). Multi-disciplinary clinical study of Smith-Magenis syndrome: (deletion 17p11.2). *American Journal of Medical Genetics, 62*, 247-254. doi:10.1002/(SICI)1096-8628(19960329)62:3<247::AID-AJMG9>3.3.CO;2-9.

Greenberg, F., Magenis, R., Finucane, B., Smith, A., Patel, L., and Lupski, J. (1996b). Smith-Magenis and its clinical overlap with Prader-Willi syndrome. Abstract presented to the American Society of Human Genetics Meeting.

Hanf, C. (1969). A two-stage program for modifying maternal controlling during mother–child (M–C) interaction. Paper presented at the Meeting of the Western Psychological Association, Vancouver, BC.

Harrington, V., Lackey, N. R., and Gates, M. F. (1996). Needs of caregivers of clinic and hospice cancer patients. *Cancer Nursing, 19*, 118-125. doi:10.1097/00002820-199604000-00006.

Hasselkus, B. R. (1988). Meaning in family caregiving: Perspectives on caregiver/professional relationships. *Gerontologist, 28*, 686–691. doi:10.1093/geront/28.5.686.

Hodapp, R.M., Fidler, D.J., and Smith, A.C. (1998). Stress and coping in families of children with Smith-Magenis syndrome. *Journal of Intellectual Disability Research, 42*, 331-340. doi:10.1046/j.1365-2788.1998.00148.x.

Kazdin, A. (2005). *Parent management training. Treatment of oppositional, aggressive and antisocial behavior in children and adolescents*. New York, NY: Oxford University Press. Kirkham, M.A., and Schilling, R.F. (1990). Life skills training with mothers of handicapped children. *Journal of Social Service Research, 13,* 67-87. doi:10.1300/J079v13n02_05.

Langrock, A. M., Compas, B. E., Keller, G., Merchant, M. J., and Copeland, M. E. (2002).

Leyfer, O. T., Woodruff-Borden, J., Klein-Tasman, B., Fricke, J., and Mervis, C. (2006). Prevalence of psychiatric disorders in 4-16 year olds with Williams syndrome. *American Journal of Medical Genetics, 141B*, 615-622. doi:10.1002/ajmg.b.30344.

Lin, N., and Ensel, W. (1989). Life stress and health: Stressors and resources. *American Sociological Review*, 54, 382-399. doi:10.2307/2095612.

Lindgren, C. (1993). The caregiver career. Image. *Journal of Nursing Scholarship*, 25, 214–219. doi:10.1111/j.1547-5069.1993.tb00784.x.

Luoma, I., Tamminen, T., Kaukonen, P., Laippala, P., Puura, K., Salmelin, R., and Almqvist, F. (2001). Longitudinal study of maternal depressive symptoms and child well-being. *Journal of the American Academy of Child and Adolescent Psychiatry, 40*, 1367–1374. doi:10.1097/00004583-200112000-00006.

Martens, M.A., Wilson, D. C., and Reutens, J. (2008). Research Review: Williams syndrome: a critical review of the cognitive, behavioral, and neuroanatomical phenotype. *Journal of Child Psychology and Psychiatry and Allied Disciplines, 49*, 576-608. doi:10.1111/j.1469-7610.2008.01887.x.

McDiarmid, M. D., and Bagner, D. M. (2005). Parent–child interaction therapy for children with disruptive behavior and developmental disabilities. *Education and Treatment of Children, 28*, 130–141. Retrieved from www.educationandtreatmentofchildren.net/.

McNeil, C. B., Capage, L. C., Bahl, A., and Blanc, H. (1999). Importance of early intervention for disruptive behavior problems: Comparison of treatment and waitlist-control groups. *EarlyEducation and Development, 10*, 445–454. doi:10.1207/s15566935eed1004_2.

Mervis C. B., Robinson B. F., Bertrand J., Morris C. A., Klein-Tasman B. P. and Armstrong S. C. (2000). The Williams syndrome cognitive profile. *Brain and Cognition*, 44, 604–628. doi:10.1006/brcg.2000.1232.

Meyer-Lindenberg, A., Mervis, C.B., and Berman, K.F. (2006). Neural mechanisms in Williams syndrome: A unique window to genetic influences on cognition and behaviour. *Nature Reviews Neuroscience*, 7, 380–393. doi:10.1038/nrn1906.

Morris, J. N., Clayton, D. G., Everitt, M. G., Semmence, A. M. and Burgess, E. H. (1990). Exercise in leisure time: Coronary attack and death rates. *British Heart Journal, 63*, 325-334. doi:10.1136/hrt.63.6.325.

Peoples, R., Frankie, Y., Wang, Y.K., Perez-Jurado, L., Paperna, T., Cisco, M., and Francke, U. (2000). A physical map, including a bac/pac clone contig, of the Williams-Beuren syndrome–deletion region at 7q11. 23. *American Journal of Human Genetics, 66*, 47-68. doi:10.1086/302722.

Plant, K., and Sanders, M. (2006). Reducing problem behavior during care-giving in families of preschool-aged children with developmental disabilities. Research in Developmental Disabilities.

Pober, B.R. (2010). Williams-Beuren Syndrome. *New England Journal of Medicine*, *362*, 239- 252. doi:10.1056/NEJMra0903074.

Querido, J. G., Bearss, K., and Eyberg, S. M. (2003). Parent-Child Interaction Therapy. In F.W Kaslow and T. Patterson (Eds.), *Comprehensive Handbook of Psychotherapy,Volume Two: Cognitive/Behavioral/Functional Approaches* (pp. 91-113). NewYork, NY: Wiley.

Raina, P., O'Donell, M., Rosenbaum, P., Brehaut, J., Walter, S. D., Russell, D.,…Wood, E. (2004). The health and well-being of caregivers of children with cerebral palsy. *Pediatrics*, *115*, 626-636. doi:10.1542/peds.114.2.e182.

Roberts, C. M., Mazzucchelli, T., Taylor, K., and Reid, R. (2003). Early intervention for children with challenging behavior and developmental disabilities. *International Journal of Disability, Development and Education*, *50*, 275–292. doi:10.1080/1034912032000120453.

Roberts, C., Mazzucchelli, T., Studman, L., and Sanders, M. R. (2006). Behavioral family intervention for children with developmental disabilities and behavioral problems. *Journal of Clinical Child and Adolescent Psychology, 35*, 180–193. doi:10.1207/s15374424jccp3502_2.

Sameroff, A.J., and Fiese, B.H. (2000). Transactional regulation: The developmental ecology of early intervention. In J.P. Shonkoff, S.J. Meisels (Eds.), *Handbook of early childhood intervention.* Cambridge, UK: Cambridge University Press.

Scallan, S., Senior, J., and Reilly, C. (2010). Williams syndrome: Daily challenges and positive impact on the family. *Journal of Applied Research in Intellectual Disabilities, 24*, 181-188. doi: 10.1111/j.1468-3148.2010.00575.x.

Schuhmann, E. M., Foote, R., Eyberg, S. M., Boggs, S., and Algina, J. (1998). Parent–child therapy: Interim report of a randomized trial with short-term maintenance. Journal of Clinical Child Psychology, 27, 34–45. doi:10.1207/s15374424jccp2701_4.

Schumann, C.M., Bauman, M.D., and Amaral, D.G. (2010). Abnormal structure or function of the amygdale is a common component of neurodevelopmental disorders. *Neuropsychologia*, *49*, 745-759. Retrieved from www.sciencedirect.com/science/journal/00283932.

Seligman, M. (1985). Handicapped children and their families. *Journal of Counseling and Development*, 64, 274-277. Retrieved from www.counseling.org/publications/journals.aspx.

Silver, E., Westbrook, L., and Stein, R. (1998). Relationship of Parental Psychological Distress to consequences of chronic health conditions. *Journal of Pediatric Psychology*, 23, 5-15. doi:10.1093/jpepsy/23.1.5.

Smith, A., Allenson, J., Elsea, S., Finucane, B., Haas-Givler, B., Gropman, A. (2006). Smith-Magenis Syndrome. Gene reviews. University of Washington.

Smith, A., Dykens, E., and Greenberg, F. (1998). Sleep disturbance in Smith-Magenis syndrome. *American Journal of Medical Genetics, 81*, 186-191. doi:10.1002/(SICI)1096-8628(19980328)81:2<186::AID-JMG11>3.3.CO;2-A.

Smith, A., McGavran, L., Waldstein, G., and Robinson, J. (1982). Deletion of the 17 short arm in two patients with facial clefts and congenital heart disease. *American Journal of Human Genetics, 34*, A410. Retrieved from www.cell.com/AJHG/.

Solnit, A.J. and Stark, M.H. (1961). Mourning and the birth of a defective child. *Psychoanalytic Study of the Child.* 16, 523-537. Retrieved from yalepress.yale.edu/yupbooks/SeriesPage.asp?Series=75.

Stagi, S., Bindi, G., Neri, A.S., Lapi, E., Losi, S., Jenuso, R. S., and Chiarelli, F. (2005). Thyroid function and morphology in patients affected by Williams syndrome. *Clinical Endocrinology, 63*, 456–460. doi:10.1111/j.1365-2265.2005.02365.x.

Stratton, R., Dobyns, W., Greenberg, F., DeSana, J., Moore, C., Fidone, G., … and Ledbetter, D.(1986). Interstitial deletion of (17)(p11.2): Report of six additional patients with a new chromosome deletion syndrome. *American Journal of Medical Genetics, 24*, 421-432. doi:10.1002/ajmg.1320240305.

Stromme, P., Bjomstad, P. G., and Ramstad, K. (2002). Prevalence estimation of Williams syndrome. *Journal of Child Neurology, 17*, 269-271. doi:10.1177/088307380201700406.

Turnbull, A. E, and Turnbull, H. R. (1986). Stepping back from early intervention: An ethical perspective. *Journal of the Division of Early Childhood, 10*, 106-117. doi:10.1177/105381518601000202.

Udwin, O. (1990). A survey of adults with Williams syndrome and Idiopathic Infantile Hypercalcaemia. *Developmental Medicine and Child Neurology, 32*, 129-141. doi:10.1111/j.1469-8749.1990.tb16912.x.

Udwin, O., and Yule, W. (1991). A cognitive and behavioural phenotype in Williams syndrome. *Journal of Clinical and Experimental Neuropsychology, 13*, 232–244. doi:10.1080/01688639108401040.

Udwin, O., Webber, C., and Horn, I. (2001). Abilities and attainment in Smith-Magenis syndrome. *Developmental Medicine and Child Neurology, 43*, 823–828. doi:10.1017/S0012162201001499.

Washington, D. (2006). Evercare study finds stress, depression, fatigue propel caregivers into downward health spiral. *PR Newswire US*. Retrieved from web.lexisnexis.com.proxy.library.vcu.edu/universe/document?_m=1b0480e5c0208787e3b172f5bc38e93cand_docnum=1andwchp=dGLbVlbzSkVband_md5=1761d99a197be3c715821320c461ecb3.

Webster-Stratton, C., and Hammond, M. (1988). Maternal depression and its relationship to life stress, perceptions of child behavior problems, parenting behaviors, and child conduct problems. *Journal of Abnormal Child Psychology, 16*, 299 – 315. doi:10.1007/BF00913802.

Webster-Stratton, C., Reid, M. J., and Hammond, M. (2004). Treating children with early-onset conduct problems: Intervention outcomes for parent, child and teacher training. *Journal of Clinical Child and Adolescent Psychology, 33*, 105–124. doi:10.1207/S15374424JCCP3301_11.

Wessel, A., Gravenhorst, V., Buchhorn, R., Gosch, A., Partsch, C.J., and Pankau, R. (2004). Risk of sudden death in the Williams–Beuren syndrome. *American Journal of Medical Genetics Part A, 127A*, 234–237. doi:10.1002/ajmg.a.30012

World Health Organization (2005). WHO Executive Board Report – Control of Genetic Diseases. Retrieved from apps.who.int/gb/ebwha/pdf_files/EB116/B116_3-en.pdf.

In: Intellectual Disability
Editors: Domenico F. Mancini and Carlo M. Greco
ISBN: 978-1-61942-298-8

Chapter 6

Cognitive Skills Enhancement in Intellectual Disability

Rosa Angela Fabio
Department of Pedagogical and Psychological Sciences, University of Messina, Messina, Italy

Abstract

Many labels refer to treatment for cognitive impairments. Most of them are referred to as "cognitive rehabilitation", "cognitive skills enhancement", "cognitive empowerment". Anyway the purpose of these treatments is to help an individual acquire the highest level of cognitive functioning and functional independence possible for that individual.

The objectives of the present chapter are to study in depth the latest theoretical approaches to cognitive empowerment in intellectually disabled children and to show that modifiability can be applied despite the presence of severe impairments in the attention, memory, reasoning and language processes of an individual.

This chapter begins with a theoretical overview on cognitive empowerment. The first part contains basic principles and theoretical standpoints of cognitive empowerment. Cognitive and biological bases of empowerment will be presented, connected to the concept of "neuroplasticity".

The second part contains operational principles of cognitive empowerment and examples of applications on case studies. Methodologies presented show how to improve attention, memory, thinking, reasoning, and present statistical data that show trends in each of the considered processes.

Introduction

Terms such as "cognitive rehabilitation", "cognitive therapy", "cognitive skills enhancement", "and "cognitive empowerment" refer to treatments that help an individual in acquiring higher level of cognitive functioning and functional independence. These terms are difficult to define and embrace numerous ambiguities, for example its refer to both a process and an outcome (Dempsey and Foreman 1997; Harris, 2000).

The empowerment of an individual with mental retardation depends on the type and extent of the underlying disorder, the associated disabilities, environmental factors, psychological factors, cognitive abilities and comorbid psychopathological conditions (Ludwik,, 2002; Kumar, Singh, and Akhtar, 2009). Cognitive Therapy with individual with mental retardation is designed to develop and enhance cognitive functions across the following domains:

- Visuospatial Skills
- Attention Skills
- Memory Skills
- Executive Skills
- Problem Solving Skills
- Communication Skill

Empowerment can be attained through one or many ways. The basic principles which inspire the intervention are modificability (Budoff, 1978; Brown and Ferrara , 1985; Vygotskij, 1978; Luria, 1961; Tzuriel, 2005; Fabio, 2007; Feuerstein, Rand and Rynders, 1992) and mediated learning. There are numerous studies that show that this modification is possible.

1. Overview on Cognitive Empowerment

Most educational interventions in intellectually disabled students have set to reaching poor goals (e.g. simply dealing with information); such a small investment prevents the development of the ability of "learning to learn". What is important, in fact, is not that the subject becomes able to reproduce information, but that he can gradually modify his underlying cognitive processes.

Cognitive empowerment has the theoretical basis on the Vygotsky's zone of proximal development theory and on the Feurstein's modifiability theory (Feuerstein, Rand, and Hoffman, 1979; Feuerstein, Rand, Hoffman, and Miller, 1980 ; Vygotskij, 1978).

The zone of proximal development, known as ZPD, is the difference between what a learner can do without help and what he or she can do with help. Vygotsky stated that a child follows an adult's example and gradually develops the ability to do certain tasks without help or assistance. Vygotsky's often-quoted definition of zone of proximal development presents it as: "the distance between the actual developmental level as determined by independent problem solving and the level of potential development as determined through problem solving under adult guidance, or in collaboration with more capable peer" (Vygotskij, 1978). Vygotsky among other educational professionals believes the role of education is meant to provide children with experiences which are in their ZPD, thereby encouraging and advancing their individual learning (Berk, 2001; Berk and Winsler, 1995). Lower limit of

ZPD is the level of skill reached by the child working independently. The upper limit is the level of additional responsibility the child can accept with the assistance of an able instructor. The ZPD captures the child's cognitive skills that are in the process of maturing and can be accomplished only with the assistance of a more-skilled person. Scaffolding is a concept closely related to the idea of ZPD. Scaffolding is changing the level of support. Over the course of a teaching session, a more-skilled person adjusts the amount of guidance to fit the child's current performance. Dialogue is an important tool of this process in the zone of proximal development. In a dialogue unsystematic, disorganized, and spontaneous, concepts of a child are met with the more systematic, logical and rational concepts of the skilled helper. This concept has been further developed by Anne Brown, among others (Brown and Campione, 1994; 1996). Several instructional programs were developed on the basis of the notion of ZPD interpreted this way, including reciprocal teaching and dynamic assessment (Fabio et al., 2008, 2009). While the ideas of Vygotsky's ZPD originally were used strictly for one's ability to solve problems, Tharp and Gallimore (1988) point out that it can be expanded to examining other domains of competence and skills. These specialized zones of development include cultural zones, individual zones, and skill-oriented zones. Of these skill-oriented zones, it is commonly believed among early childhood development researchers that young children learn their native language and motor skills in general by being placed in the zone of proximal development.

In the Feuerstein view to help these students learn, it is not enough to expose them to a rich world of colours, objects of different forms, sounds, and movements, without changing their relation with these stimuli so that they do not remain superficial. In order to change an experience into a source of learning, some components are necessary. These components induce the individual to classify, make comparisons, group, label and convey meaning to his current experience, putting it in relation to previous ones. This active way of experiencing the world is the result of a form of interaction, the so-called "experience of mediated learning". "Mediation" means that a change can be caused by another human person (H) that puts him/herself with an active behavior and with precise intentions between the other person (O) and a stimulus (S); therefore, he/she has the role of a mediator. Thanks to an experience of mediated learning, the organism (O) that is directly exposed to the stimuli (S) receives them and answers them with adequate competences only after their features have been selected, framed, modified by an adult human mediator (H).

All that the individual will learn is organized by the adult mediator who determines the relations among stimuli. In other words, in educational and rehabilitative relationships the educator should select some stimuli, set them into a time sequence (before and after) and according to purpose, put them into a causal and spatial system, attach a special meaning to certain stimuli, propose them many times, cancel other ones, highlight associations among some stimuli and avoid other ones.

Finally, it is important that this kind of intervention takes place at three levels: cognitive, emotional, and behavioral. In effect, the basis underlying this methodology is human relationship. The relationship is intended both as an instrument of mediation to improve RS student's abilities and as a way to restore a meaning to the world itself through the interaction with the adult.

2. Biological Bases of Cognitive Empowerment

The biological bases of cognitive empowerment are normally referred to the concept of "neuroplasticity" (also referred to as brain plasticity, cortical plasticity or cortical re-mapping).

Neuroplasticity is the changing of neurons and the organization of their networks and so their function by experience. As known, the brain consists of nerve cells or neurons (and glial cells) which are interconnected, and learning may happen through changing of the strength of the connections between neurons, by adding or removing connections, or by adding new cells. "Plasticity" relates to learning by adding or removing connections, or adding cells.

New findings on neuroplasticity suggest all areas of the brain are plastic even after childhood. Hubel and Wiesel (1963, 1969, 1978) had demonstrated that ocular dominance columns in the lowest neocortical visual area were largely immutable after the critical period in development. Different studies determined that environmental changes could alter behavior and cognition by modifying connections between existing neurons and via neurogenesis in the hippocampus and other parts of the brain, including the cerebellum.

According to the theory of neuroplasticity; thinking, learning, and acting actually change both the brain's physical structure (anatomy) and functional organization (physiology) from top to bottom. Recent advancements in brain imaging techniques allow neurologists and other scientists to peer into a living brain and to see the differences in structure resulting from life experiences (Douglas, 2004).

Using positron emission tomography, Silberstein et al. (1993) have made movies of this blood flow as it occurs in different regions of the brain. An interesting result, easily seen using his techniques, is that in a person who learns to solve a particular problem effectively, when asked to do the problem over again, the blood flow is much less intense. Indeed, as we know, when a problem has been solved repeatedly, we solve it without effort. We interpret these results to indicate that once structures have been formed, much material and energy are no longer required; the process of learning stops. What has been learned is strengthened by repetition (Fabio, 2008).

Sometimes we solve a familiar problem without even realizing we have done so. In these circumstances, our brain seems to have a mind of its own. We drive our automobile from point to point and have difficulty remembering the route we took. We remember a familiar tune but not the words. We also are aware that we have some bad habits and resolve to change them. Why is it so difficult to change what our brains do effortlessly? It takes a conscious effort to make a change in the structure of our brain. Sometimes we find that the effort is so great it seems to be beyond our ability to make the change, as any smoker can attest. We make a conscious effort and fail, but through repetition we can reach automatism.

As Touretzky (1990) and Touretzky and Leen (1995) suggest, it is known that many parts of the mammalian brain contribute to incremental learning. Although the cortex may play a central role, other brain areas known to make vital contributions include the basal ganglia, hippocampus, amygdale, and cerebellum. It is important to understand the roles of these various areas and their interactions with each other during learning. The development of theories of incremental learning will provide a better understanding of how the process occurs and may result in improved approaches to the development of skills in both humans and machines.

The authors underline that in general, enriched environments increase the number of brain connections. Connections are created when an individual becomes curious about something and is free to explore that curiosity. At such times, brain cells sprout thousands of new connectors—dendritic spines that grow out like tree branches. Each cell can generate hundreds of thousands of connectors during its lifetime. The brain makes the new connectors available for the processing of sensory data and for incorporating that data into prior knowledge constructions. Enriched environments, varied experiences, and piqued interest around a central topic stimulate the production of connectors, thus allowing for more storage options in response to the experience. Even a slight change for a learner, such as changing to a new seat in the classroom, will cause the brain to generate new dendritic branches and spines as it attempts to incorporate the new viewpoint and new relationships that the learner experiences among objects and people in the classroom. The brain adapts itself in order to cope with changes it encounters in its environment.

New connectors are not necessarily permanent. They gradually become permanent by being revisited—repeating the activity (practice), exploring the activity with some variation (rehearsal), or reflecting on the activity by talking about it.

If the connections are not revisited, they may disintegrate and be lost forever. The adage "use it or lose it" applies most certainly to the establishment and retention of connectors within the brain. The quality of the connections and the extensiveness of the connections within the brain's systems constitute how well something is understood or how well an individual can perform. Evidence indicates that the more connections you have, the better you are able to solve problems, think clearly, and understand events. The number of connections the brain constructs depends on the individual's interest in participating in an experience.

Generating the growth of dendrites, the threadlike extensions that grow from neurons (brain cells), is important. When dendrites grow, neurons make more connections to other neurons. When information within a dendritic system is reinforced through practice or rehearsal, the connections gradually become stable, permanent, and usable.

Increasing proper connections among the brain's neurons results in a better functioning brain. These connections result, in part, through inherited growth patterns within the genetic makeup of a person. They also develop in response to stimuli in the environment that the brain encodes as nerve impulses. The implication here for educators is obvious. Since brains increase dendritic growth as a result of enriching experiences, and since growth is stabilized by practice and rehearsal, the school environment can and should provide such experiences. Doing so will help students retain what they have learned and increase the likelihood of their being able to apply that learning to new situations.

3. The Assessment of Processes and Abilities

Before starting a cognitive empowerment program it is important to know exactly the abilities and the processes that a child is able to perform. This procedure is called assessment. In assessment procedure we have to refer to both underlying cognitive processes and abilities.

Below we will shortly refer to the physiological functioning of cognitive processes, continue with the Feuerstein model of cognitive deficits at each of these levels and finally, task analysis procedure will be presented.

Human information processing theory deals with how people receive, store, integrate, retrieve, and use information. Cognitive processes can be divided into three phases: input, elaboration and output.

During the input phase, learners are gathering information. They are registering and making sense of what they read or are told, and organizing it in their minds. Input may be a sound, a sentence, a picture, an idea, a smell, a taste, or a task to be done. Normally the input phase is studied through perception and attention processes. Perception is the ability to take in information via the senses, and process it in some way. Vision and hearing are two dominant senses that allow us to perceive the environment. Attention is the selection of important information. The human mind is bombarded with millions of stimuli and it must have a way of deciding which of this information to process. Attention is sometimes seen as a spotlight, meaning one can only shine the light on a particular set of information.

During the elaboration phase, learners are developing this organization. They become aware of relationships and patterns in the information they receive (which they may relate to previous experience), and form concepts. Elaboration by the learner leads to the 'Aha' experience, the "Aha" experience refers to the moment when a new idea is grasped for the first time. In Piagetian terms, the learner is engaged in assimilation and accommodation. This is the most difficult phase to access and change, but its quality can be enhanced by improving input and output processes and by drawing attention to common elaboration strategies. Examples of cognitive processes included in the elaboration phase are memory and reasoning. Memory allows us to store information for later retrieval. Memory is often thought of consisting of both a long-term and short-term store. Long-term memory allows us to store information over prolonged periods (days, weeks, years). Short-term memory allows us to store information over short time scales (few seconds or minutes). Reasoning is the process of drawing conclusions from facts or evidence, and in general, to make relationship between facts and concepts. Others auhors have expanded on these definitions by adding the transfer process. The transfer process may involve using what one has learned in one situation in other situations, which can differ in some ways from the training situation (Broad and Newstrom, 1992; Holton, Bates and Ruona, 2000).

During the output phase, learners have to select from what they know in order to solve a problem or answer a question. They have to show or tell what they know, by means of a sign, a word, a sentence, or an essay. They may be asked to explain, discuss, demonstrate, draw or take action A with language. Language is a system for encoding and decoding information. In its most common use, the term refers to so-called "natural languages", the forms of communication considered peculiar to humankind.

This model is helpful in teaching and assessing cognition because it breaks up thinking into stages. Teaching may be about the processes typical of the Input phase, or of the Elaboration phase, or of the output phase. The model is also valuable as a means of identifying where learners have difficulties.

4. The Evaluation of Cognitive Processes

With reference to the evaluation of underlying cognitive processes, as in the model above presented, Feuerstein categorizes deficits related to them into three dimensions, or phases, of the mental act: input, elaboration, and output.

Input deficiencies, seen as most problematic, were 1) blurred and sweeping perception; 2) unplanned, impulsive, unsystematic exploratory behaviour; and 3) impaired receptive verbal tools and concepts. Blurred and sweeping perception is seen in imprecise details, poor clarity, and a haphazard, hurried, impulsive approach to work. Students may not read directions and do not develop steps for beginning a task or for asking for help when needed. With unplanned, impulsive, unsystematic exploratory behaviour, the student lacks an information gathering system, does not routinely read directions, look for commonalities, or summarize. Many students have problems because they have impaired receptive verbal tools: because of insufficient vocabulary, they misunderstand words in problems and directions as well as in general subject content.

As an example we can think of a child who touches anything, who always runs around the room: when we try to speak with him, he is not able to attend information because of too much excitement.

The *elaboration phase* involves what we do with collected data. It is the heart of problem solving. Teachers see the following as particularly problematic for their students: 1) lack of, or impaired, planning behaviour; 2) narrow mental field; 3) episodic grasp of reality; and 4) lack of, or impaired, need for pursing logical evidence. The first of these involves a bridging between the present and the seemingly non-existent future. Students with deficient planning behaviours have difficulty setting goals and determining steps to reach these. They lack organization and do not follow steps to achieve goals. When narrow mental field is evident, students are unable to remember and manipulate multiple pieces of information simultaneously. As they try to deal with a new piece, they lose earlier information. They depend on concrete rather than abstract thinking and often have difficulty following complex directions. Episodic grasp of reality is perhaps the most devastating of the cognitive deficiencies. When it is present, the individual views each object/event as a unique, isolated phenomenon. Something learned in one setting is seen as applicable to that setting only. It is not obvious to the student that correct grammar will be important in a social studies paper as well as in an English composition. A child may not see the need to apply knowledge of fractions in computing measurements to reduce a recipe. This can manifest as a behavioural problem as well when students do not see the relationship of cause and effect between their actions and the consequences of those actions. Students who have a lack of, or impaired need for pursuing logical evidence do not seek explanations for incompatibilities. They may simply say, “Because,” when asked to give a reason. Things appear to them to “happen” without reason. They do not connect events or establish relationships. Asked why they like a particular movie or school subject, they often respond with a tautological answer, "It's my favourite!" The notion of supporting thoughts with logic is unfamiliar to them. They do not expect things to make sense.

In the *output phase* of the mental act, we state the answer, complete the paper, solve the problem, or make the decision.

The two most prevalent deficits at this level were 1) egocentric communication modalities and 2) trial and error responses. Students with egocentric communication modalities see things only from their own perspective. They therefore do not provide enough detail, precision, or argumentation. They assume that the listener knows what they know and they expect others to read their minds. A student may begin an elaborate narrative without first explaining that this is the plot of a television show. The student may give directions to a school visitor saying that the library is located "where the guidance room was last year." With trial and error responses, students are distracted by irrelevant information and answer quickly with what appear to be random guesses. There is no system for achieving goals. If one answer is not correct, they immediately substitute another, without reflecting on the source of the error. Impulsivity plays a big part in this, as does lack of confidence. Students often feel that there is one right answer to every question and that it is their job to continue guessing until they happen to hit upon it.

5. The Assessment of Abilities

To assess the abilities of intellectually disabled children we can use the procedure of task analysis. Task analysis refers to what a user is required to do in terms of actions and/or cognitive processes to achieve a task. Task analysis is used most often with those who have problems mastering complex behaviours (e.g., individuals with autism, people who are mentally retarded or mentally ill, young children).

Method for analysing tasks is task decomposition. The aim of 'high level task decomposition is to decompose the high level tasks and break them down into their constituent subtasks and operations. This will show an overall structure of the main user tasks. At a lower level it may be desirable to show the task flows, decision processes and even screen layouts. The process of task decomposition is best represented as a structure chart (similar to that used in Hierarchical Task Analysis). This shows the sequencing of activities by ordering them from left to right and from bottom to up. In order to break down a task, the question should be asked 'how is this task done?. If a sub-task is identified at a lower level, it is possible to build up the structure by asking 'why is this done? The task decomposition can be carried out using the following stages:

1) Identify the task to be analysed.
2) Break this down into subtasks. These subtasks should be specified in terms of objectives and, between them, should cover the whole area of interest.
3) Draw the subtasks as a layered diagram ensuring that it is complete.
4) Decide upon the level of detail into which to decompose. Making a conscious decision at this stage will ensure that all the subtask decompositions are treated consistently. It

may be decided that the decomposition should continue until flows are more easily represented as a task flow diagram.

5) Continue the decomposition process, ensuring that the decompositions and numbering are consistent. It is usually helpful to produce a written account as well as the decomposition diagram.

6) Present the analysis to someone else who has not been involved in the decomposition but who knows the tasks well enough to check for consistency.

Examples of task analysis may come from different areas: cognitive, behavioural and emotional abilities. A method of systematic task analysis is applied to the problem of designing a sequence of learning objectives that will provide an optimal match for the child's natural sequence of acquisition of mathematical skills and concepts. Resnick, Wang, and Kaplan (1972) begin by proposing an operational definition of the number concept in the form of a set of behaviours which, taken together, permit the inference that the child has an abstract concept of "number". These are the "objectives" of the curriculum. Each behavior in the defining set is then subjected to an analysis that identifies hypothesized components of skilled performance and prerequisites for learning these components. On the basis of these analyses, specific sequences of learning objectives are proposed. The proposed sequences are hypothesized to be those that will best facilitate learning, by maximizing transfer from earlier to later objectives. The paper concludes with a discussion of the ways in which the curriculum can be implemented and studied in schools.

Another type of task analysis is cognitive task analysis: it identifies aspects of system design that place heavy demands on the user's cognitive resources including memory, attention, and decision-making (Barnard and May, 2002). It is used to determine thought processes that users follow to perform tasks at various levels, from novice to expert (Hanser, 1995). Cognitive task analysis looks at the system from the viewpoint of the user performing a specific task. The information gathered allows the designer to focus upon the system features that the user will find hardest to learn and be likely to make the most errors. Included in the analysis is examination into past critical incidents that may have occurred to shape the users feelings or expectations about the task (Schrraagen, Chipman, and Shalin, 2000). By identifying and highlighting where potential challenges could occur, designers can create a system that leaves more time for the user to perform the given task rather than struggle with using the interface (Barnard and May, 2002).

There are many different methods for conducting cognitive task analysis. At a minimum, cognitive task analysis should include the same steps of task analysis of mapping out the task, identifying the critical decision points, clustering, linking, and prioritizing them, and characterizing the strategies used (Klein, 1993). Cognitive task analysis relies on the technique of Data Driven Knowledge Elicitation (DDKE) to extract information about cognitive events, structures, and models. In depth interviews are used to probe into the cognitive processes of users who are performing the task. However, interviews are often very subjective, so the data collected may not present a complete and accurate representation of the cognitive processes involved. To account for this bias, controlled observation methods are also recommended. Controlled observation uses verbal protocol analysis of expert's responses to the task when instructed to think out loud. An advantage of controlled observation is that key features of the task can be manipulated and data can be automatically collected by the system (Klein, 1993).

We can make assessment of all behaviours of the person with which we are working or we can use also assessment present in the specific literature, such as Portage method or Vineland scales.

Assessment of both processes and abilities lead to define cognitive, emotional and behavioural objectives that are unique for each intellectually disabled person. For example, if we discover that a child is not able to turn off the gas, our proximal objective is to teach him that. If we discover that he is able to read figures but not symbols, our proximal objective is to teach him that. Aims are normally organized at three levels: behavioral, emotional and cognitive.

6. Basic Methods of Cognitive Empowerment

Unconditional acceptance of the child is the first method here considered. This is the most important concept for the development of the child. In the educational intervention the relationship with adults is based upon the following methods: unconditional acceptance, rules, reinforcement, containment, shaping, fading, prompting, hierarchy, automatic process, abstraction, economy.

1. *Unconditional acceptance.* Unconditional acceptance means that the child is supported in all that he is, no matter what that might be. This does not mean that the child is supported in acting out all that he is, rather that he is supported in expressing whatever he has inside, no matter what it is and no matter what it might trigger in the facilitator. Given unconditional acceptance, the child at some point begins likewise to unconditionally accept him/herself — all of him/herself. In the view of Adzema (2000) unconditional acceptance, therefore, is the indispensable element of a primal therapy whose stated goal is to get people real. It may also be why some other therapies succeed, to an extent, in helping a person to be more real, in that they grant unconditional acceptance. For these reasons, it is very important that teachers and caregivers have a disposal of unconditioned acceptance of the students, to make them feeling loved despite their difficulties in daily interactions.
2. *Rules.* Rules are very important keys in this intervention, since they can convey order to the external world, which otherwise would be perceived as chaotic and disorganized-disrupted. Rules can work if they are constantly and repeatedly used in a right manner; rules must be few and given in an affirmative way (“keep hands still” instead of “do not move your hands”) and must be concrete and given at the right moment.
3. *Reinforcement.* Response strength can be assessed by measures such as the frequency with which the response is made (for example, a child may raise from the bench more times during the lesson), or the speed with which it is made (for example, the child may read a book page faster than another child). The environment change contingent upon the response is called a reinforcer. Reinforcements are nice events that are able to keep or increase the probability that the subsequent behaviour will be shown again (Foxx, 1986).

There are different type of reinforcement. A primary reinforcer is a stimulus that does not require pairing to function as a reinforcer and most likely has obtained this function through the evolution and its role in species' survival. A secondary reinforcer is a stimulus or situation that has acquired its function as a reinforcer after pairing with a stimulus which functions as a reinforcer.

4. *Containment.* when students present stereotypes or unplanned, impulsive, unsystematic exploratory behaviour, they should be bodily-physically contained to enhance their attention process. For instance, their hands have to be kept separate in order to interrupt hand stereotypes and their attention should be driven to the work to be done.
5. *Shaping.* shaping or modelling consists in reinforcing every approximation that is much more similar to the desired behaviour, until the student shows a meta-behaviour (a behaviour that is close to the desired one) that was not in his behavioural repertoire (Foxx, 1986). Shaping involves gradually modifying the existing behavior into the desired behavior. If the student engages with a rabbit by hitting it, then he or she could have their behavior shaped by reinforcing interactions in which he or she touches the rabbit more gently. Over many interactions, successful shaping would replace the hitting behavior with patting or other gentler behavior.
6. *Fading.* Fading consists in giving many helps in the beginning of the work and then in gradually removing them, so that the student becomes able to do that work without any help. As an individual gains mastery of a skill at a particular prompt level, the prompt is faded to a less intrusive prompt. This ensures that the individual does not become overly dependent on a particular prompt when learning a new behavior or skill.
7. *Hierarchy.* Hierarchy means to learn from simplest objectives to more complex ones. As presented in the example in the second chapter, a child has to learn before the + (plus) sign and when he masters it, he can go over to learn the X (multiplication) sign.
8. *Automatism.* Automatism refers to the dynamics from controlled processing to automatic processing of attention. In any starting step of a task, initially we use controlled processes of attention to learn and so performance is slow, awkward and prone to errors. We can say that the full amount of our memory load is engaged, we can say also, in other words, that all our cognitive resources are engaged to solve the new learning.

   For example we can think of a child that is learning to sum up two numbers. It is very difficult initially for the child to bear in mind the first number, to memorize the second number, to recall the first and to sum up both. It is difficult also to understand that the plus sign means "to add", "to join"... but also "become bigger", "go on"... and so on. So, when the teacher asks him to join the toys of Mary with the toys of Marc, he thinks hardly, he does it slowly and then reaches the result. During his problem solving, if someone asks him something else he makes mistakes in the calculation and forgets the result.

   As training proceeds, performance requires less vigilance, becomes faster and errors decrease, a transformation that can be defined as "automatism". With learning, the attentive strategies that once needed control become automatic.

   Coming back to the above mentioned child, as learning proceeds, he becomes able to think of the plus sign faster and reaches the result easily. He becomes able to reply

also to someone who asks him something else. In other words the child automates learning of the plus sign. In the model below we are positioned in the A level, when automatism appears and discharge of cognitive load on A level takes place.
Later the child has to learn how to multiply, or how to sum up and subtract some quantity. If he were totally (or even partially) engaged in the A level, it would be difficult to access to more complex tasks. He can now have access to the execution of subtraction and summing up (B level) thanks to the fact that he assumed the A level as an automatic subroutine.

9. *Abstraction.* Abstraction refers to the passage leading from concrete experience to symbolization. In effect it is important that learning involves not only symbolic learning, but also concrete learning. To understand the symbolic value of the concept of numerical quantity a child has to be trained before in counting concrete materials and things.
10. *Economy.* Economy refers to the fact that in any learning setting it is better to try to give the smaller possible help, so that the subject is stimulated to autonomy. Sometimes educators help too much learners and this let them to be dependent from the educator itself.
11. *Specificity.* Specificity is related to the economy principle and refers to the enhancement of cognitive processes. It means that if a child or an adult with a disability has a specific deficit in the input phase (eg processes of attention), the empowerment action has to take place selectively on the process of attention and not on others like for example on the logical or linguistic processes.

7. Examples of Methodologies Based on Cognitive Empowerment

An examples of case study in which cognitive empowerment methodologies was applied will be presented. It is an example of intervention and training in girls with Rett syndrome (Antonietti, Castelli, Fabio, Marchetti, in press).

Reading-Writing Ability Training

Communication is a very important goal in girls with Rett Syndrome. Rett Syndrome (RS) is a genetic disorder with a specific biological marker for its diagnosis: its aethiology is due to the genetic mutation of gene MECP2 on the x-chromosome (Amir et al., 1999). This developmental disorder in females results in severe mental retardation and neurological disability. In late infancy, after a period of superficially normal but subtly flawed development (Nomura and Segawa, 1990) RS girls undergo striking developmental regression (Hagberg, 1993; Moeschler, Charman and Graham 1991). There is a characteristic loss of pre-existing hand use such as object reach, grasp, and manipulation, and the appearance of distinctive hand stereotypies (hand wringing, tapping, and mouthing). Post-regression, though severely retarded, patients often regain social interest and are relatively stable for an extended period before progressive motor deterioration occurs in the form of weakness, wasting, and dystonia (Hagberg, 1993). During this period, crude self-feeding capabilities may be retained, but voluntary hand use is generally limited and hand stereotypies are pervasive (Fontanesi and Haas, 1988). Some studies (Witt Engerstrom, 1990) show that patients often remain visually attentive to objects and people, tracking their movements and even showing preferences by means of "eye pointing".

The authors in a single case study had the aim to teach to the RS girl to communicate through abstract symbols, such as our common letters, starting from images in order to allow them to communicate through writing or pointing. It consists of two phases:

First Phase

- evaluation of pre-requisites;
- discrimination of images of familiar objects and people.

Second Phase

- discrimination of the image-word associations;
- biunivocal correspondence between word and image (direct correspondence) and between image and word (indirect correspondence);
- separation of words into syllables and reconstruction;
- separation of syllables into letters and reconstruction;
- construction of sentences;
- communication.

FIRST PHASE

1. Evaluation of pre-requisites: the girl had learnt a way of communication: she got accostumed to the presentation of two stimuli, to the request of looking at them and to choose the requested one either by looking at it and touching it. As far as the pre-requisites of the reading-writing ability training, the most relevant one is the girl's ability of reading images. Therefore a group of about twenty images was chosen: they were photos of important persons (parents, siblings, teachers…) and of relevant objects (food, animals, toys…) in the dimension of an A4 paper sheet.
2. Discrimination of photos and images of familiar persons and objects. The girl was presented one photo (target) with a distractor; she was asked to look at them and to choose the target. Stimuli were presented in the randomized right-left order and only when the girl had reached the criteria for each image (she intentionally chose the target, so that the possibility of casual choices could be excluded) the other photos could be introduced with the same procedure. Once this step was reached for all twenty photos, they were reduced to the dimensions of 5x5, following the same methods and criteria. Finally photos were substituted by drawings. For instance the photo of the girl's dog was substituted with the drawing of a dog and gradually other images could be introduced, provided that they were part of the girl's world (a chair, a bed, a phone…). The discrimination procedure was the same as for photos.

SECOND PHASE

3.Discrimination of the association image-word . The work with words started in this phase. Twenty bysillable words were chosen: they must be words that interest the girl (such as "dad") and that are different in the letters (it is better to avoid words that start with "c" and "g" or with "p" and "b" as they are hard to be discriminated). Each word was written on a white sheet reporting also, in the first letter, the corresponding image and was presented with a distractor (a white sheet): the girl was asked to choose the stimulus with the word "dad". The procedure and the criteria were always the same.

4.Biunivocal correspondence between word and image and between image and word. This work provided another proof of the intentionality of the girl's choices, as it allowed to exclude casual choices. In the direct correspondence the girl was presented one word, for instance "dad", and near it the images of dad and of another object. The girl was asked to choose the right image that corresponded to the word. In the indirect correspondence the girl was presented one image, for instance "dad", and near it the words of dad and of other objects (for instance: the word "dad" and another word). The girl was asked to choose the right word that corresponded to the image. Since the girl's fine motor skills were good, she was also asked to take the right image and put it on the word and viceversa; otherwise the girl can be helped by the educator.

5.Separation of words into syllables and reconstruction. The words that the girl had learnt were cut into syllables. The verb "cut" is used here literally: the girl watched the educator cutting words with scissors. For instance "father" was cut into "fa" and "ther": the girl worked with syllables 1. She was asked to look at two syllables (the target syllable "fa" and a distractor syllable) and to choose the target one. In this way the girl learnt the first syllable, then the second, then the two target syllables were presented togheter and so on for every syllable of each word. After this step, the girl was asked to reconstruct the word: she was given the first syllable ("fa") and she was asked to choose the following syllable that completed the word "father" chosing it between two syllables or even among three ones. Finally the girl had to make this work without the initial help of the first syllable: she was given some syllables and she was asked to build the word "father". At the last step, the girl was asked to build also new words that she had not learnt in the training but that were made up of the syllables she had learnt.

6.Separation of syllables into letters and reconstruction. The same work with words and syllables was reproduced with letters: syllables were cut into single letters.The previously described procedure was followed also with letters and at the end the girl was asked to build new words using letters.

7.Construction of sentences. The girl learnt to build short sentences using only two words, for instance she was asked to build the sentence "dad eats" choosing the right letters from a group of many ones. At the beginning the girl needed plenty of time, since she had to choose among 21 letters put in front of her; then she gradually became faster as the position of letters did not change; moreover, sentences gradually became longer.

8.The quality jump: communication. Initially the girl was asked simple questions, such as "What is your name?", "Is mum here with you?", "What is mum's name?" and she was encouraged to answer using letters. In this case the quality jump occurred: letters were not used to reproduce what the educator said anymore, but they were used for the production of an autonomous answer. Finally the single letters were sticked on a big paper, that became the alphabetic table the girl used to communicate. It can be easly rolled up and transported everywhere.

M. now composes words using her forefinger, as if the table is a computer keyboard; it is important that neither the educator nor the mother touch the girl's hands and arms while she is writing, as she has to do it by herself.

She has become very familiar with this kind of communication. We have to say that she generally answers questions, but she hardly never makes questions. She does it only in those situations that are very important for her and emotionally charged for her, as the following episode can confirm.

M.'S Performances in the Reading Ability Training

M.'s performances in the most important phases of the reading-writing ability training is now presented:

1.reading words
2.reading syllables
3.reading letters

The procedure of the training, as well as the evaluation of M.'s performances, were always the same in each phase. M. was submitted to the training three or four sessions a week: in each session she was presented the item (word or syllable or letter) for five times and the criteria that allowed to proceede to the next step was five correct answers produced consecutively for five sessions. Performances concerning reading words are described in figure 1.

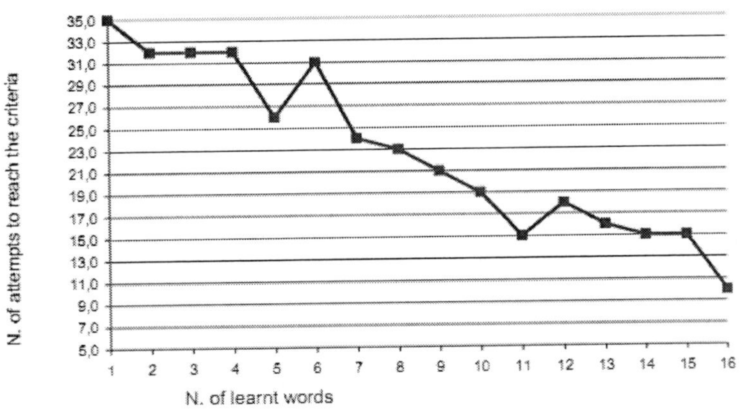

Figure 1. Number of attempts to reach the criteria for each word.

As figure 1 shows, M. learnt sixtheen words: they were names or nicknames of family members ("dad", "mum", "efi", "uncle"), names of familiar objects ("bike", "ball", "wine", "sun", "moon"), of simple animals ("frog", "mouse") and so on. 2 To learn the first word ("dad"), M. made 35 attempts to reach the criteria, so she needed seven sessions of work, that correspond about to two weeks of training.

Test C has been used in order to control the statistical significance of the reading words intervention. In this case the obtained value is $Z\ (16) = 4.02$, $p<.05$. The trend of this intervention, the reading of words, is a decreasing trend, thus confirming that this training does not only allow the ability of reading words, but also allows the girl to "learning to learn". In other words, the girl did not only learn to read some words, but she actually "learned to learn": while the training was going on she was able to learn words faster and sooner. Performances concerning reading syllables are described in figure 2.

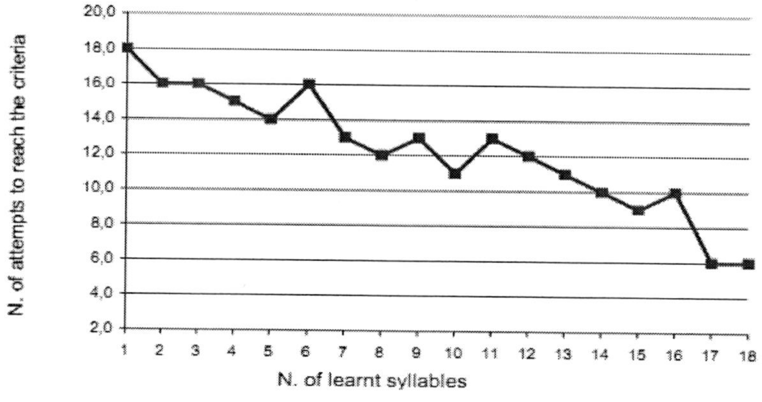

Figure 2. Number of attempts to reach the criteria for each syllable.

As figure 2 shows, M. learnt eightheen syllables, derived from the words she had learnt in the previous training. To learn the first syllable ("bi" form "bici"), M. made 18 attempts to reach the criteria, so she needed three sessions of work, that correspond about to one week of training.

Test C has been used in order to control the statistical significance of the reading syllables intervention. In this case the obtained value is $Z\ (18) = 3.72$, $p<.05$. The trend of this intervention, the reading of syllables, is a decreasing trend, thus confirming that this training does not only allow the ability of reading syllables, but also allows the girl to "learning to learn". In other words the girl does not only learns to read some syllables, but she actually "learns to learn": while the training was going on she was able to learn syllables faster and sooner. Performances concerning reading letters are described in figure 3.

As figure 3 shows, M. learnt ninetheen letters. To learn the first letter ("a"), M. made 8 attempts to reach the criteria, so she needed two sessions of work, that correspond about to one week of training.

Test C has been used in order to control the statistical significance of the reading letters intervention. In this case the obtained value is $Z\ (19) = 1.94$, $p<.05$. The trend of this intervention, the reading of letters, is a decreasing trend, thus confirming that this training does not only allow the ability of reading letters, but also allows the girl to "learning to learn". In other words the girl does not only learns to read some letters, but she actually "learns to learn": while the training was going on she was able to learn letters faster and sooner.

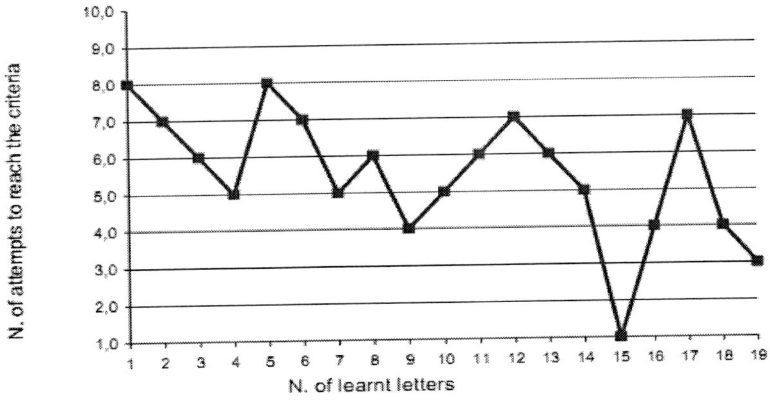

Figure 3. Number of attempts to reach the criteria for each letter.

Conclusion

In this chapter several particular active research areas within the context of the cognitive empowerment have been surveyed, focusing on studies concerning the dynamic perspective, id est the modifiability of processes and abilities of intellectually disabled children.

We revised a definition and theoretical and up-to-date overview on cognitive empowerment.

We showed that cognitive empowerment and modifiability in intellectually disabled children can be applied despite the presence of severe impairments in the individual or of hard hindrances in his/her living conditions. This was the case of girls with Rett Syndrome in which it is confirmed that it is possible to modify RS girls' cognitive structure, thus improving the quality of their life, as well as the quality of people who live with them.

References

Adzema, Michael. (1985). A primal perspective on spirituality. *Journal of Humanistic Psychology*, 25(3), 83-116.

Amir R. (1999), Rett sindrome is caused by mutation in x-linked MECP2, encoding methyl-CpG-binding protein 2, in *"Nature Genetics"*, 23, pp. 185-8.

Antonietti A., Castelli, I., A., Fabio R.A., Marchetti, A. (in press), Training communication abilities in Rett Syndrome through reading and writing, *Brain and Developments*, submitted.

Barnard, P. and May, J. (2002). *Cognitive task analysis.* June 5, 2002 from the World Wide Web: http://www.mrcbu.cam.ac.uk/amodeus/summaries/ CTAsummary.html.

Berk, L and Winsler, A. (1995) "Vygotsky: His Life and Works" and "Vygotsky's Approach to Development." In *Scaffolding Children's Learning: Vygotsky and Early Childhood Learning*. National Assoc. for Education Of Young Children.

Berk, L. E. (2001). *Development through the lifespan*. Elmsford, NY: Pearson.

Bluma S., Shearer M., Frohman A., Hilliard J. (1990), *Il metodo Portage*. NY Ed.

Broad, L.M. and Newstrom, W.J. (1992). *Transfer of Training*. New York: Addison-Wesley.

Brown A.L., "Domain-specific principles affect learning and transfer in children", *Cognitive Science*, 14 (1990), pp. 107-133.

Brown A.L., "Knowing when, where, and how to remember: A problem in metacognition",., in *Advances in instructional psychology*, Hillsdale, HJ, Erlbaum, eds. Glase R.,1978, pp. 77-165.

Brown A.L., Ferrara R.A., "Diagnosing zones of proximal development", in *Culture, comunication, and cognition: Vygotskian perspectives*, Writsch J. V., London and New York, Cambridge University Press, 1985, pp. 273-305.

Budoff, M. (1987). Measures for assessing learning potential. In C. S. Lidz (Ed.), *Dynamic assessment: An interactional approach to evaluating learning potential* (pp. 173–195). New York: Guilford.

Demeter K. (2000) Assessing the developmental level in Rett syndrome: an alternative approach? in "*European Child and Adolescent Psychiatry*", 9, pp. 227-33.

Dempsey, I., and Foreman, P. (1997). Toward a clarification of empowerment as an outcome of disability service provision. *International Journal of Disability, Development,* and Douglas F. (2004). *The Other Half of the Brain. Scientific American,* V 290 N 4, pg 54. Education, 44, 287-303.

Fabio R. A. "Dynamic assessment of intelligence is a better reply to adaptive behaviour and cognitive plasticity", *Journal of General Psychology*. 2005, 23, 12-45.

Fabio R.A., Antonietti A., Marchetti, A., Catselli, I (2009). Attention and communication in Rett syndrome, *Research in Autism Spectrum Disorders,* 3, 329–335.

Fabio R.A., Giannatiempo S., Antonietti A., Budden S., (2008), The role of stereotypies in overselectivity processes in Rett Sindrome, *Research in Developmental Disorders*, 2008, 23, 56-69.

Feuerstein R., Rand, N., Hoffman, G., and Miller P. (1980). Instrumental enrichment: *An intervention program for cognitive modifiability*, Baltimore, University Park Press.

Feuerstein, R. Rand, Y., and Rynders A. (1979). Don't Accept Me as I Am: *Helping 'Retarded' People to Excel.* Plenum Press.

Feuerstein, R., Rand Y., Rynders J. (1992). *Non accettarmi come sono. Un nuovo approccio per affrontare la Sindrome di Down*. Milano: Rizzoli

Fontanesi J., Haas R., (1988), Cognitive profile of Rett Sindrome. *Journal of Child Neurology 1988;*3:S20-S24.

Foxx R. M. (1986), *Tecniche base del metodo comportamentale. Sviluppare abilità e ridurre comportamenti problema in persone con handicap grave o autismo*, Erikson, Trento.

Hagberg B.(1993), Clinical criteria, stage and natural history, in Hagberg B. *(ed): Rett Syndrome-Clinical and Biological Aspects*. London, Mackeith Press, pp 4-21.

Hanser, L. M. *Traditional and Cognitive Job Analyses as Tools for Understanding the Skills Gap*. Berkeley: National Center for Research in Vocational Education, University of California, 1995. (ED 383 842).

Harris, B. (2000). Psychology. In A. Hassenbruch (Ed.), *Reader's Guide to the History of Science* (pp. 607-608). London: Fitzroy Dearborn.

Holton, III. E. F., Bates, R. A., and Ruona, W. E. A. (2000). Development of a generalized learning transfer system inventory. *Human Resource Development Quarterly*, 11(4), 333-360.

Hubel, D. H. and Wiesel, T. N. 1969 Anatomical demonstration of columns in the monkey striate cortex. *Nature* 221, 747–750.

Hubel, D. H. and Wiesel, T. N. 1979 Brain mechanisms of vision. *Sci. Am.* 241, 150–162.

Hubel,D. H. and Wiesel, T.N. 1963 Shape and arrangement of columns in cat's striate cortex. *J. Physiol.* (Lond.) 165, 559–568.

Klein, G. A. (1993). *Naturalistic decision making: Implications for design.* Crew System Ergonomics Information Analysis Center.

Kumar, I., Amool, R., Singh, L., and Akhtar, K. (2009). Social development of children with mental retardation. *Industrial Psychiatry Journal*, 18(1): 56–59.

Ludwig M, (2002). *Pregnancy and Birth after Assisted Reproductive Technologies.* Springer Verlag, Berlin, Heidelberg, New York.

Luria A.R., Higher cortical functions in man, New York, Basic Books, 1961.

Moeschler JB., Charman CE., Berg SZ., Graham JM. (1991), Rett Syndrome: A review of currente knowledge. *J. Autism Dev Disorder* 1991; 82:1-10.

Nomura Y., Segawa M. (1990), Clinical features of the early stage of the Rett Sindrome. *Brain dev.*12:16-19.

Resnick L.B., Wang, M.C., Kaplan, J. (1973). Task analysis in curriculum design: a hierarchically sequenced introductory mathematics curriculum. *J. Appl. Behav. Anal..,* 6, 679–709.

Schraagen, J. M., Chipman, S. F., and Shalin, V. L. (2000). *Cognitive task analysis.* Mahweh, NJ: Lawrence Erlbaum Associates, Inc.

Silberstein R.B., Ciorciari J., Schier M.A., Pipingas A., Wood S. (1993). The steady state visually evoked potential and topography and vigilance. Proc XVth Annual Conference of the Australian Society for the Study of Brain Impairment. In: B.G.Frost, M.Watson and H.P.Pfister (eds). *Brain Impairment: advances in applied research.* Australian Society for the study of brain impairment. 267-274.

Tharpe, R. G. and Gallimore, R. (1988). *Rousing minds to life. Cambridge*, MA. Cambridge University Press.

Touretzky, D. S., and Leen, T. K., . (1995). *Advances in Neural Information Processing Systems 7,* Cambridge, Massachusetts; London. MIT Press.

Touretzsky, D. S., (1990). *Advances in Neural Information Processing Systems* 2, Cambridge, Massachusetts; London. MIT Press.

Tzuriel D., "Dynamic assessment of young children : Educational and intervention perspectives", *Educational Psychology Review,* 12 (2000), pp. 385-435.

Tzuriel D., Kaufman R., "Mediated Learning and cognitive modifiability: dynamic assessment of Young Ethiopian Immigrant Children to Israel", *Journal of Cross-Cultural Psychology*, 30-3 (1999), pp. 359-380.

Vytgosky, L. S. (1978). *Mind in Society. The development of higher psychological processes.* Cambridge, MA: Harvard University Press.

Witt-Engerstrom I., (1990), Rett Syndrome in Sweden: Neurodevelopment-disability-patholophysiology. *Acta Paediatr. Suppl.,* 1990;369:19-26.

In: Intellectual Disability
Editors: Domenico F. Mancini and Carlo M. Greco
ISBN: 978-1-61942-298-8

Chapter 7

EMERGING TRENDS OF RESEARCH ON NEW TECHNOLOGIES ON COGNITIVE SKILLS ENHANCEMENT IN INTELLECTUAL DISABILITY

Rosa Angela Fabio
Department of Pedagogical and Psychological Sciences, University of Messina, Messina, Italy

Intellectual disability is a lifelong condition with multiple aetiologies (Harris, 1995). There are no specific personality or behavioural characteristics that are specific to intellectual disability (American Psychiatric Association, 1994). Severe levels of intellectual disability or syndromes may be associated with motor disability. In these cases there are even more limits in social and adaptive functioning. In Rett Syndrome for example initially the child looks normal and seems to follow a normal development. It is at about 18 months of age that a subtle regression in the evolutive acquisitions begins, opening the path to the clinical stages described by Hagberg and Witt-Engerström (1986). Loss of the previously acquired language skills and of purposeful hand use, increasing difficulties in motor abilities (dyspraxia), and mental retardation are the most clear signs of the regression involved in RS. Other typical signs of RS appear meanwhile: hand stereotypies - such as hand-washing, hand-wringing, hand-mouthing - breathing disorders (breath holding and hyperventilation), ataxia, agnosia, bruxism. Since persons with Rett Syndrome are not able to communicate occupational therapy can include assistive technology devices, such as pointers and switches that activate toys or a simple cause/effect computer activity (Pizzamiglio et al., 2008). Lack of expressive and receptive language is also a large part of Rett syndrome.

Today technology-based solutions that address cognitive disabilities can range from very simple low-tech, low-cost solutions such as a picture-based instruction set or schedule of events (AbleNet Technologies, Inc; Attainment Corporation, Inc.), to high-tech, high-cost computer based environmental control systems, auditory prompting systems (AbleLink Technologies, Inc), and communication aids for individuals who have significant expressive/receptive communication deficits (Saltillo Corporation, Prentke Romich, Inc.; Dynavox Systems, Inc.). Communication systems and augmentative and alternative communication devices are often used to increase communication skills. Some of these systems include eye pointing, communication boards (pictures, facial expression, gestures, and the activation of switches). However, little research has been done to cultivate communication and literacy in girls with this condition (Skotko et al., 2004). Some of the research that has been done showed the successful use of switch-activated augmentative communication devices, computers with graphics to make requests and eye pointing with picture communication symbols. Story book reading was found to facilitate meaningful communication for girls affected with Rett syndrome as well (Skotko et al., 2004).

To overcome difficulty in examining and empowering the abilities of people with Rett Syndrome, Eye-Tracker technology may be helpful (Fabio et al., 2009a; 2009b). Eye-tracker consists of an instrument that is transportable, works without further equipment and can be used in normal room light conditions. It measures either the point of gaze ("where we are looking") or the motion of an eye relative to the head. It can be useful in helping researchers to better study attention and cognitive processes in RS girls. One of the first studies using eye tracking technology was the one by Baptista et al. (2006) who used eye gaze in 7 girls. The experimenter presented two stimuli at a time, a target and a distractor stimulus, and asked the child to choose the target stimulus during three cognitive tasks: (1) verbal instruction condition (look at picture X), (2) recognition and matching of pictures (look at the one that is the same), and (3) categorization of pictures (look at the one that is similar). Comparing fixation times of target and distractor stimuli revealed a higher percentage of correct alternatives. Of the seven children assessed, only one did not present predominance of fixations on the correct alternatives in any one of the tasks. One child did well in all tasks while six responded correctly to the verbal instructions task. The rate of correct answers suggests that there is measurable and intentional gaze in RS girls and it can be used as a path to explore their cognitive performance. Three years later, in a study that used the same cognitive tasks, De Lima, Alves de Araùjo, and Schwartzman (2009) recommended re-evaluation of the method because a small group of 10 girls with RS (aged 4–12 years) did not manifest recognition of the target stimulus within a fixation time of 4 seconds, even if they argued that the low age of the sample and the brief fixation span could have interfered with the results.

In another recent work Fabio & Giannatiempo (2010) report 22 cases of girls with Rett syndrome aged between l0 and 20 years, involved in a psvchoeducational intervention based on cognitive empowerment through the multimedia eye-tracker. Participant were assigned either to the multimedia training setting or to the traditional instruction setting. Results show that hypermedia instruction produce higher cognitive performance than traditional instructions.

Traditional instruction setting:

The size of the black circle show the fixation time: in the first card the target (happy girl) is focused for a longer time.

Means of fixation time of the target and of the distractor before and after training:

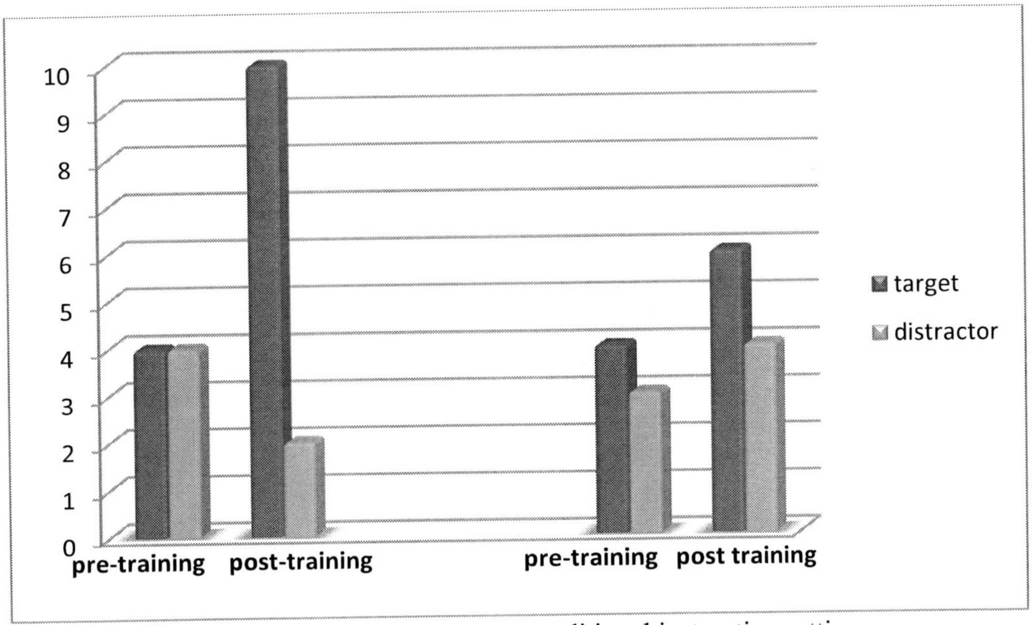

multimedia training setting traditional instruction setting

This type of hypermedia instruction is an approach that may help people with Rett Syndrome or people with both cognitive and motor deficit to overcome their limits.

References

American Psychiatric Association, (1994). *Diagnostic and Statistical Manual of Mental Disorders.* 4th Edition, Washington DC, American Psychiatric Association.

Baptista, P. M., Mercadante, M. T., Macedo, E. C., & Schwartzman, J. S. (2006). Cognitive performance in Rett syndrome girls: A pilot study using eye tracking technology. *Journal of Intellectual Disability Research, 50*, 662–666.

De Lima Velloso, R., Alves de Araùjo, C., & Schwartzman, J.S. (2009). Concepts of color, shape, size and position in ten children with Rett syndrome. *Arquate Neuropsiquiatria, 67*, 50–54.

Fabio, R.A., Antonietti, A., Marchetti, A., & Castelli, I. (2009a). Attention and communication in Rett syndrome. *Research in Autism Spectrum Disorders, 3*, 329–335.

Fabio, R.A., Giannatiempo, S., Antonietti, A., & Budden, S. (2009b). The role of stereotypies in overselectivity processes in Rett syndrome. *Research in Developmental Disabilities, 30*, 136–145.

Fabio, R.A., Giannatiempo, S. (2010). Cognitive empowerment and communication: a multimedia proposal. Proceedings of the 1st European Congress on Rett Syndrome. From research to treatment: new perspectives in Rett Syndrome, Milan, 5-7 giugno, p. 34.

Hagberg, B., Witt-Engerström, I. (1986). Rett syndrome: a suggesting staging system for describing impairment profile with increasing age towards adolescence. *American Journal of Medical Genetics, 24,* 247 - 252.

Harris, J.C., (1995). Developmental neuropsychiatry, assessment, diagnosis and treatment of developmental disorders (pp.91-126) Vol II New York: Oxford University Press.

Pizzamiglio, M.R., Nasti, M., Piccardi, L., Zotti, A., Vitturini, C., Spitoni, G., Nanni, M.V., Guariglia, C., & Morelli, D. (2008). Sensory-motor rehabilitation in Rett syndrome. *Focus on Autism and Other Developmental Disabilities,* 23, 49-62.

Skotko, B.G., Koppenhaver, D.A., & Erickson, K.A. (2004). Parent reading behaviors and communication outcomes in girls with Rett syndrome. *Exceptional Children,* 70, 145-166.

INDEX

C

D

E

F

G

H

I

K

L

M

N

O

P

Q

R

S

T

U

V

W

X

Y

Z